What Vets Don't Tell You About Vaccines

Catherine O'Driscoll

Also written by Catherine O'Driscoll

The Golden Retriever Companion - *a chronicle of joy*

First published - February 1997; reprinted January 1998

Second edition - October 1998

Published by Abbeywood Publishing (Vaccines) Ltd,

PO Box 1, Longor, Derbyshire, SK17 0JD, England

ISBN 0 9523048 3 X

Dedication

*'Beloved, let us love one
another; for love is of God, and
he who loves is born of God and
knows God.'*

1 John 4: 7

*This book is dedicated to all the
humans and dogs and cats,
horses, cattle and sheep, who
have loved, and all those born of
God who have grown in spirit
through living the pain of
vaccine damage. We are the
voice of the voiceless.*

Acknowledgments

This book could not have been written without the advice freely given by a number of vets. I am therefore very grateful to Christopher Day, Jean Dodds, Peter Gregory, John Saxton and James Newns. Other vets have helped, too - you know who you are, and you have my sincere thanks. I also thank Dr Viera Scheibner, who has given practical support and advice so that our experiences with the animals can be recorded and added to the catalogue of human tragedies associated with vaccines.

Dr Tony Page has been a friend to me and to the animals. Hylda Reynolds and June Goose are two special animal lovers: they would not be quiet when they were told. Both have been more than generous, and have shared a great deal of their work. Leslie Kaufman, Chrissie Mason, Jean Collinson, Heather Peterson, Sally Cronk, Sylvia Kolkowski, Paul Kolkowski, Alison Lovell, Barbara Burgess, Rosamund Walters, Lin Delamar, Hilary Jupp, Ed and Sandy Dorosz, Alex and Sandra Brigola, Ann Martin, Dave and Rosemary Woodworth, Karen Matthews, Brian James, Sheila Hamilton-Andrews, Karen Brown, Gaile Ward and Wendy Volhard (all of gracious spirit), as well as others too numerous to mention, have been supporters and champions of the animals.

Big 'thanks' go to the people who have taken part in the Canine Health Concern vaccine survey, and who will be moved to do so in the future, and to the people who went from door to door to ask people to complete vaccine survey questionnaires. This work will continue until life comes before profits.

To my husband, John, who vigorously pursues the truth, and whose statistical skills have enabled us to scientifically measure vaccine damage. He is my rock.

And to all the people and all the dogs who gave their stories to this book, so that their suffering would not be in vain.

Table of Contents - What Vets don't tell your about vaccines

Prologue

Who Killed the Darling Buds of May?

We went to collect Prudence from the kennel. Pat Bartlett led us in to the puppies. There were about eight of them - fat squidgy little bundles of incoordination, rolling and lolloping around with sleep in their eyes; falling and stumbling onto one-another, and fearlessly rushing to our eager outstretched arms. And then Oliver took hold of my finger in his tiny little mouth, and Prudence sat before John and gave a sweet little bark, and both Oliver and Prudence became the heart magnets, and John and I were the metal filings.

Oliver and Prudence were our darling buds of May, born in the spring and plucked in full bloom.

Soon after John and I got married, we welcomed a Golden Retriever called Chappie into our home. Then Sophie, then Oliver and Prudence. These, our canine children, filled our home with happiness. It was idyllic. So many people long for a dog, but they work and wouldn't leave the dog on his own all day. Or they live in a flat, or in a city with no fields nearby, so they wait, and they wish.

But we were blessed: our dogs came to the office with us - John and I ran our own marketing business. Our dogs were our receptionists and paper shredders, and well-known stars in the town where we walked and played at lunch time. One day an elderly man passed us in the park. He yelled: "Those are the happiest dogs in Northampton," and I thanked God, because he may have been right.

Each day in my office, Chappie would lie by the window, Sophie at the foot of my desk, Prudence by my side, and Oliver, well Oliver lay on my feet or in the middle of the doorway. He would; he was like that. And there was always a smile and a warm welcome for every visitor; there was always laughter, and always love in the room.

Then, one morning, John woke me as usual with a cup of tea. But something was missing. Oliver wasn't beside me on the bed. "Where's Ollie?" I asked, bleary eyed. In the four years I had known Oliver, he had never allowed me to welcome the day without his sunshine in my heart.

"Catherine," said John, looking very worried, "there's something wrong with Oliver. He can't stand up. His back legs are paralysed." So I got up, and I went downstairs to where Oliver was lying.

You know, there was once a programme running on the TV called, 'The Day That Changed My Life,' and this was the day that changed my life. It unfolded ahead of me like a nightmare, and I still haven't woken up. John, too, will never be the same.

So there was Oliver lying on the floor in the sitting room. And Prudence, Chappie and Sophie were giving him a wide berth. They wouldn't come in the room. I know now that dogs can sense death, and they leave the dying alone. But I didn't know that then. Because if I had known, we wouldn't have done what we did on that day.

I sat down next to Oliver and I talked to him, using all the consoling sounds I could muster. And I stroked his head and his neck, and his tummy because he liked that, and I kissed him, and I told him not to worry, that we would take him to the vet, and the vet would make him better. And I waited for John to get washed and dressed, and then John came down and sat with Oliver while I went upstairs to get washed and dressed. And then we made a stretcher of some blankets, and we carried Oliver to the car.

We must have known this was serious, deep inside, because I climbed in the back of the estate with Ollie, and I rested his head upon my lap, and I talked to him as the car lurched and bumped along the road. At one point, Oliver got it into his head that he wanted to sit up and look out of the window, but he couldn't manage it, so I calmed him down and I stroked his neck, and I said, "It's all right Oliver. Don't you worry. You'll be all right. Mummy will look after you."

And his eyes locked into mine. That was the moment that changed my life. His eyes locked into mine and he decided to believe me, to trust me, to take my word for it. And in that look was all the love in the Universe. The most knowing knowingness that has ever been known.

So we arrived at the vet's, and we carried Oliver out of the car, and the vet was there waiting for us and he ushered us immediately into his room, and we laid our darling Oliver on the table. You know, Oliver always used to shake and quiver when he was at the vet's. He was always beside himself with fear. But today he was calm. He was serene. There was an emanation of peace rising from him, and he laid there on that table, and he waited patiently while the vet tried, and tried again, and again, to find a vein to take a blood sample, and Oliver wasn't in the least bit worried.

And now I think, I don't know but I think, that Oliver always knew he was going to die in that veterinary surgery.

So Oliver is lying on the table in the veterinary surgery, and John and I are worried because it isn't the normal vet, it's a locum, a young whippersnapper, and we hope that he knows what he's doing. But he smiles, and he tells us not to worry, and he tells us that he thinks Oliver has a virus on his spine, and he needs to stay with them so he can put a drip into Oliver's body, a steroid drip, and Oliver should be better in a couple of weeks.

And the young vet is wearing a white coat, and we don't know what else to do anyway, so we leave Oliver at the veterinary surgery. And while they're carrying him out to the kennels behind the surgery, Oliver looks at me, and he lunges the front half of his body towards me, and he says with his eyes, "Please mummy, please don't leave me. Let me come home with you." And I say, "It's all right Oliver. You'll be all right. We'll see you later." And then John and I walk out of the surgery and I collapse against the wall in tears. Because my head is telling me that Oliver will be all right, and my heart knows he will not.

And, God damn it, I listened to my head. And I listened to the vet. And I didn't listen to Oliver.

So John and I went away, and we tried to carry on with our work. But I kept phoning the surgery. Who cares if they think I'm a neurotic dog owner? I am, anyway. So I kept phoning the surgery, and I kept asking if the senior vet could please take a look at Oliver because, you see, he is very dear to us. He's a special person. And we need to make sure that the senior vet has seen Oliver. And the receptionist kept telling me that the senior vet hadn't arrived yet. And then she's been too busy. And I keep phoning the surgery. And John calls in and gets told to go home. And then I call again, and the locum comes on the phone, and he keeps umming and ahhing and I wait silently for him to tell me that Oliver is all right.

"Are you still there?" he asks. And I make a noise so he can know I am still there, and I wish, and pray, that he will tell me Oliver is all right. And then he says that Oliver is dead.

I want to hit the vet, and at the same time I want to put my arms around him because he is a young vet and he needs his confidence if he is to save lives, so I just sit there crying on the end of the phone. John is standing beside me, so I hand the phone over to him. And John says no we don't want a post-mortem, we don't want our Oliver to be cut up, as if he was just a lump of meat or something. And then we get in the car to bring Oliver home, where he should have been all along. And then we are acting the parts of the people in the veterinary surgery, the ones who are crying while the clients sit and watch and look embarrassed, and Oliver is put on a stretcher and we take him out through the back door and somehow drive him home.

Then we're in our back garden, looking for a resting place for Oliver's body. We lived in a modern house, and the builder had laid our lawn on builder's rubble. And John couldn't get through it to dig Oliver's grave. So he's standing there with a shovel in his hands and the tears are streaming down his face, and he can't get through the damn rocks and bricks and plastic bags, and I'm standing there beside him with the tears running down my face, and the sun is beginning to go down, and Oliver's body is waiting in the car and the time is running out. So John asks me to go and find a neighbour who will lend us a pickaxe.

I go walking down the lane, tears streaming from my eyes, sobs wrenching themselves from my body, and I'm wandering around, wondering whose door I can knock on with tears streaming down my face, and I'm wondering how I'm going to manage to speak the words that convey to my neighbour that I need a pickaxe.

Ian and Sue, from the cottage next door, they're doing the washing up, and they see me walk by, and they see the tears and they come rushing out. Your neighbours aren't supposed to see you like this. They're supposed to see you calm and confident, with everything going well in your world, but Ian and Sue saw me sobbing in the lane, and they came rushing out. They said, "Oh no, not Ollie," because they knew that Oliver was a special dog. And my heart and my head, they kept saying, "Oh no, not Ollie."

So Ian told me to go home. He said he would find me a pickaxe. And Ian brought the pickaxe to John, and John dug a hole, and we buried Oliver in the twilight.

It's strange how Chappie, Sophie and Prudence reacted. Sophie sat at the other end of the garden, smiling and laughing and looking cheerful. She was trying to cheer us up. Prudence wandered around worrying. And Chappie came to the grave where we had placed Oliver, and he said his last goodbyes. For the first time in his life, Chappie howled at the moon. And for months afterwards, Chappie went out into the garden, and he sat on Oliver's grave.

Somewhere in the middle of all this, my stepmother phoned, and I cried on the phone and told her about Oliver, and said I couldn't speak. Then my sister Leslie phoned, because Leslie loves dogs, and she understood, and a friend sent us flowers. And everyone else thought that Oliver was just a dog. It seemed strange to me, that. I mean, I really thought that my heart was going to explode, and my stomach ached, and my head ached, and the inside of my body was like a pressure cooker. If the lid had come off, I would have started screaming and I might never have stopped, but when I told people that Oliver had died, they said 'Oh' and started talking about something else. As if Oliver was just a dog.

But I will never forget Ian and Sue who came rushing out when they saw me with tears streaming down my face. Because I know that most people would draw the curtains and not want to get involved.

And Oliver was only four years old.

Two years later, when Prudence was only six, we were told she had leukaemia; that she had two months, at most, to live. This time, the loss was not sudden - we had time to say goodbye. We had time to tell her how much we loved her. Time to thank her for the love she had given us. We had time - thirty days - to watch the life weep out of her, like a tyre with a slow puncture. And we had time to hope and pray, and watch her go.

And we had time to listen to Prudence. During those last few days, Prudence told me many things. She began by dragging her weary body, with great determination, to each house in the village inhabited by the children she had loved. Pru's heart was as large as the Universe, and she had to tell everyone how very much she loved them. Before she left us. And she led me to every person we passed in the street; and she lay down contented as soon as we began to talk.

A few days before she died, Prudence walked to the village community centre. She peered in through the windows, and told me she wanted to go inside. But dogs weren't allowed in there so I led her home again. And the next day she set a determined course to the community centre, and she peered inside. So we went in. And she lay down next to me and next to Sheila, and she waited for me to get the message.

For Prudence asked me to do one thing before she died: she asked me to tell you - you who love life - why our dogs are dying, why our children are dying, why animals and people all over the world, are dying. And crying. So that we can learn to care for one-another, as she cared for us. Prudence has asked me to be her voice, and the voice of all the animals and all the children, all the people whose hearts are breaking, whose bodies are suffering.

Prudence told me that she died, and Oliver died, to prove to the world that man is killing the planet and the life on it. I know you're going to think this is crazy, but I have to tell you this.

You know, people say that animals are not conscious. They say that their minds and emotions are limited to bodily needs. They think that human beings are the only ones who are capable of complex emotions; that if we think otherwise, we are anthropomorphosising. Yet when elephants grieve, we can see their tears. And when Prudence died, I saw her tenderness towards me, and her concern for me.

Pru's illness was a cruel illness; we tried to save her, and sometimes she would perk up and we thought she was on the mend, and then she would slide downhill again, only to rally round the next day. The night before Prudence died, she asked to come upstairs with me to lie on the bed. I had been sleeping next to her on the floor downstairs. But this night she asked to go upstairs, so John carried her up to the bed.

I lay there talking to her as she struggled to breathe, and I noticed that her paws were icy cold, and I knew that Prudence was dying. So I spoke to her: I said, "You've always been such a good little girl Prudence, and I love you very much. You've protected Chappie and Sammie, and you've played with Sophie, and you've looked after me and John. You're such a good little girl. I don't want you to go, but if it's too much for you, I will understand."

Prudence looked at me, and she let out her little hissing, effervescent sound, like a bottle of lemonade with the lid coming off; the sound she always made when expressing love and gratitude. She looked into my eyes; her eyes were a brown million miles. She was thanking me for letting her go, and telling me that she loved me too. The next morning, before the vet arrived, John carried Prudence into the garden and he told her the same thing. It took us two years to admit to each other that we had each, separately, given Prudence permission to leave us.

Three years after Pru's death, I read the following passage in Sogyal Rinpoche's 'Tibetan Book of Living and Dying':

"If you are attached and cling to the dying person, you can bring him or her a lot of unnecessary heartache and make it very hard for the person to let go and die peacefully . . for such a person to be able to let go and die peacefully, he or she needs to hear two explicit verbal assurances from loved ones. First, they must give the person permission to die, and second they must reassure the person they will be all right after he or she has gone, and that there is no need to worry about them.

"When people ask me how best to give someone permission to die, I tell them to imagine themselves standing by the bedside of the person they love and saying with the deepest and most sincere tenderness: 'I am here with you and I love you. You are dying, and that is completely natural; it happens to everyone. I wish you could stay here with me, but I don't want you to suffer any more. The time we have had together has been enough, and I shall always cherish it. Please now don't hold onto life any longer. Let go. I give you my full and heartfelt permission to die. You are not alone, now or ever. You have all my love'."

You know, that night with Prudence, lying on my bed watching her die, was perhaps the most tender moment in my life. I wasn't sharing the last few hours of an inferior life. I was sharing the last few hours of a noble life; the life of a dog whose primary motivation was to care for others. And Prudence, right to the very end, wanted only to please me, and she needed my permission before she would die. A few days later, I picked up a book and opened it at random. The following words stared out at me from the page: "I am sorry I had to leave you, but the pain was too hard to bear." I don't know, but something inside me tells me that this was a message from Prudence. We should listen to the animals; they are conscious.

Oliver and Prudence, when they came to live in my heart, each lit a small candle. Everyone lights a candle. It is the candle of love and light. Together - the dogs and the cats and the cattle and the sheep, and even the humans - we can spread light where there is darkness. For we have made a crazy world, and now we must make it sane. It is time.

The dogs have come to remind us.

Introduction

We had four Golden Retrievers, and two died before they had reached middle age. Chappie and Sophie were still with us, but Chappie had thyroid disease and ruptured cruciate ligaments which rendered him a cripple, and Sophie, at only six years of age, developed arthritis so bad that she didn't want to get out of bed in the morning.

After Oliver died, Samson came to live with us. When he was only two we discovered that he had autoimmune disease, where the body's own immune system attacks the host. Then, after Prudence died, Gwinnie arrived on the scene. She was so allergic that, if you touched her back, it would ripple. She used to chew at her flesh and her paws; she was in allergic agony.

We asked the vet why Oliver had died. He didn't know. So I took to wailing why? out to the heavens. Eventually, though, we found a homoeopathic vet who ventured an opinion about Oliver's death. He told us that it sounded like a classic vaccine reaction: that Oliver had probably been killed by a vaccine. Then, after Prudence died, a friend, Susan Rezy, sent us an article written by an American vet called Jean Dodds. Dr Dodds also seemed to be implicating vaccines in Oliver's death, and there was a link with Pru's death, too.

When you bring a puppy home with you, you believe you are hugging your dreams. But John and I were hugging our nightmares. We thought we must be the worst dog owners in the world: why were our dogs so unhealthy, and why were they dying?

You know, when each of us suffers a personal tragedy that is almost too hard to bear, we have a choice. We can allow that suffering to make us bitter; we can look for someone to blame and seek revenge. Or we can rise above that suffering, as the mystics would do. The third choice is to transmute that suffering into a force for good: to use the knowledge gained

1

through our experience to help others in a similar position. We thought that if we could at least find out where we were going wrong, other dogs might fare better.

Jean Dodds' article told us, for the first time, that we weren't alone, and we weren't particularly unusual. Thousands, if not millions, of dogs and dog owners around the world had been through our pain. In fact, Dr Dodds explained that there has been a significant increase in the frequency of autoimmune and allergic diseases in the pet population since the introduction of modified live virus vaccines. According to Dr Dodds, a most eminent vet and researcher, autoimmune diseases have four main 'triggers': genetics, virus or vaccines, sex hormones and stress.

The first of these is the animal's or human's genes. In scientific terms, of the more than 40 diseases of autoimmune nature, susceptibility to almost all is strongly influenced by genes associated with the class I or class II major histocompatibility complex. In lay terms, our dogs are inheriting a susceptibility to pain and premature death - but this inherited trait must be 'triggered' by something else.

This is how the genetic predisposition works: 'Histocompatibility' is the degree to which the immune system of an animal will tolerate the presence of foreign tissue. Class I group serve as markers for lymphocytes (white blood cells), which attack and destroy body cells that are virus-infected or whose surfaces bear foreign antigens. Class II antigens have a pronounced role in governing intercellular co-operation, and are sometimes found to influence the reactivity of individuals to certain antigens (an antigen is a foreign invader, such as a toxin or invading organism).

According to Pedro Luis Rivera, DVM, type II hypersensitivity reactions result in tissue injury, i.e., pemphigus (blisters and ulcers to the skin, which may be life-threatening), arthritis, fibromyalgia (tissue), and kidney and liver damage. Examples of type III hypersensitivity reactions are Lupus erythematosus and rheumatoid arthritis. And type IV hypersensitivity reactions sensitise T cells causing inflammations.

In plain English, some of our dogs - as many as 50 breeds of pedigree dogs and their crossbred offspring - are genetically susceptible to autoimmune diseases due to the way in which their bodies reacted to foreign invaders. However, we have to acknowledge that we are all of us genetic weaklings. Some human families are more prone to cancer than others; some of us are besieged by allergies and asthma; some of us seem to inherit behavioural problems. In most cases, though, we need a trigger to set it off. Pollen and hay fever come to mind - you don't have hayfever all year round.

I was sitting on a plane next to a man who was reading a scientific paper, and I started talking to him. He turned out to be a toxicologist working for ICI. I explained to him about certain breeds and lines of dogs having hypersensitivity reactions to vaccines. He told me that you don't actually need a genetic pre-disposition to react to a vaccine. Vaccines, he said, can actually cause T cell immunodeficiencies.

Autoimmune disease is any disorder involving inflammation or destruction of tissues by the body's own immune system. According to the Oxford Concise Veterinary Dictionary, 'such disorders result from the activity of lymphocytes primed to act in response to 'self antigens'; antibodies, complement, hypersensitivity reactions, and other immune mechanisms may be directed against 'self' tissues'. In other words, if the body is subjected to a foreign body it doesn't like, it might go crazy and start attacking itself.

The following diseases are autoimmune disorders:

- Hashimoto's thyroiditis
- Addison's disease
- Rheumatoid arthritis
- Lupus erythematosus
- Idiopathic thrombocytopenic purpura
- Haemolytic anaemia
- Chronic active hepatitis
- Diabetes mellitus
- Hypogonadism
- Myasthenia gravis
- Pemphigus, vitiligo (skin inflammations)
- Glomerulonephritis
- Alopecia
- Grave's disease
- Hypoparathyroidism
- Seizures and other neurologic manifestations
- Uveitis and other immunologic eye diseases

The Oxford Concise Veterinary Dictionary adds polyarteritis nodosa, an inflammation of the wall of one or more arteries, which is often found in a virus infection.

So, logically, a vaccine could trigger autoimmune diseases in animals (and humans). It is, after all, a 'foreign body', injected directly into the system, which has the potential to invoke a hypersensitivity reaction which can lead to autoimmune disease. Any organism (animal or human) could have a bad reaction if it comes into contact with a virus or toxin. Our dogs are injected with a number of different live viruses, such as parvovirus, distemper, rabies, hepatitis, and parainfluenza, as well as a dead bacterin (toxin), viz., leptospirosis. We are counselled to inject our dogs with these foreign proteins every year.

It is well documented in the human field that some people have bad reactions to vaccines. The difference with our dogs, cats and horses, is that they face the risk of a reaction year after year after year until many of them drop. This is because we are told by vets that animals must have boosters every year.

The common vaccines used today are MLV - modified live virus - vaccines. MLV vaccines are 'attenuated', which means they are supposedly rendered harmless, and they are designed to multiply in the host, with the aim of stimulating a more effective immune response. Dr Dodds wrote: "However, the MLV vaccine can also overwhelm the immunocompromised or even a healthy host that is continually bombarded with other environmental stimuli."

Dr Dodds adds that underlying autoimmune thyroid disease pre-disposes a dog to other immune-mediated diseases affecting other target tissue and organs, especially the bone marrow, liver, adrenal gland, pancreas, skin, kidney, joints, bowel, and central nervous system. "The bottom line," she writes, "is that viruses capable of inducing immune dysregulation in genetically susceptible stock can initiate autoimmune thyroid disease". In another paper, Dr Dodds list parvovirus, retroviruses, cytomegalovirus, measles and distemper viruses, and hepatitis viruses as capable of stimulating autoimmune diseases and - specifically - the frequent use of MLV vaccines for parvovirus, distemper, hepatitis, Lyme's disease, Bordetella and rabies.

In plain English, if your dog has underlying thyroid disease, a vaccine can trigger other life-threatening diseases. The problem with thyroid disease is that it often goes undetected. Coat loss, hormonal imbalances (irregular seasons), behavioural problems . . these and other conditions can be symptoms of thyroid disease but they are usually treated at face value without establishing the underlying cause.

Interestingly, thyroid disease is said to be 'inheritable'. This means it is caused by something, and is then passed down the line; there is a fine but important difference between inherited and inheritable.

Homoeopaths have contended for many years that vaccines go into genetic memory and cause problems for offspring. The correct homoeopathic term for this is `miasm'. It can legitimately be argued that vaccines cause thyroid disease, which gets passed down the line and then makes progeny more susceptible to autoimmune diseases triggered by vaccines: a self-defeating circle in the real sense of the word.

In yet another paper, Dr Dodds stated: "Immune-suppressant viruses of the retrovirus and parvovirus classes have recently been implicated as causes of bone marrow failure, immune mediated blood diseases, haematological malignancies (lymphoma and leukaemia), dysregulation of humoral and cell-mediated immunity, organ failure (liver, kidney), and autoimmune endocrine disorders - especially of the thyroid gland (thyroiditis), adrenal gland (Addison's disease), and pancreas (diabetes). Viral disease and recent vaccination with single or combination modified live virus vaccines, especially those containing distemper, adenovirus 1 or 2 and parvovirus, are increasingly recognised contributors to immune-mediated blood diseases, bone marrow failure, and organ dysfunction."

You can imagine my alarm when I first read Jean Dodds' papers. If you listen to most vets, they will tell you that vaccines are perfectly safe, have passed rigorous safety checks, etc., etc., but they won't tell you that a vaccine is capable of causing death: leukaemia, bone marrow failure, organ failure, diabetes, and so on. But, of course, reactions like these are very, very rare. Aren't they?

According to one vaccine manufacturer, only 15 dogs had suffered adverse vaccine reactions in three million of their administered doses. If the vaccine manufacturer is right, then the probability of one of my six dogs experiencing a vaccine reaction is about five in a million. The chances of three of my dogs having a vaccine reaction is about one in fifty billion tera-doses. Six out of six, like three out of six, is mathematically impossible. So someone is mistaken.

- Chappie: thyroid disease.
- Sophie: arthritis.
- Prudence: leukaemia.
- Oliver: paralysis and death.
- Samson: autoimmune disease.
- Gwinnie: allergies.

You will find, as you read through this book, that there is substantial scientific evidence to show that all of the above diseases can be initiated by vaccines. Six out of six, and all diseases have been associated - by scientific heavyweights - with vaccine damage.

It must be invalid for a vaccine manufacturer to claim that its experience of fifteen reported reactions is representative of real life probability. For a start, the claim supposes that unless all reactions happen immediately after the jab, they don't exist. Mathematically speaking, my own experiences mean that the real probability, whatever it is, is vastly higher than the manufacturers care to admit. It is significant, however, that the veterinary vaccine manufacturers' adverse reaction admission is five times higher than that acknowledged in human reactions.

Of course, Dr Dodds listed other possible triggers for autoimmune disease. She wrote that sex hormones might play a part, advising dog owners not to vaccinate their bitches whilst pregnant or during or close to their seasons. She said that stress might play a role: don't vaccinate your dog while he's under stress (i.e., fresh from his mother and litter mates and introduced to new surroundings, or straight after heavy physical exercise).

Dr Dodds also mentions that nutritional influences might be involved in vaccine reactions: the diet might be nutritionally deficient or imbalanced, or the food might contain harmful chemical preservatives or toxins. She's right there - John and I have since changed our dogs to an entirely natural diet (real food rather than artificial pet food) and, as a consequence, we have managed to help our dogs overcome their disabilities. As I write, Chappie is a fifteen-year-old swinger, and Sophie is fourteen. Of course, they haven't been vaccinated since the truth flew our way, and this helps enormously.

Adverse drug reactions are another trigger - some drugs, such as some of the sulfa antibiotics, can be recognised by a genetically susceptible host as foreign invaders and trigger autoimmune disease.

Even the vaccine manufacturers themselves advise that successful vaccination relies upon a competent response from the dog's immune system, and that if the dog's diet is 'wrong', he may not be able to mount an immune response. Similarly, certain drugs, such as steroids, suppress the immune system, and these, too, can prevent the dog from responding adequately to the vaccine.

John and I, in our loss, were confused. Why, then, do vets recommend annual vaccination in the face of such risks? We had no idea that certain dogs might be genetically susceptible to vaccine-induced disease. Why did no-one warn us, and how do you know if your dog is at risk? In fact, what we find is the veterinary profession and vaccine manufacturers continually playing down the risk. According to most of them, vaccine reactions are very, very rare.

We spoke to Chris Day, our homoeopathic vet. He told us that, in his opinion, the damage caused by vaccines might now outweigh the good the vaccines are doing. Dr Dodds explained that killed vaccines might be safer - but MLV vaccines were cheaper for the manufacturer to produce and appeared to last longer. Chris also introduced us to the homoeopathic nosode, a safer alternative to vaccines - more of this later.

By a series of chance coincidences I was introduced to a lady called Sally Cronk. Sally had lost a dog - Sadie - to autoimmune Haemolytic anaemia and was on the same trail as us. She, too, had seen Jean Dodds' work and was raising money to help the Royal Veterinary College study the harrowing disease that took Sadie. Sally introduced us to other people who had experienced the devastation we had experienced. All of us were asking questions about vaccines and photocopying articles and sending them around to each other.

But all of us, with few exceptions, were being stonewalled by the veterinary establishment. Ordinary vets and August bodies were denying the vaccine-autoimmune disease connection. Very few vets seemed to be prepared to stand up and say what they thought about vaccines, others appeared not to know the risks.

Remember, we had our own experience to go by, and we also had a growing group of friends whose dogs had suffered - they thought - from the prick of the needle. June Goose had experienced horrendous grief and loss due, she thought, to vaccines. Hylda Reynolds had lived through a nightmare with her dog Jamie. People were writing to the vaccine manufacturers, and their fears about vaccines were often flatly denied. Vets were using strong words in defence of vaccines, saying our dogs would die without them and we would be irresponsible to take the risk of not vaccinating. And all the while, the suspected damage was being denied or - we thought - under reported.

As business people, John and I immediately suspected some sort of cover up was going on to protect commercial interests. Sai Baba, the Indian Avatar, said: "Greed is the seedbed of grief", and I had a feeling that he was right. We felt that independent research was needed: research that could only be conducted by dog lovers for their dogs; by the people who had nothing to lose, either financially or professionally, if vaccines were found to be more harmful than helpful. We started a group called Canine Health Concern and invited dog lovers from around the world to take part in independent research.

We didn't, however, just set out to test vaccines. We wanted to test all the areas implicated in our dogs' sorry state: diet, environment, chemicals, stress . . . a massive questionnaire was the result. We contacted veterinary colleges across the country, asking for support. They told us to go away.

We contacted individual vets: vets who had bees in their bonnets about their own specialised areas. Vets who blamed processed pet food; vets who blamed in-breeding for the show ring; vets who eschewed modern pharmaceuticals and favoured 'alternative' therapies instead. Eventually, we had an impressive team of vets from around the world, all with their own theories, plus alternative practitioners, as well as behaviourists who would help us to test the stress theory.

The next step was to enlist the support of dog lovers and get them to take part. We thought that this would be the easiest part - but it turned out to be the hardest. To begin with, we were relying upon the dog magazines to help us reach the public and tell them what we were trying to do. With few exceptions, we found that the dog magazines weren't interested. Ostensibly billed as magazines for people who loved dogs, it soon became clear that the magazines were reliant upon big business for their survival. Without advertising revenue, the magazines would fold - and if they published the theories CHC was testing, the advertising revenue would, we thought, soon dry up. And would they be sued if they published our questions, based upon maverick veterinary opinion?

Even when we did manage to get publicity for the research, dog lovers simply weren't taking an interest in the numbers we required. We were getting nowhere. Ordinary dog lovers didn't know what we were on about. After all, if you have one dog and he dies of an autoimmune disease, you just think you're unlucky. It's not until you have several dogs and they all start dying or getting ill that you begin to believe something is going on. We found that the people whose lives had been touched by the tragic early demise of a much-loved pet sometimes responded. But we also needed healthy dogs to compare them against, otherwise the research would be limited.

So I decided to write a book to explain to dog lovers why this research was so crucial. In it, I intended to explore each of the theories: diet, vaccines, genetics, environmental chemicals, pharmaceuticals, stress . . . but the vaccine issue itself jumped up and shouted at me: there was no single source of information concerning the pros and cons of vaccination for pet owners. And vaccination, it seemed from the research material I was gathering, was probably the most significant destructive factor in our pets' health.

Also, there seems to be an awful lot of passion, bigotry and bias surrounding vaccination, and it is so dreadfully easy for people to make up their minds without knowing all the facts. Ask someone who has seen a dog die of distemper whether the vaccine regime should be changed: they will invariably answer no. Ask a typical vet who believes that vaccines have halted epidemics. And then ask someone whose dog died of autoimmune haemolytic anaemia or heart failure within hours or days of their annual booster shot.

We all of us want the best for our dogs - but the question is, what is best? I have to admit a certain bias: I would no longer be party to vaccinating another dog; neither would I allow myself to be vaccinated, nor any child I loved. Whilst running away from deadly human and canine diseases, I believe we have created and caused other diseases in their place - diseases that are no less horrendous and tragic than the diseases we first tried to prevent.

Worse, when our dogs are killed by a vaccine, we are rarely able to answer that question, 'why?'. It's not as though we can say that our dogs picked up a virus and died. Instead, we have to say that for some inexplicable reason, our dog had a fit and died, or his back legs were paralysed and he died, or he died of cancer or leukaemia. But we don't know what caused these things - except that some scientists do, but they aren't letting on; or maybe the men and women in the street don't have ears to hear.

But there are many people like me who want to avoid the mistakes of the past; who want to ensure the best possible health for their new dogs.

Since the first edition of this book was published, I have been made aware of other species that are also being killed by vaccines. Cat owners, like dog owners, are encouraged to vaccinate annually against panleukopenia, calcivirus, rhinotracheitis, leukaemia, FIVS, FIP and rabies in some countries. Horses must be vaccinated in order to compete in events - often as frequently as every six months. Depending upon the local risk, horses will be vaccinated against potomic horse fever, flu, Eastern/Western/Venezuelan influenza, rhino, Lyme, strangles and rabies. So distressed are some horse owners at the reactions they're seeing, that I have been told that they are paying vets handsomely to go around issuing certificates whilst squirting the vaccines down the drain.

As I write, an advisory panel sits in the UK to decide whether pet owners are to be forced, by law, to vaccinate their pets against rabies every year. I present to you here overwhelming evidence to explain why this legal compulsion would be immoral, and why animals in countries where vaccination is mandatory are being unfairly treated.

Vets and scientists tell us that only a tiny minority of dogs (and horses and cats and humans) suffer adverse vaccine reactions. I want them to realise what the words 'tiny minority' mean to the people and animals who vaccines have harmed. Besides which, as this book will show, it is not a tiny minority. Annual vaccination is causing far-reaching and widespread damage to countless individuals - individuals who are innocent and do not deserve to be the victims of greed.

Vets and vaccine manufacturers, as stated earlier, tell us that only a tiny minority of 'organisms' suffer adverse reactions to vaccines. Perhaps because the risk is thought to be tiny, the average pet owner who visits the vet is rarely warned of the risks associated with vaccination. Vets, however, are advised by the vaccine manufacturers that adverse reactions might occur if:

* the dog is genetically defective
* there is something wrong with the dog's diet
* the dog was unhealthy when vaccinated
* the dog was stressed at the time of injection
* the dog's immune system is incompetent
* the dog is exposed to the virus within a given time frame before or after vaccination
* the dog is taking immune-suppressive drugs
* the vet stores and handles the vaccine inappropriately
* a puppy still has maternal antibody in his system, which could interfere with the effectiveness of the vaccine.

These bullet points were taken (and translated) from vaccine manufacturers' own data sheets.

In fact, the Merck Manual, the doctors' bible, goes further. If you put on your Sherlock Holmes hat and do a little sleuthing, you will discover why it is that humans and animals react to vaccines in so many different ways.

Talk to most people about vaccine damage, and they will find it hard to understand how one little needle can produce epilepsy, arthritis, cancer, leukaemia, behavioural problems .

. . a whole myriad of different dis-eases. After all, it's not like pricking your finger and you bleed.

But, it seems, that the term, 'vaccinosis' (a morbid reaction to vaccines) is indeed a whole range of symptoms - and different people (animals or humans) can exhibit one, several, or even all of the symptoms as a direct result of vaccination.

The Merck Manual tells us that, "Patients with either B or T cell immunodeficiencies *should not be given live vaccines* because of the risk of vaccine-induced illness, and family members should not receive live polio virus vaccines."

So already we know that a class of people - with B and/or T cell immunodeficiencies - should simply not be given live virus vaccines; and this information comes from Merck, a vaccine manufacturer. The information contained here is not hedged in any way; it is not watered down by get-out clauses or the claim that reactions only happen in a minority of cases. Merck states, directly, that patients with B or T cell immunodeficiencies *should not receive live virus vaccines.* But how can you tell whether a patient (animal or human) has B or T cell immunodeficiencies?

Merck says, "Associated features of B cell deficiencies include respiratory or food allergies; features of T cell deficiencies include heart disease; and features of combined T and B cell deficiencies include dermatitis, neurological deterioration, and eczema".

This means that if your dog, cat or horse has allergies, heart disease, skin disease, or neurological problems, a live virus vaccine could present a serious threat to him. In fact, Merck takes this one stage further, and advises that children from families prone to these conditions should not be vaccinated with live virus vaccines. It states: "Children with known or suspected immunodeficiency diseases should not receive any live virus vaccines, since they could *initiate a severe or fatal infection* . . . Children receiving

14

immunosuppressive agents (corticosteroids, antimetabolites, alkylating compounds, radiation) may have aberrant responses to active immunization procedures . . . Children with fluctuating or progressive neurologic disease should not be immunised until their condition has been stabilised for at least one year."

In short, Merck advises that vaccines can initiate severe or fatal infection - to be precise, a vaccine can kill a child. As dogs, cats and horses also have T cells and B cells, and immunodeficiency diseases, it stands that vaccines can also kill them, too. You might ask, as I did, what these severe or fatal infections resulting from MLV vaccines might be - and this question will be answered throughout this book.

The question we must also all ask is, "how great is the risk?". Would it be safer to protect our animals against viral infection, or does the vaccine represent an equal or greater threat?

The trouble is, everyone I have spoken to confirms one thing: vets routinely vaccinate animals whether or not they have skin disease, heart disease, allergies, or are taking immunosuppressive drugs. At the top of most vaccine data sheets (issued by the manufacturers), vets are advised to vaccinate healthy animals only. But vets routinely vaccinate unhealthy animals. In countries where rabies vaccination is mandatory, the owners must become criminals if they refuse to play Russian roulette with their friends' lives. And all the while, the authorities yawn at our concerns while those who make money from vaccines obscure the evidence upon which informed choices can be made.

As an example of this deliberate obscuration, *Veterinary Practice Nurse* published an article in 1996, written by a vaccine manufacturer, saying, "Despite scaremongering amongst certain canine journalists, there is no evidence for the mythical disease coined 'vaccinosis' in boosted dogs, and there is no evidence of harm in any breed of cat or dog from giving a full booster every year'.

As Merck has shown us, this is a fundamental untruth - an untruth that misleads professional caregivers who subsequently mislead their clients. Could it be that the vaccine manufacturer is unaware of even the most basic information? And if so, is this not negligence? Or does this type of propaganda have a more sinister backdrop?

'Veterinary Review', again in 1996, published another article to promote vaccinations. In it the author wrote: "Small animal vaccinations are a vital contributor to practice income. . . Do you **ALWAYS** point out to clients when being consulted about some other matter that their animal is not vaccinated or its booster is overdue? Do your nurses **ALWAYS** ask about previous vaccinations when accepting animals for routine surgery and dentals? . . . Watch out for non verbal signals (body language) by yourself or your staff that YOU think full vaccination of cats is expensive, and don't decide in advance what your client wants. Give them the message, but don't get "heavy", and let them decide. You may well be surprised.

"As well as booster reminders, manufacturers will provide all manner of printed personalised material to send to your clients. The impact may not be massive, but it won't cost you much! . . . Have you got your own practice video playing in the waiting room? The impact of television is massive, use it to get your own message across. Vaccine manufacturers can be persuaded to sponsor your own video, as they clearly see the benefit of this form of communication. If you experience a local outbreak of disease, make sure the local press know about it. Write them an article.

"The vaccination fees of differing practices will be sought by a small proportion of potential clients. The wisdom of being the cheapest is debatable. Do you want to attract the clients who are primarily or only interested in cost? How many 'new' sales will you gain by competitive charging and will they offset your reduced profit? . . . Therefore the fee for vaccination should be at least your normal consultation fee plus the cost price of the vaccination used plus your normal markup plus VAT . . . It may be reasonable to make a small reduction where more than one animal is vaccinated, but don't undervalue your time."

We all need to realise that vaccines represent a significant source of income for vets, and we all need to bear this in mind when they advise boosters. Alongside this, we need to understand that vets are not taught to look for vaccine reactions. As far as they are concerned, a vaccine reaction is where the dog falls down and dies immediately after the jab. No-one has told them that chronic diseases can be vaccine-induced.

A system exists in England whereby vets must notify the Veterinary Medicines Directorate if they suspect an adverse reaction to a drug. Most countries have similar schemes. However, the whole scheme in the UK hinges on the word 'suspect'. This means that, for example, if a dog has an epileptic fit within 20 minutes of being vaccinated, but the vet doesn't know that the vaccine can cause epilepsy, then he will not report this coincidence to the Veterinary Medicines Directorate. Worse, if a dog develops, say, arthritis within nine months of being vaccinated, the vet is highly unlikely to suspect a link between the vaccine and the disease, and will consequently fail to report the 'reaction' to the VMD. Canine Health Concern's vaccine survey, however (detailed in chapter eleven), shows that arthritis typically develops in dogs - in a cluster - nine months after a vaccine event.

It is my contention that vaccine reactions are grossly under-reported, and highly unlikely to be diagnosed in the first place. Recently in America, when a group of dog owners got together to sue a vaccine manufacturer, the court demanded that the vaccine company's records be made available for scrutiny. It was discovered that the vaccine company was under-reporting known vaccine reactions by a factor of ten. And what about all the reactions the company didn't know about because the vet was so ignorant of the potential adverse reactions that he didn't think to report them?

Indeed, interim results from the Canine Health Concern vaccine Survey show - scientifically - that as many as one in every hundred dogs has an adverse reaction to vaccination. This reaction can be sickness and diarrhoea, all the way through to chronic (long lasting) disease such as arthritis and epilepsy, and it can also be death. So now study the evidence, and make your own informed choice.

But before doing so, consider this: the first edition of this book was published in February 1997. By April of the same year, a vaccine had claimed the third of my special friends. Samson died, aged five, on April 12th, 1997. If you notice a little anger as you read through these pages, please forgive me. You see, Samson, Oliver and Prudence all fell into the category described by Merck - they should never have been given live virus vaccines. Nobody told me, and only a small elite knew. All the canine vaccine manufacturers choose to share with us, and with vets, is the phrase, 'immunocompetence may be compromised by a variety of factors'. Is that good enough when the result could be death?

Having read the first edition of this book, some people have said that they will no longer give their pets annual booster shots - because it is neither necessary nor safe. But they wonder whether, perhaps, they should give the puppy jabs and the first year's booster because, understandably, they want to give their pets some modicum of protection. Sammie died to tell you that *this is all it takes*.

When Samson was a tiny puppy, we took him to the vet for his second puppy shot. The next day we found him lying in the garden with paralysed rear legs and dysentery. In those days we had no idea that vaccines could do this to anyone. We were still reeling from Oliver's death, and we thought - Oh God! - that Samson was going the same way. So because we didn't know that vaccines could do this, I went running round the neighbouring farms, asking if anyone had put poison down.

But Sammie recovered, and the next year he went off for his booster - because we loved him, and wanted to protect him. When we awoke the next morning, Sammie was running around the house screaming, his head swollen to the size of a large football. We rushed him to the vet where he was given an injection and, again, it never occurred to us that the vaccine might be involved. Before the next booster, we thankfully had attended Chris Day's surgery, and Sammie was never vaccinated again. But the damage had been done.

Previously, when Prudence died, I panicked, and had all the living dogs checked-over by Chrissie Mason, a radionics practitioner. Sammie, on the surface, seemed a perfectly healthy two-year-old, but Chrissie's analysis caused her enough concern to recommend a blood test. When the results came back we were horrified to discover that our apparently healthy dog had autoimmune disease. Chris Day phoned with the results, saying, "his immune system is waging a war with itself".

Intensive homoeopathic and nutritional therapy ensued. Blood tests were taken regularly, and we seemed to be winning the battle. Meanwhile, Sammie endeared himself to my heart - he with gigantic heart and brain. Then one day, when Samson was five, John came back from the morning walk with a worried look on his face. "Sammie isn't right," he said. "He was lagging behind on the walk".

Most dog owners wouldn't think too much of this - but I burst into tears. My inner Self knew exactly what was to come. I've made you cry enough; suffice to say that Sammie had an enormous cancer on his spleen and he had an emergency operation to remove his spleen. Again we thought we'd won the battle. Christmas came and went, and Sammie seemed happier than he had been for months. But then he stopped eating, and then he died.

All it took was one puppy shot - paralysed rear legs and dysentery - followed by one booster - hypersensitivity reaction - to set Sammie up for an early death. Samson was killed the day a vaccine destroyed his immune system.

Over the past few years, I have spent many hours on the telephone, listening to people sob their hearts out while they tell me how their dogs died. Many of us take years to come to terms with the unnecessary and cruel death of a very special friend. Since the publication of the first edition, I have spent even more time on the phone listening to people sobbing. So numerous have these calls become, that many of the 'victims' have joined forces to help counsel others whose experience they share. We have formed an international network, with the aim of warning others of the dangers that the so-called 'experts' will not voice.

For we have a right to know the truth. It is wrong that 'experts' should make decisions on our behalf, accepting that a proportion of all dogs, horses, cats and humans will suffer adverse vaccine reactions. Life should not be measured by scientists in terms of numbers. And no-one should take it upon themself to hide the full truth knowing that others will have their lives shattered as a result.

I want vets to know what 'a tiny minority' really means. Not because I am blaming anyone, but because the truth has the power to set us all free. Science can do as it wishes and go its way without emotion, but it is my contention that emotion - in its highest form of love - is the driving force behind all life. Science, after all, is there for the benefit of man, and not the other way round - and human beings have no other purpose except to love. All else is vanity.

Animals mean a great deal to people. As Chief Seattle wrote: "What is man without the beasts? If all the beasts were gone, man would die of great loneliness of Spirit, for what happens to the beasts soon happens to man. All things are connected."

The aim of this book is to help a consumer revolution along its way; a revolution that is happening all over the world, in every sphere. This revolution says that consumers - ordinary people - are not stupid, and they have a right to know the truth. This truth is very often, in fact invariably, obscured by the big businesses who hold the advertising budgets and the sponsorship money and the research grant purse strings. We believe, more often than not, what scientists say - but I have discovered that scientists regularly say what they are paid to say, and others are too frightened to step outside the accepted norm.

For this reason, a book exposing the dangers of vaccination has had to come from an 'ordinary dog lover': someone who can't be hounded out of business for upsetting the status quo. But it has also received the support and practical help of very many scientists and vets.

You may, after reading this book, decide to continue vaccinating your dog each year. This is your choice - but at least it will be an informed choice. As I look back over the years, and mourn for Oliver, Prudence, and Samson, I am convinced of one fact: we should at least be told.

Summary:

* MLV vaccines should not be given to those with B and/or T cell immunodeficiencies
* MLV vaccines should not be given to those with allergies, skin disease, heart disease, neurological problems
* MLV vaccines can stimulate autoimmune diseases
* In addition to 'faulty genes', environmental factors can render vaccines harmful
* Vaccines can overwhelm even a healthy host if negative environmental factors exist
* We question the assertion that only a tiny minority of animals are affected
* Vets have not been taught the full truth about vaccines

Your notes

Chapter One

The principle of vaccination

The following words appeared in Dog World (UK) magazine on June 28th, 1996. They were written by Steve Dean, a vet.

My final letter is from a lady worried by all the scaremongering about vaccination. At the risk of suffering the wrath of the homoeopathy lobby, let me set her mind at rest. There is no evidence which suggests that annual booster vaccines produce disease in normal healthy dogs.

Some breeds and individuals have a predisposition to disorders of the immune system which vaccines may trigger; however these are in the tiny minority.

My reader rightly states that distemper is now rare, as is hepatitis, and they are so because of the tremendous success of the vaccines. In fact parvovirus is also dwindling for similar reasons. It is against this background of low incidence that other schemes such as homoeopathic nosodes flourish, for if there is no infection then even water will work!

I have, however, seen the results of a distemper outbreak in a rural community where vaccination was allowed to lapse, and it was not a happy event. In addition, kidney disease is still a major problem in dogs and I would lay money on the likelihood that leptospirosis is the chief criminal in this.

So stop vaccinating if you wish but be prepared to suffer the consequences in years to come.

My reader is, however, more reasonable than this. She asks is every other year sufficient? Yes for distemper, hepatitis and parvovirus, but not for leptospirosis. Is it harmful to vaccinate old dogs over ten years - no, in fact they probably need boosters as much as any dog as they become more vulnerable to disease as they get old.

It may well be that we can expect lifelong vaccination for some of the classic diseases, like distemper and hepatitis, some time in the future and I am on record as saying we should look into this possibility. However with current knowledge, we would still need to boost immunity to leptospirosis annually. A final comment in this reader's letter intrigued me: "I have just heard that there used not to be boosters at all after initial jabs!" Who invents such misinformation I do not know.

The problem has always been getting people to have booster vaccinations for their dogs. They were always recommended. In my earlier veterinary years the uptake on boosters was less than 25 per cent and now it is much better. Perhaps that is why we see so little of the classic diseases in the modern dog in the UK.

However, whichever way you look at it, this triumph over disease is because of effective vaccines, which I use for my dogs annually, and so far not an autoimmune symptom to be seen in any of them.

Steve Dean will, I hope, forgive me for using him as the representative of the veterinary world, but his views are pretty standard for the average vet. Dog owners whose dogs suffered reactions to vaccines might disagree with him. Others, who have heard the 'rumours' about the dangers of vaccines, will perhaps be comforted by Mr Dean's words. Others, still, who are about to bring their puppy home and wish to do the best for him, will perhaps be interested in the issues surrounding vaccination. Others, of course, will simply trust the experts who - it must be said - tend to treat dog owners like mushrooms: keeping us in the dark and throwing manure at us from time to time.

So, unlike Steve Dean and some vets, I - a fellow mushroom - will attempt to throw some light upon the whole vaccine issue. In the clear light of day, we shall be better able to protect our dogs from unnecessary disease.

Why vaccinate?

It is most likely that the majority of all vets are currently in favour of vaccination. The arguments for vaccination are straightforward: they protect against some mild diseases and some deadly diseases. The vast majority of doctors and vets believe that vaccines prevent or control the outbreak of viral epidemics. Historical statistics are used to prove that vaccines are efficacious, and that vaccines control disease.

Vaccination in England was born in 1798, when Edward Jenner discovered that those who worked close to cows didn't get smallpox. He found that if you inject cowpox into humans, the humans were prevented from getting smallpox (although I have to tell you that Edward Jenner's son was one of his father's first guinea pigs, and he died of tuberculosis at the age of 21; his son's friends, who were also involved in the experiment, also died in their twenties). But the medical profession was delighted with the concept of miracle vaccines and, soon, the human race had the benefit of typhoid vaccines, tuberculosis vaccines, diphtheria, tetanus, influenza, polio and other vaccines.

At the time of the American Civil War, Louis Pasteur discovered that it was possible to attenuate (render less harmful) bacteria, and produce vaccine in quantity. Pasteur put on a public display in June 1881, when twenty-five sheep, six oxen and a goat were vaccinated in public. A few days later they were publicly inoculated with virulent anthrax bacteria, along with another twenty-five sheep, four cows, and a second goat, none of whom had been given the protective vaccination. A few days after this, there was another public gathering, and the onlookers saw that all the unprotected animals were dead or dying of anthrax, whilst all those that had been vaccinated were healthy. (*Cured to Death*, Melville and Johnson)

Pasteur thus gave a boost to anti-infective medicine: immunology. Vaccines were considered to be of inestimable value. Indeed, it is claimed that the great diseases which ravished Africa and Asia may well have exacted far more death than is the case, were it not for vaccines. This point is quite interesting considering Pasteur's historically documented last words, uttered on his deathbed. He said:

"Seed is nothing, soil is everything," meaning the germ is nothing, the host's resistance is everything.

However, Dr Viera Scheibner - an eminent scholar who fights against the vaccine regime - comments: "This example cannot be accurate. The vaccinated animals could not have been perfectly healthy at that time. It is known that administration of vaccines is followed by the so-called negative phase (Wright, A.E., 1901 - on the changes effected by antityphoid inoculation in the bacterial power of the blood. *Lancet*, September 14). It is quite possible that he might have switched the unvaccinated for the vaccinated animals. Pasteur was a well-known plagiarist and swindler."

There is substantial research material available to support the belief that vaccines are harmful. Indeed, researchers have contentiously shown that:
* Vaccines do not prevent disease or immunise, *they sensitise.*
* Vaccines cause encephalitis, an inflammation of the brain.
* Encephalitis has many diverse symptoms, ranging from acute to chronic.
* Vaccines are deadly poisons.
* Vaccines can cause the diseases they are designed to prevent.
* Vaccines are shed into the environment, spreading disease.
* Vaccines disarm the immune system.
* Vaccines unbalance the immune system

Our starting point - The Merck manual - tells us that vaccines can cause or exacerbate encephalitis (inflammation of the brain), epilepsy, skin disease, behaviour problems (from brain damage), and autoimmune diseases (which include Addison's disease, rheumatoid arthritis, Hashimoto's thyroiditis, Lupus, haemolytic anaemia, chronic active hepatitis, diabetes mellitus, Grave's disease,

Hypoparathyroidism, skin inflammations, Uveitis, and other immunologic eye diseases).

And yet despite this, vets and doctors routinely deny that what we - the parents and animal guardians - see as vaccine reactions, are anything to do with vaccines. I have coined this malady, "vaccine-associated ostrich disease". If we cannot make them acknowledge or even see it, then we must become informed ourselves, and decline their invitation to the needle.

Summary

* Vaccines are designed to protect from viral and bacterial disease
* Pro-vaccinators claim that vaccines have halted epidemics
* Anti-vaccinators claim that vaccines can cause the diseases they are designed to prevent
* Anti-vaccinators, and The Merck Manual, say that vaccines can cause other life-threatening diseases
* Many vets claim that annual booster vaccinations are necessary.

Chapter Two

Adverse reactions to vaccination - case studies

Many dog, cat and horse owners have reported adverse reactions to vaccination. A few examples are included here, with explanations, and many similar examples are included in chapter nine. These case stories are not exhaustive - it was necessary to draw a line when the same sorry story cropped up time after time. When I speak at seminars, I can see the coins dropping, as people realise that their animals and children - who first became ill shortly after vaccination - are victims of vaccinosis.

I have grouped the reactions together under general headings because this illustrates an emerging pattern. However, many of the animals exhibited a range of symptoms. Because 'vaccinosis' (a morbid reaction to vaccines) is not generally recognised by the average conventional vet, many of the vets cited have failed to establish a link between the vaccine and the reaction. This may be because the vaccine and the reaction were, indeed, not connected, or it may be due to the fact that, not expecting a link, no link was sought. It took humanity, after all, 85 years to link death and observed side-effects to the smallpox vaccine.

The following case studies cannot be held up as scientific evidence - not, at least, in the conventional sense. Science requires controlled studies, and these examples were not controlled. However, they do represent real life experiences which, I contend, are valid for the purposes of observation. In fact, it is my view that personal experience is more valid than science would have us believe - because it is glaringly clear that scientific research is only as good as the way it was conducted and the people who know about it!

Importantly, all reactions illustrated here occurred within minutes, hours, or a few days of vaccination - and there comes a point where coincidence must become evidence. Besides which, there is plenty of scientific research to show that the reactions listed here have, indeed, been positively associated with vaccine damage.

Many, many cases of suspected vaccine reaction cannot be included because the reactions occurred weeks or even months after the vaccine, although there is evidence that delayed reactions are possible.

Anaphylactic shock/hypersensitivity/allergic reactions:

Mrs JR Briggs took her miniature Dachshund for her annual booster each year with no problems until she was four years old. The dog was vaccinated in the morning and by late afternoon she was rubbing her face on the carpet. She was very hot, and her face was swollen. Mrs Briggs took the dog back to the vet who gave the dog an injection and said that she had been stung by a wasp. "I was not convinced," says Mrs Briggs, "and asked him if it could have been the vaccination. He said no."

Mrs Briggs chanced the booster again the next year, explaining to the vet what had happened the year before. By the afternoon, the same symptoms repeated themselves. Bonnie was rushed back to the veterinary surgery, where the vet agreed this time that it must have been the annual booster. Bonnie still lives, and Mrs Briggs counts herself very lucky. The dog will not be vaccinated again.

The homoeopathic vet Peter Gregory tells of a cat who started sneezing five days after her booster. She had persistent respiratory problems, runny eyes, and ulcers on her eyes for a year until she received homoeopathic treatment for vaccinosis. She is now free of symptoms.

Ann Townsend routinely had her top show ponies vaccinated against equine flu and tetanus. During 1998, her pony was clearly ill on the morning following his vaccination. He had a massive oedema the size of a honeydew melon on his neck, he was dejected and off his food. In spite of being given antibiotics and anti-inflammatories, the pony did not respond. Ann says, "He wasn't able to put his head or neck down so he couldn't graze, roll or lie down; this lasted for four weeks and everything had to be fed at chest height or above."

The oedemas spread to various parts of his body and, at one stage, Ann says he had legs like an elephant. He had lost 40kgs (10%) of his body weight, which Ann says frightened her rigid. He then developed signs of liver and kidney failure and was showing the early signs of jaundice. Ann was despairing at this stage, as nothing in the conventional medicine chest was making an impact. Ann turned to Indian Herbs, and the pony started to improve, although the neck oedema took three months to disappear completely.

Ann says, "I was involved in direct conversations with the veterinary advisors of the vaccine company, but I was less than satisfied with what I was told. They couldn't guarantee that, having had a violent reaction this time, he wouldn't have one again. I was told that the risk of such a reaction, from the results of their clinical tests, was only one in ten thousand. But when I asked about the control sample used in their tests, this meant that just 0.04 of a horse showed a reaction. I questioned the validity of the statistics quoted to me. Either a whole horse shows a reaction or it doesn't! At the time my pony was so desperately ill, I knew of three other animals in different parts of the country which were in a similar state as a result of their annual vaccination, and I have to say that my circle of friends does not extend to 30,000 people yet I know of four cases of seriously ill animals.

"Subsequent research has revealed that many horse owners have experienced similar problems in recent years. It seems that the adjuvant of the vaccine, which makes it work more effectively, had to be strengthened as a result of an equine flu outbreak in vaccinated horses. The boosted adjuvant was, it seems, the reason behind the increased incidence of adverse reactions even in animals previously exposed to the same sort of vaccine."

Mushroom Commentary

Anaphylactic shock and/or hypersensitivity (allergic) reactions are well known by vets, vaccine manufacturers, and doctors as one possible sequel to inoculation. Vaccine manufacturers recommend that adrenaline be used in severe cases (to prevent the animal/human from dying). Indeed, medical practitioners, who are routinely vaccinated, always have adrenaline standing by for themselves.

As shall be explained later, anaphylactic shock and hypersensitivity reactions may be easily overcome by an organism; or they may lead to chronic (long lasting) disease; or they may result in death.

Most people whose dogs are vaccinated can, if they look, notice that their pets are 'under the weather' after vaccination. This is because the animal's body is doing what it should do: fighting the challenge presented by the vaccine. In the majority of cases it is assumed that the dog has made a full recovery and has become immune to the diseases he was vaccinated against.

Conversely, it is believed by some that the vaccine is capable of harming an organism by setting off an imbalance in the body that can cause diseases such as cancer, allergies, skin complaints, and so on, months or years later. Indeed, Christopher Day, Honorary Secretary of the British Homoeopathic Veterinary Association, has noticed that many dogs succumb (die), or display symptoms of chronic disease, within three months of vaccination (as happened to Oliver).

At present, most vets will discount the vaccine as a cause of disease if the reaction hasn't taken place within hours or one or two days of the jab, and they will often deny a link even when it has occurred immediately.

It is interesting to note here that the necessary research has not even been conducted where vaccines for humans are concerned. In an editorial in the *British Medical Journal* of 9

March 1996, it is stated that: "pre-licensure randomised placebo controlled trials are too small to detect rare events", and that current data are "inadequate to accept or reject a causal relation".

Indeed, the British Committee on Safety of Medicines stated, following a mass vaccination campaign in 1994, when seven million children were vaccinated in the national measles/rubella campaign: "serious reactions to the vaccine were very rare", but the Committee then admitted that 530 serious reactions had been reported. The parents of damaged children who had formed various action groups cited examples in the JABS summer newsletter that children had been paralysed and severely disabled for life by vaccines, but were not considered to be damaged enough to receive compensation from the Vaccine Damage Payment Unit. So the word 'rare' must be taken as a highly subjective word.

The Merck Manual states that, "children should not be given the DTP vaccine *again* if a child develops encephalopathy within 7 days; a convulsion within 3 days; persistent, severe, inconsolable screaming or crying for three hours or an unusual, distinctive, high-pitched cry within 48 hours; collapse or a shock-like state within 48 hours, and immediate severe or anaphylactic (allergic) reaction to the vaccine".

Epilepsy/fits:

On the 19th June 1993, Mrs B Grant's ten-week-old puppy received her first vaccination. Six hours after the jab, the puppy sat up on her bed. Mrs Grant thought the puppy was being sick as there was saliva on her mouth. The second vaccine was administered on the 3rd of July. Thirteen hours later, the puppy sat up on her bed again. Her front legs were stiff and, once again, Mrs Grant thought she had been sick. However, the longer it went on, Mrs Grant began to think that the puppy was having a fit. Her husband disagreed. The puppy was taken to the garden before going to bed and she looked as if she was drunk.

The next morning, at 5.30, the puppy was yowling. When they went downstairs, the Grants found her staring at the wall. "She didn't seem to hear us coming into the room and the kitchen was a total mess," says Mrs Grant. "We presumed she had been fitting. Her front legs were wet through with saliva. We rang the vet and he told us he would meet us at the surgery at 8.30. He wondered if it could be vaccine related, and then he weighed her."

The vet gave the puppy Phenobarbitone tablets to take at home and charged the Grants £30. The puppy had four more apparent fits. Mrs Grant phoned the vet at 1pm and was told to double the tablet dose. She had five more fits and the vet called in at 5pm, saying he was in the area, and asked how the dog was.

The vet then left, telling the Grants to phone him if the puppy got any worse. He then rang at 9pm and told the Grants to take the puppy to the surgery at 10.30pm, and he and his wife took her home for observation. The vet returned the puppy the next day, saying that she only had two fits, but she was very agitated. The puppy slept for three hours and, on waking, was ravenously hungry but not thirsty.

At 7.30pm the puppy ran outside and stood rigid with her tail between her legs. She looked afraid. At 8.45pm she repeated this pattern, but passed a motion and shook. The same happened at 9.15pm. By 10.15pm she was rigid and producing a lot of saliva. She passed a motion, ran in circles, and snapped at a chair.

At 10.45 the same occurred, except she was running in circles snapping her jaws. At 12 noon the fits seemed to have disappeared, but the puppy was producing a lot of saliva and she was running around yowling and snapping. She reminded Mrs Grant of a rabid dog. At 12.35am she had a long fit, passed a motion, and snapped at Mr Grant. Another long fit followed at 1.05am, and she was still running around snapping.

At 2am Mr Grant rang the vet and asked him to fetch the dog. The vet offered to sedate her, took the dog away with him, and told the Grants to phone him the next day. When they did so, the vet advised them not to have the dog back as her temperament had completely changed and she was still snapping.

"We rang the vet on Wednesday," says Mrs Grant, "and told him to put the puppy out of her misery and suffering."

Mushroom Commentary

According to Merck, "Noninfectious causes of encephalitides (inflammation of the brain) include . . . vaccine reactions: many." Merck also states that epilepsy can be caused by, "CNS (central nervous system) infections (meningitis, AIDS, encephalitis . . .)"; and also by a foreign serum or drug allergy (vaccines contain serum), or by convulsive or toxic agents - and vaccines, as shall be explained later, contain a variety of toxic agents.

When you examine the other case stories relating to epilepsy and fits (found in chapter nine), you will see that the dogs became epileptic at different times after vaccination. This phenomenon is explained later by Hans Selye's 'Non-Specific Stress Syndrome'. The time differences can be accounted for by the fact that each organism has the ability, in greater or lesser degree, to mount a defence against an offending substance (such as a vaccine). A defence is mounted, the dog becomes exhausted, recuperates, and mounts another defence, and this cycle continues until the dog recovers, or develops a chronic disease (in this case epilepsy), or succumbs (dies). Time delays can therefore be accounted for by the fact that the animal or child is able to do battle against the vaccine to greater or lesser degree.

Differences in vaccine manufacture should also be considered.

Also bear in mind that modern vaccines - multiple live virus vaccines - are designed to multiply in the host. This is because vaccine manufacturers must tread a very fine line between attenuation and virulence (attenuation is where the vaccine is rendered harmless, and virulence is where the virus is active and will cause disease). Accordingly, MLV vaccines are designed to multiply in the host slowly, until such time as an immune response has been successful. Day ten appears to be a crucial day as far as many of our testimonies are concerned: it is quite possible that they have multiplied to the point where the host is overcome by them, rather than able to combat them. Alternatively, it could be because vaccines contain serum (blood product). Veterinary manuals talk openly about serum reactions ten days after administration.

In the case of long-term epilepsy, we shall demonstrate later that the vaccine has permanently damaged the dog's brain: epilepsy is essentially a neurological condition. Merck defines epilepsy as, "A recurrent paroxysmal disorder of cerebral function characterised by sudden brief attacks of altered consciousness, motor activity, sensory phenomena, or inappropriate behaviour caused by abnormal excessive discharge of cerebral neurons. Any recurrent seizure pattern may be termed epilepsy. Convulsions may recur at intervals if there is a permanent lesion or scar in the CNS (central nervous system), in which case a diagnosis of epilepsy is made."

Dr Jean Dodds lists epilepsy as an autoimmune disease. There is some evidence to say that epilepsy is an hereditary condition - but it is necessary to remember that not all genetically pre-disposed dogs develop the condition. There seems to be a tolerance threshold beyond which an organism succumbs to its genetic faults. Vaccines are known to be one such trigger. As Merck says, live virus vaccines should not be given to children (or dogs, cats, horses), who have, or are suspected to have, immunological deficiencies. These individuals are not suited for vaccines - MLV vaccines are not designed for them - and they shouldn't be given.

Recent British government research shows that the DTP (diphtheria tetanus pertussis) and MMR (measles mumps rubella) vaccines can increase the risk of seizure five-fold. Even thought the American government has been busy reassuring the country that the measles vaccine is perfectly safe, its Public Health Laboratory Service Statistics Unit has found that the combined two produced seizures three times more than was previously reported, and that the DTP schedule is responsible for a four-fold increase in seizures. (*What Doctors Don't Tell You*, vol 1, no 8.)

US evidence, incidentally, shows that the DTP vaccine caused convulsions in infants less than a year old, usually three days after they had been given the dose. The MMR vaccine took longer to cause convulsions - between 15 and 35 days afterwards. *The Lancet*, in 1989, reported that one in 400 children given the MMR vaccine will suffer convulsions; and in 1995, that children given the MMR jab were three times more likely to suffer convulsions than those who didn't receive it. It should be noted that the measles and distemper viruses are, to all intents and purposes, the same virus.

I don't know about you, but I often wonder why they continue to give these known convulsion-inducing agents. In the remarkable book by Neale Donald Walsch, entitled, 'Conversations with God', God says: "A lawyer's career would end tomorrow were there no more litigation. A doctor's career would end tomorrow were there no more illness. A philosopher's career would end tomorrow were there no more questions. We, all of us, have a vested interest in keeping the game going. Your medical establishment understands this. That is why it staunchly opposes - it must, it has to for its own survival - any new miracle drug or cure - to say nothing of the possibility of miracles themselves."

A paper prepared by AIP McCandlish, et al, and published in the *Veterinary Record* during 1992 (130, 27-30), says: "Post-vaccinal encephalitis is a recognised complication of the administration of certain strains of live attenuated canine distemper virus vaccine (Hartley 1974, Bestetti and others 1978, Cornwell and others 1988)." The paper describes a five-year-old Labrador bitch who had whelped 10 pups three days previously and was then given a booster vaccination against distemper, adenovirus, parvovirus, parainfluenza virus, and leptospirosis: "No abnormalities were noticed until the pups were 22 days old, when three of the litter developed nervous signs with crying or screaming, convulsions and twisting of the head and neck." Five of the pups were ultimately destroyed. The cause of the nervous disease was found to be canine distemper and the paper suggested that the vaccine rather than a field virus was responsible.

It seems strange to me that vets can discount the possibility that vaccines can cause epilepsy in dogs despite the published research - but this happens repeatedly in our case studies.

Animals contracting the disease they were vaccinated against:

Mrs Sue Boone had great plans for her Afghan puppy, Daniel. Sue had waited six years to buy another Afghan, as it had taken her this long to come to terms with the death of her previous and much-loved Afghan David. Sue says, "From the moment we met Daniel, we knew he was the right little boy for us. He had such a friendly, outgoing nature. He very quickly stole our hearts and made great friends with all of our other animals. Daniel was loved so much by everyone that it was a privilege to know that he was our little boy."

Sue and her husband Eddie took Daniel for his follow-up vaccination when he was twelve weeks old, along with the couple's older King Charles Cavalier Spaniel, George. The vet appeared quite distracted, talking about the ill health of a close relative. Eventually, Eddie asked the vet whether he was going to inoculate the older dog, and the vet showed surprise, thinking he had already done so.

Daniel was vaccinated on a Saturday, and by the Monday he was showing signs of being off colour. He was listless, lacking his usual vivacity, and refusing water. The couple telephoned the vet for advice, and were told it might be an adverse reaction to the vaccine. The vet suggested the Boones give the puppy glucose water. By Tuesday, Sue was getting very concerned. She telephoned Eddie at work and waited for him to come home. By the evening Daniel had bad diarrhoea. As their own vet wasn't on duty, they went to another vet who indicated that Daniel should be put down immediately. But Sue and Eddie persuaded the vet to treat Daniel, and he was left at the surgery on a drip, where he stayed for three days and nights. The Boones' own vet took over the treatment after the third day. The Boones took Daniel home during the night-time, but he was returned to the vet and put on a drip each day.

Sue and Eddie spent the next five weeks trying to keep Daniel alive. At his funeral Sue read out the following words: "We were all so very proud of Daniel and, in return, he gave us so much happiness, albeit for such a short time. We will never know why our little Daniel had to suffer this terrible illness. He always had the best of everything and he was never put at any risk. We were all so protective of him. Only God knows why Daniel was called to Heaven.

"We would like to offer our sincere gratitude to our vet and all of his staff for their help, support and kindness during the past five weeks. His door was open 24 hours each day for Daniel, and also for Daniel's brother Sebastian when he also came down with the parvovirus. Without the quick action of the vet and his staff, we could also quite possibly have lost little Sebastian. We would also like to thank all those people throughout the country who prayed and who lit candles for Daniel and Sebastian.

"For five long weeks, Daniel fought for his life. Some days he seemed so much better, other days we were filled with despair, but throughout all of this time, our little boy was so brave. He had so many drips put into his little legs that his veins collapsed and he could take no more. But he never complained and he always had a wag of his tail and a lick for everyone. When he was too weak to eat or drink, we fed him through a tube, and Daniel never offered to bite or become aggressive. He just put up with his lot.

"Daniel became too ill to play with his toys or his friends or his brother. He just sat on his chair and watched the world go by. Throughout his illness, we clung to the hope for Daniel's recovery. We really thought that he would make it, he fought so bravely and for so long that we just couldn't accept that he wouldn't pull through.

"We were therefore filled with desperation and despair when Daniel became so much worse during the early hours of Christmas Eve. We knew that our baby was losing his fight. He almost died in his daddy's arms, but once more we pulled him back to life. We knew then that we had to let our little boy go to heaven. His poor little body could take no more and we couldn't let him suffer any more. Our brave little fighter fell asleep in his mum's arms on Christmas Eve, 1993.

"We know that Daniel will not be alone, he will have David to play with in heaven. Such a tragic waste of a little life. We will never understand why it should happen to our little boy. We wanted to do so much with Daniel - to take him to shows and Afghan racing, and just to share our lives with him.

"Daniel will always remain in our hearts, thoughts and memories, along with David. We know that one day we will hold them both in our arms again. Until that day, we must say goodbye to Daniel. We love you so very much."

Sue discovered the truth after Daniel had been laid to rest by speaking with an eminent specialist at a university, where Daniel's blood samples had been sent whilst the Boones were trying to keep the puppy alive. Sue never received written confirmation of the information she received from the specialist, although she did receive a letter of sympathy from him. The specialist appeared originally to be suspicious of Sue's telephone call, but when Sue told him that she wasn't looking for revenge, that she just needed to know why Daniel had died, he became more lucid. Sue took notes.

As the man was originally unwilling to even speak to Sue, it didn't seem worthwhile contacting him to ask if I could quote him in this book. It has been my experience, while trying to find out why our dogs are dying, that science, far from being an open quest for the truth, is far more often a tight-lipped attempt to protect the status quo, professional status, and commercial interests. I have worked, instead, from the notes Sue took during her telephone conversation with the specialist.

Dr X told Sue that Daniel had contracted parvovirus from the vaccine. It is quite possible, although not proven, that the puppy received two inoculations in error (as the vet hadn't been concentrating). Nevertheless, a blood sample taken six days after inoculation showed that Daniel had in excess of 4,000 units of antibodies in his blood, more than double the number Dr X would expect. Dr X advised Sue that this total would be acceptable two weeks after the jab. Further, faeces tests showed that there was no parvovirus in Daniel's system.

Sebastian, Daniel's litter mate, contracted parvovirus from Daniel (he had been brought into the home during the initial days of Daniel's illness, as Sue had been advised that Daniel was only suffering from enteritis). The faeces tests also showed that there was no salmonella or enteritis in Daniel's system. Dr X advised Sue that Sebastian was showing classic signs of parvovirus, and that he would either fully recover or die; eight out of ten dogs survive parvovirus.

Dr X told Sue that Daniel did not show classic signs of parvovirus. He said that internal damage was very unlikely in 'normal' parvo. Sue had been told by her vet that Daniel had died of liver damage. Dr X refuted this, saying that Daniel died of a word Sue wrote down in her notes: `interception'. Dr X explained that this was where the bowel dissolves into the body because excessive parvo had eaten the bowel.

(I have been advised that Dr X was probably trying to explain that Daniel was suffering from intussusception, where the bowel telescopes into itself.)

Astoundingly, Dr X told Sue that when the results were known on the sixth day of illness, Daniel should have been put to sleep. He said that it was clear Daniel stood no chance, and he had never known a dog to go on for as long as five weeks. Dr X told Sue he had been an expert on parvovirus since the late 1970s, and that he could cure natural parvo, but not vaccine-induced parvo. Dr X felt that it was unethical of Sue's vet to allow her to pursue such a useless cause.

Sue had arranged for Daniel to be buried in a pet cemetery. However, when the cemetery staff went to collect Daniel from the vet's, they were advised that Daniel was now 'clinical waste' and could not be buried; he would have to be incinerated. When Sue mentioned this to Dr X, she was told that Daniel was not clinical waste, he could have been buried. Furthermore, he felt a post-mortem should have been carried out at his university.

Sue sent me a scrap book containing the shreds of Daniel's life. Photographs, letters from loving friends, vaccination certificates, diet sheets, get well cards, Daniel's pedigree, veterinary bills for medicines and emergency call-out charges, and a photograph of a strapping Daniel carrying a bone and pushing his way through a dog flap the day before the parvo injection. At the end, Sue had written: *"Why Daniel? We loved him so much."*

A vet, who has asked to remain anonymous, told me of a case where a cat contracted hepatitis shortly after vaccination. The cat was quickly hospitalised to undergo intensive treatment. After about six weeks, the cat recovered. The next year, at booster time, the vet discussed with the owner whether the cat should be vaccinated again, but because the owner was in contact with a lot of cats (although her own cats were kept indoors), she wanted to go ahead. Within a few weeks of the shot, the cat was down with hepatitis again but this time failed to respond to intensive treatment. "In my view," says the vet, "the vaccine caused hepatitis in this cat. I wanted to put in an adverse reaction report but the owner was too distraut, so it never got reported."

The anonymous vet explained that she wished to remain anonymous as she was opening her own practice and feared repercussions from new competitors who might take the opportunity to 'shop' her to the RCVS for not completing an adverse reaction report. "This is sad but true," she said, "and I do not want to commit professional suicide by providing them with ammunition. Hope you understand - unfortunately it's a political jungle out there and I HATE politics . . ."

The anonymous vet further added: "The RCVS Guide to Professional Conduct states . . 'All veterinarians should accept as a serious ethical obligation the reporting of suspected adverse reactions to medicinal products in both animals and man. Any observation which might lead to suspicion of an adverse reaction should be subject to careful professional judgment.' This is from the RCVS Guide, 1996, Chapter 4, Section 3, Paragraph 21 (p 77)."

Mushroom Commentary

A number of people have commented that they would rather risk the side-effects of vaccination than the terrible diseases we vaccinate against. It is therefore one of life's cruelest jokes that the vaccine itself should cause the disease, but, apparently, in an incurable form.

When an animal dies of a condition, or suffers the symptoms of a condition, he was vaccinated against, vets usually suggest that the animal must have been incubating the disease at the time of the jab; or that, in the case of young animals, maternal antibodies interfered with the vaccine's efficacy; or that the vaccine failed, and the animal subsequently went out and picked the virus up. Alternatively, it is possible that the animal is not suffering from the disease he was vaccinated against, but from some other condition. But there is another possibility: the vaccine has indeed caused the disease it was designed to prevent.

In fact, Tom R Phillips and Ronald D Schultz clarify this possibility for us in an article appearing in Current Veterinary Therapy XI, 1992: *"Incomplete vaccine attenuation or vaccination of an immunosuppressed host can result in modified live vaccines causing the disease they are designed to prevent. Examples of this problem are feline respiratory vaccines causing a mild upper respiratory tract disease after immunisation, and the development of post vaccinal encephalitis subsequent to canine distemper vaccination. An even more alarming example is vaccine induction of clinical rabies (Esh et al., 1982, Pedersen et al., 1978)."*

Daniel's short life has now revealed its meaning for Sue. He came to tell us that it is possible to give a puppy parvovirus from the vaccine. Dr X told Sue that there was one chance in a thousand of this happening. If this was an accurate, rather than a chance, remark, then the odds sound pretty high to me - the World Health Organisation contends that a one-in-ten-thousand reaction is too high where humans are concerned. Three years later, Sue cannot talk of Daniel without crying.

The Canine Health Concern telephone line is red hot these days. Dog lovers phone constantly to share their worries and experiences. One lady phoned in tears. She told me that her dog had received a faulty vaccine and that it induced distemper in him. He recovered, but not before infecting a puppy in the house. The puppy died, and the vaccine manufacturer admitted liability and paid the vet bills. Now, ten years on, this lady had another puppy in the home, and having seen distemper, she didn't want him to get it. So she vaccinated him.

She was crying because the puppy had stopped eating and was losing weight rapidly. The logic of all this confuses me: if the vaccine caused the disease, why did the lady vaccinate again because she was frightened of the disease? Personally, I'd have been more frightened of the vaccine. At the end of the conversation, she wailed: "And my pup's got to have his second shot next week, and I don't know what to do".

We are so brainwashed into thinking that we must vaccinate at all costs, that even though a dog shows signs of being unsuited to vaccines, we do it again and again . . . because a man in a white coat tells us we must.

Autoimmune diseases:

Mrs J Matless says that, although unconfirmed by her vet or the drug company, she feels her 10 month-old Springer Spaniel suffered a reaction to her vaccine. Ten days after her second injection, her eyes and face swelled up and she had a very high fever. The puppy was admitted to the veterinary hospital and after four days stabilised on antibiotics and high-dose steroids.

Some six weeks later, after considerable 'pushing' by Mrs Matless, 'auto-immune deficiency' was mentioned. The vaccine company paid for blood tests, and the results confirmed that Cassie had autoimmune disease. "I was told she would have to stay on steroids and must never be vaccinated again," Mrs Matless says. "What does that say?"

Today, Cassie is in good health; her medication has been reduced to quite a low dose. Mrs Matless has been told that Cassie won't make 'old bones'.

Mrs P Fox took her youngest Sheltie, then aged two, for his booster in June 1995. By the end of the evening, he appeared to be very ill and his condition worsened over the next few days. He was taken to the visit the vet, who confirmed that the dog was seriously ill with a temperature of 106.5°F.

Mrs Fox says that over the next few weeks it was 'touch and go', and the dog was referred to a veterinary college and hospitalised for two weeks. After numerous tests, the Sheltie was diagnosed as having immune-mediated polyarthritis, but it could not be proven that the vaccine was the cause of this.

The dog can now walk for three-quarters of an hour, but he never plays with Mrs Fox's other dogs and has great difficulty in standing up from the lying position. Mrs Fox says, "Before his booster he was a fit and active dog who loved nothing better than racing around and playing with my other dogs. The onset of his illness was so sudden following his booster that there is no doubt in my mind that the booster was the cause of it. He is still far from well and under medication. I have been in touch with the vaccine manufacturer - so far without success - although they say they are investigating the matter."

Mrs and Mrs M Roberts' beautiful cocker spaniel died one week after having his booster injection. He was boosted on the Friday, and became ill on the Monday evening. He was taken to the vet on Tuesday morning, and the vet told the couple that the dog had a very high temperature and a swollen spleen. A blood test was taken, revealing that his blood count was very low and that the red blood cells were breaking up. The vet administered steroids.

Mr and Mrs Roberts say that the dog deteriorated very rapidly from here, and the vet suggested a blood transfusion on Thursday, bringing his own dog into the surgery to donate the blood. However, the vet advised that the transfusion would only give the cocker a few days longer, and a match donor would need to be found to give the dog a better chance. Mrs Roberts says that her dog was in a very poor state at this stage, and the couple agreed that it would be kinder to have him put down. Although it was a terrible decision to have to make, they didn't want to see him suffer any more.

The dog was seven years old. He was diagnosed by the vet as having haemolytic anaemia. The couple suggested that the booster might have caused the condition, but the vet flatly denied this.

Mushroom Commentary

We know from Dr Dodds' work and The Merck Manual that vaccines can cause autoimmune diseases (where the immune system attacks itself). Speaking in 'Vet Med Today', the Journal of the American Veterinary Medical Association, Dr Ronald D Schultz, a top American immunologist, stated: "Immune-mediated disease has developed in human beings following vaccination, as was seen with cases of Guillain-Barre syndrome following swine flu vaccinations, and rheumatoid arthritis following influenza vaccination. In many cases it is impossible to show a direct connection between the damage and a vaccine, since it is the accumulation of many antigens over many years that results in clinically evident disease."

Merck, I think, can expand on this: "autoimmune diseases may be initiated by the encephalitis that can follow rabies vaccination in which an autoimmune cross-reaction probably is initiated by animal brain tissue in the vaccine". In fact, all sorts of vaccines in addition to the rabies vaccine are typically cultivated on dog, cat and monkey brains and kidneys; chick embryos, hamsters and guinea pigs - all of which can be described as 'foreign protein', which can cause an allergic reaction, autoimmune disease and encephalitis.

Further, the Merck *Veterinary* Manual confirms that modified live parvovirus vaccines are suspected to cause autoimmune haemolytic anaemia in dogs (an autoimmune disease).

Dr Schultz later goes on to state that, on the subject of over-vaccinating, "The client is paying for something with no effect or with the potential for an adverse reaction. I believe that adverse effects are increasing, because we are putting more and more components into these animals."

In a paper entitled, *"Effects of Vaccines on the Canine Immune System"* by Tom R Phillips, et al, published in *Can J Vet Res*, 1989, it is stated: " . . . the results of this study demonstrate that the majority of polyvalent canine vaccines significantly suppress lymphocyte responsiveness to PHA. . . . in certain circumstances, even a relatively short duration of suppression could become clinically significant especially if the animal was in a partially immunosuppressed condition (e.g. nutritional deficiency). . . This is the first report of individual vaccine components which are not immunosuppressive by themselves causing an immunosuppression when inoculated in combination. Thus, the results of this study may have implications for other species which receive polyvalent vaccines".

Translation: combined vaccines (distemper plus parvo plus adenovirus plus leptospirosis plus whatever else you want to throw in there) seem to work together to suppress the immune system temporarily and leave animals and humans open to disease.

International pharmaceutical concern, Merck, states in 'The Merck Veterinary Manual': "Some viruses induce immunological deficiencies, usually via effects on the bone marrow. Examples are human immunodeficiency virus (the cause of AIDS in man) . . . . . and human and canine parvoviruses . . .

"Bone marrow suppression with transient (21 day) or chronic/latent erythroid dysplasia in the presence or absence of thrombocytopenia and neutropenia, Coombs' positive haemolytic anaemia, and immune-mediated thrombocytopenia have been associated with (i.e., may prove to be caused by) both retroviral and parvoviral infections in man and other species. Also, *modified live parvovirus vaccines in dogs . . . are suspects as causes (in genetically susceptible animals) of such haematological diseases. (emphasis added)*

To translate for Merck, if a dog dies of an autoimmune disease, or contracts an autoimmune disease, shortly after vaccination, there is every reason to believe that this could have been caused by the vaccine. At the very least, for those who would prefer to blame 'irresponsible breeders', there is evidence to support the view that the vaccine contributed to the situation. Despite this, many of the vets quoted in the anecdotal evidence (here and later) claimed that there was no possible link between vaccines and autoimmune disease (although I concede that the dog owners could be misrepresenting the views of their vets). Do vets deny vaccine damage because they haven't been taught properly, or because vaccines represent around 40% of their practice income? After all, to be accepted to study in a veterinary college, you need to be academically pretty bright. Could it be that, armed with a qualification, most of us think there's no need to continue learning?

Another piece of evidence to confirm that autoimmune diseases can be initiated by vaccines is supplied by the insert within the Rabdomun rabies vaccine box. This states: "Because Rabdomun is produced on an established cell line, it has safety advantages over inactivated brain-origin rabies vaccines. *Tissue-origin vaccines contain extraneous protein in addition to rabies antigen that can lead to autoimmune disease."* *(emphasis added)*

I was put in touch with a Fellow of the Institute of Biological Sciences, a man who heads a pathology lab. The man, who has asked not to be named because he is frightened of upsetting his clients (vets) and thereby losing business, told me: "I have seen several cases of autoimmune haemolytic anaemia, some of which ended in death. This disease is not uncommon. What is striking about this disease is that it always seems to occur, in my experience, a day or so after vaccination.

"I have been in touch with the vaccine manufacturers, and they tell me that it is pure coincidence. This really irritates me, because they don't say 'that's interesting, we'll have to look into this,' they just flatly deny any connection.

"In my opinion, this instant denial is highly unscientific. I expect an open mind from my scientific peers - but the vaccine manufacturers won't even look. It's all down to money, of course. You can't beat them when there's so much money involved.

"As for the vets, they occasionally fill in an adverse reaction form, but you have to remember they're running a business and these forms take time. Anyway, the amount of time involved in an adverse reaction report is rarely rewarded because it only gets shelved by the drug company."

However, *The Journal of Veterinary Internal Medicine*, Vol 10, No 5 (September-October) 1996, published a paper entitled: *"Vaccine-Associated Immune-Mediated Haemolytic Anaemia (IMHA) in the Dog"*. The paper states: "This study provides the first clinical evidence for a temporal relationship of vaccine-associated IMHA in the dog."

The study showed a marked difference in frequency of IMHA (also known as AIHA) between the first month after vaccination and subsequent months which was not seen in the control group. "This temporal relationship strongly supports that vaccination can trigger IMHA in dogs. Although reactions are frequently reported to vaccine manufacturers, these companies consider this to be proprietary information and are hesitant to release such data."

Interestingly, the paper goes on to state: "Because vaccine components can remain in the body for extended periods of time, chemical reactions caused by these vaccine components may continue to occur later than with other drugs that are excreted or metabolised more quickly." This statement in its own right would appear to support the belief that vaccines can cause reactions some time after the jab.

Later the paper states: "Vaccine-associated IMHA has been reported after diphtheria-pertussis-tetanus vaccination in children."

And later: "The vaccines reported in this study are commonly used canine vaccines (DHLPP, rabies, Borrelia, Bordetella and coronavirus). They included modified live viruses, killed viruses, and killed bacterins. Any of these components, as well as the adjuvants used in these vaccines, may stimulate or disrupt the function of the immune system or elicit increased antibody production that could lead to IMHA."

The authors conclude that, because not all cases are reported to the manufacturers (none of the cases in this retrospective study had been reported), the prevalence of vaccine-associated IMHA is likely to be underestimated.

I would like to emphasise here that the study concluded that live virus vaccines, killed virus vaccines, and killed bacterins - as well as other constituents of vaccines - may disrupt the immune system to the extent that the killer disease IMHA/AIHA can be induced. In short, no vaccine is without risk.

Behaviour changes:

Mrs A Stubbs' bitch, Berry, was "a gorgeous, healthy, and very intelligent pup and was no trouble in any way until she was inoculated at 13 weeks of age".

The day after the vaccination, a large lump appeared at the needle site and later lengthened out down Berry's back. She appeared very unwell, with a lack of appetite, and she was very quiet. She was taken to the vet the next day, and her temperature had risen to 105°F. The vet administered antibiotics. Berry lay as if dead for four days and then recovered. A small lump came up a month later after her second injection, but it soon went down on its own. Berry was a little listless.

For a while, Mrs Stubbs says Berry seemed perfectly normal. She then went a little moody and came into season at six months, rather early for a GSD. Her short season was followed by a phantom pregnancy. This was repeated four months later, and she also had 'strange turns'. "When running in the wood I heard her cry out," says Mrs Stubbs. "She crawled to me, swaying and sitting down. I thought someone had run into her or she'd had an accident, but she soon recovered."

A few days later this strange behaviour repeated itself. This time Berry seemed to pass out for a few seconds. "It always seemed to happen when they had put up a rabbit or had an extra-mad run," Mrs Stubbs observed. "I concluded that it was an inability to get enough oxygen. So I took her for less exciting walks."

Mrs Stubbs says that Berry has never been as trainable or sensitive as she would have expected from her breeding, or from the brief time she knew her before inoculation. Her seasons have continued to be short and close together followed by phantoms, and three attempts at mating her have failed.

Berry had a booster a year after her first jabs. There was no illness, no swelling, but two weeks later another session of fainting fits. One was particularly bad, lasting for half an hour. For the last two years, Berry has had neither boosters nor 'funny turns'.

"Physically she is very well," says Mrs Stubbs, "but she never seems to have matured mentally. It's very hard to get any concentration with her, and she gets obsessions over objects. Of course, this may be her natural way, but from what I know of her relatives, I doubt it."

Mrs Rippard's Springer Spaniel bitch was a pleasant happy puppy until she received her vaccine jab. "Her behaviour became unpredictable," says Mrs Rippard. "She would snap when stroked, even though she had come to you for a fuss. She never changed in all the years we had her. She had to be put down due to her behaviour. I don't blame the vet - she was doing her job. But it put me off having our present dog vaccinated. He is 11 now and healthy."

Mushroom Commentary

Some people laugh at the people who consult the so-called `dog shrinks'. We imagine that it's the owners who must be nuts. Yet we have moved from a world with ordinary people whose dogs seemed fine without professional training, to dog 'trainers', to canine behaviourists. We now have 'problem dogs'. Dogs who can't be left in the house on their own without destroying it; dogs who are aggressive for no apparent reason; dogs who are disobedient . . . nervous dogs; highly-strung dogs; clingy dogs. Dogs, in fact, who are suffering from vaccine-induced encephalitis: brain damaged dogs.

Those in their eighties can often be heard to say that dogs didn't used to be like this. Is this true, or are these people distorting experiences from youth? Is it the case that dog owners these days don't have a clue and are screwing their dogs up, or are dogs' minds less robust than they used to be?

A friend came to see me with her beautiful Golden Retriever. She admitted, shamefacedly, that Arthur (I have used a pseudonym) had taken to biting my friend's grandchildren and other people without provocation. She had taken him to a behaviourist who had recommended a change in diet as, he believed, the dog suffered from food allergies which were causing this behaviour.

My friend told me that Arthur had terrible skin problems that were being alleviated with the new diet. Arthur laid down on his back and I began to rub his tummy. His legs began to paddle. Having just finished reading a book by Dr Harris L Coulter called, 'Vaccination, Social Violence and Criminality', I felt sure that Arthur's problems stemmed from encephalitis induced by vaccination: sudden unprovoked aggression, digestive disorders and hypersensitivity (a dog with a tickly tummy = hypersensitivity) are, according to Coulter, vaccine reactions.

I suggested to my friend that she take Arthur to a homoeopath (as conventional vets do not recognise the conditions I describe as being linked to vaccines). My friend chose not to. This may be because she is a Christian, and someone in the fundamentalist church has been releasing tracts saying that homoeopathy is connected to the devil.

Now, if I was the devil, the first thing I'd do is join the church and start spreading misinformation from within! As Christ was a healer and was accused of being associated with the devil for healing, I'd have thought the Church would have more sense than to accuse any other healing art as satanic. The devil, I would think, destroys, whereas God heals.

Interestingly, the word 'vaccination' numero logically adds up to 666 - the Antichrist . . . simply assign multiples of six to each letter of the alphabet (A = 6, B = 12, C = 18, and so on), and add up the numbers relating to the letters, and, hey presto, 666 (spooky, eh).

Meanwhile, I strongly suspect that much of the aggression in the modern dog has its root in vaccine damage - as do many of the behaviour problems we are experiencing.

In fact, good old Merck can help us out again. Merck describes encephalitis as: "An acute inflammatory disease of the brain due to direct viral invasion or to hypersensitivity initiated by a virus or other foreign protein. Encephalomyelitis is the same disorder affecting spinal cord structures as well as the brain.

"Secondary encephalitis, usually a complication of viral infection, is considered to have an immunologic mechanism. Examples are the encephalitides following measles, chickenpox, rubella, smallpox vaccination, vaccinia, and many other less well defined viral infections."

The manufacturer of the Servier flu vaccine reports in the Data Sheet Compendium that encephalitis had been associated with an earlier brand of vaccine it had manufactured. Maybe all vaccines can induce encephalitis - I believe so. It is the process, and not the specific virus or bacterin, which is the problem.

Merck continues: "Noninfectious causes of encephalitides include . . . *vaccine reactions: many.*"

A paper appearing in the *Veterinary Record* (AIP McCandlish, et al, 1992) states: "Post-vaccinal encephalitis is a recognised complication of the administration of certain strains of live attenuated canine distemper virus vaccine."

Merck continues: "Symptoms of encephalitis: may be associated with cerebral dysfunction (alteration in consciousness, personality change, seizures, paresis) and cranial nerve abnormalities. The distinction between aseptic meningitis and encephalitis is based on the extent and severity of cerebral dysfunction . . ."

Interestingly, Dr Jean Dodds has discovered that dogs brought to her with problems of aggression screen positively for thyroid disease in a high number of cases. As you know, Dr Dodds asserts that vaccines are one of the triggers that causes autoimmune disease in genetically susceptible animals, including the autoimmune disease Hashimoto's thyroiditis. The CHC vaccine survey (see chapter eleven) seems to show that an awfully high number of dogs are inheriting thyroid disease. The vaccine isn't triggering it, it's there already, probably because we've been vaccinating generations of dogs now.

Because thyroid disease is 'inheritable' rather than 'inherited', this means that something causes thyroid disease, and it can then be passed down the line. The first large-scale study of thyroid disease was in Japan after the dropping of the atomic bomb, and there is also a very high incidence of thyroid disease in the surrounds of Chernobyl.

Immune-mediated thyroid disease can also be initiated, according to Dodds, by a vaccine. It is one of many examples of widespread systemic disruption caused by vaccination. It may also be that dogs who test positive for thyroid disease also have encephalitis. Maybe thyroid damage and encephalitis go hand in hand? Or maybe dogs with thyroid disease should not receive live virus vaccines because the vaccine can initiate severe or fatal reactions in them, such as encephalitis. What is clear, is that some dogs exhibit the personality changes, alterations in consciousness, etc., described by Merck after they are vaccinated. Knowing that vaccines can cause encephalitis, it would be preposterous to discount behavioural problems in dogs as vaccine-associated problems, especially when these behavioural changes occur immediately after vaccination.

Also, as an aside, consider the role of diet and thyroid disease. Three commonly-used artificial pet food preservatives - ethoxyquin, BHA and BHT - are known to destroy selenium and vitamin A. Selenium and vitamin A are essential for healthy thyroid function. Fluoride, added to our drinking water, is also damaging to the thyroid. And do not forget that the vaccine manufacturers themselves warn that dietary deficiencies can compromise an animal's immune system, and thus render vaccines harmful. (They don't actually go so far as to say that vaccines can be harmful if an animal is 'immunocompromised', but safe inoculation relies upon the animal mounting an immune response, without which the animal can die.)

Death:

One of Mr RP Steer's two nine-year-old Airedales collapsed within ten minutes of receiving his booster in August 1995. He died the next day. Mr Steer's vet contacted the vaccine manufacturer, who wrote to the vet, and Mr Steer later passed the correspondence to Hylda Reynolds after she had urged members of the public to share information relating to suspected vaccine reactions.

The individual working for the vaccine manufacturer wrote that he was very sorry to hear about the tragic death of the dog, and was happy to share his thoughts about the case from the details the vet supplied.

In his letter, the vaccine company representative said that he felt that the history and clinical signs, particularly the very high body temperature of 107°F, would indicate to him that heat stroke/hyperthermia was the most likely cause of the problems.

The vaccine company representative admitted that allergic reactions are occasionally recorded against vaccines, pointing out that this was stated in the data sheet. However, he said that vaccine reactions to this particular brand of vaccine were very rare. He explained that, if such a reaction manifests itself as generalised anaphylaxis, then symptoms such as collapse and generalised shock may ensue shortly after vaccination. This, he said, is due to the release of histamine and other inflammatory mediators from hypersensitised mast cells and, he maintained, is a rare over reaction to the presence of an antigen that the immune system has previously been exposed to. "Such reactions produce vasculogenic shock (i.e., blood volume is normal but circulatory capacitance is increased by presence of histamine, leading to relative hypovolaemia)."

The vaccine company representative went on to explain that shock is characterised by pale mucous membranes, tachycardia, cold periphery, delayed capillary refilled, collapsed superficial veins and reduced levels of consciousness. Without treatment shocked animals often become hypothermic. He pointed out that Rula was showing a very high temperature, whereas, if it was a vaccine reaction, she would show a very low temperature.

The vaccine manufacturer's representative said that some dogs who show anaphylactic reactions to vaccines recover on their own, but severe cases need rapid attention and usually respond quickly and well to adrenaline and/or soluble steroid therapy.

Finally, he understood why Mr Steer should be concerned about the possible involvement of the vaccine, but from the signs described he felt it unlikely that the vaccine was involved.

As the representative said he was happy to discuss the case further, and expressing an interest in any post mortem or histopathology reports, Mr Steer wrote to him directly.

Mr Steer was not seeking any restitution in any way, and told the vaccine manufacturer this, but as he had been present throughout, he felt he could give a thorough account of what happened.

Mr Steer wrote that he couldn't agree with the reason given for Rula's death: overheating. The dogs had been given their morning exercise at 9.30am and spent the rest of the day at home with the family. The Friday of that week was the coolest day of the summer and the appointment at the vet's was at 6pm. Mr Steer wrote, "When taking the dogs to the surgery Rula was her usual boisterous and inquisitive self, she leapt into the back of our van full of life and vigour. The journey took six minutes and we drove with the windows open."

Mr Steer left Rula in the car, with the windows wide open, while he went into the surgery with his other dog. One other patient was waiting to see the vet. After waiting for five minutes, he took the first dog in to see the vet. He then returned to the van to collect Rula, saying that she had been waiting there for no more than 14 minutes. When he opened the door of the van, she jumped out as usual, literally pulling him into the surgery. "There was nothing apparently wrong," he wrote.

Mr Steer says that the vet then administered the injection into Rula while stroking her, and he asked Mr Steer what he fed her because he'd never seen such perfect teeth in a nine year-old dog.

Mr Steer claims that the vet was looking at Rula all the time he was talking to him and, when they left, Rula jumped into the van. Within 600 yards she had collapsed. As the vet had left at the same time as Mr Steer, he felt it was pointless returning to the surgery. Instead, he returned home. By this time, Rula was nearly unconscious. Her tongue and gums were a purple colour, which made him believe she had suffered a heart attack. She was also having great difficulty in breathing. Mr Steer rang the vets' 24-hour service and was told to take Rula to another practice.

Mr Steer says that when they arrived at the surgery, the vet took Rula's temperature and that it was very high. "The vet there would not listen to me," he wrote, "and assumed that she had been locked in a vehicle for some considerable time. While they did everything possible to save her, I feel that if the original vet had been present he could have given her an antidote."

Mr Steer said in his letter to the vaccine company representative that the symptoms he had described in his letter were exactly the same as Rula's symptoms, with the exception that he said she was suffering from hypothermia. He asked why the first vet didn't notice this and do something about it while he was handling her. Either she wasn't hypothermic and something else contributed to her death, or she was and the vet was at fault.

Finally, Mr Steer asked whether the vaccine manufacturer offered any guidelines about taking a dog's temperature before vaccinating an animal, saying that his previous vet always did this but it had never been done in his presence in the current practice.

The vaccine company representative replied to Mr Steer, explaining that he could only comment in broad fashion because he didn't have first hand experience of the case. He admitted that it was not possible to rule out a component of vaccine reaction in this case, but it would be highly unlikely in view of the clinical signs that had been reported, and particularly the very high temperature which is typical of heat stress, and the opposite of what is seen in anaphylactic reactions.

He added that the signs of heat stroke can come on very quickly - once a dog loses its ability to balance the body's production and loss of heat, the dog's temperature can soar uncontrollably to life threatening levels. Even rapid and intensive therapy may fail in these cases, he said.

The vaccine company representative said that he understood from the vet in the second practice that soluble corticosteroids were administered as part of the intensive treatment of this case. He explained that these drugs have many uses, including the treatment of anaphylactic/allergic reactions (i.e., they are one possible `antidote' to a suspected vaccine reaction).

In the vaccine company's experience, vaccination does not predispose to heat stress; the representative claimed that this was the only case of this nature that had been brought to their attention that summer.

And finally, he said that there are no specific recommendations for vets to take an animal's temperature before vaccinating the animal with any of the vaccines then on the market. He did, however, say that animals should be healthy before vaccination, but it is up to individual vets and practices as to how they carry out examinations. In his experience, some vets routinely take temperatures, and some do not. He did, of course, express his sympathies.

Mushroom Commentary

Most, if not all of the vaccine manufacturers warn, within the data sheets accompanying their vaccines, that dogs can suffer hypersensitivity reactions following vaccination. They further advise that adrenaline be administered in this event. (Adrenaline is used therapeutically to treat anaphylactic reactions, reducing broncho constriction and counteracting a drop in blood pressure brought about by histamine release.) Adrenaline is there for use in life or death situations. In other words, when an organism mounts a huge allergic reaction to a foreign invasion, the reaction itself could lead to death (see Seyle's non-specific stress syndrome later).

Although the vaccine company representative believes that an elevated temperature is inconsistent with anaphylactic shock, Seyle's non-specific stress syndrome describes 'deranged' temperatures (high or low temperatures) as symptomatic of a reaction to a stress. However, it appears from Rula Steer's experience that we would be unwise to have our dogs vaccinated in hot weather, as the expert opinion in this case tells us that hot weather was the cause of her demise.

(Vaccine manufacturers warn that immunocompetence may be compromised by, amongst other things, stress. It has been clearly demonstrated here that hot weather is a stress.)

An allergic reaction to vaccines, which would appear similar to Rula's reaction except for the temperature difference, is not dissimilar to, say, a person who is allergic to chocolate or peanuts. These people, in certain circumstances, can die if they accidentally eat peanuts or chocolate, and they carry adrenaline or antihistamine with them just in case.

It is clear that only a small number of dogs react this violently to the vaccine jab. If all dogs reacted in this way to the vaccine, none of us would - hopefully - have our dogs vaccinated. It is, though, my contention that vaccine reactions are vastly under-reported, and that there is a huge spectrum of disease lying between `slightly queasy' and death.

As stated earlier, vaccines remain in the system for a long time - so chemical reactions caused by these vaccine components may continue to occur later than with other drugs that are excreted or metabolised more quickly.

I must also add that, in my view, vets and vaccine manufacturers have escaped serious scrutiny in relation to vaccines because 'ordinary people' often have difficulty in understanding the medical excuses given to them. Further, they are often so distraught at their animal's death, that they simply don't have the heart to take matters further. We also have a tendency to view vets as gods, and they to view us as stupid.

Cattle farmers, though, adopt a different approach when their livestock die unnecessarily. Dr Ed Dorosz,a vet who works with cattle and other large animals in the Canadian Prairies, tells me that he has seen instances where cattle were vaccinated, walked three steps, and dropped dead.

"These people aren't going to stand by while their livelihood dies in front of them," says Ed. "In fact, the vaccine companies realise this and have paid out without any argument."

Heart failure:

At the end of 1990, Mrs A Batson says she had two healthy, lively, happy Cavaliers. At that time, they both had their boosters. Mrs Batson says, "The reaction was horrendous. They were dragging their back legs around and greatly distressed for about 24 hours."

One of the dogs, Jamie who was seven, deteriorated from then until ten months later when he had to be put to sleep. He had developed a very serious heart murmur. The younger dog, Marty, later developed the same problem and Mrs Batson says it broke her heart to say goodbye to another beloved, sweet, friend. The vet suggested that the vaccine was from a bad batch.

Bet Hargreaves is a breeder of Cavaliers. She has been trying for many years to work out why it should be that Cavaliers seem to have a deterioration to their heart condition about a month after their boosters. "It is a fact that Cavaliers have a pre-disposition to Sinus Arhythmia (irregular heartbeat)," says Bet. "Since I believe no research has ever been carried out on Cavaliers already suffering from a heart condition, should vets, when giving Cavaliers vaccinations, pay particular attention to Cavaliers with heart trouble and record any adverse reaction to their heart problem? It is now accepted by the vaccine company that certain families of dogs do have allergic reactions to their vaccinations."

Bet further points out that research in Sweden showed that 31% of Cavaliers have Thrombocytopenia, a low platelet count. "After giving the live parvo vaccination, their platelets drop on the third day, and then again around a month later.

I have pedigrees of Cavaliers already suffering from heart trouble and some did seem to have adverse reactions to their boosters about a month later, when their heart condition had deteriorated and they died shortly afterwards.

"Yet other Cavaliers, also with heart conditions, had their yearly boosters and lived onto normal old age. Could it be that the Cavaliers who seemed to have had an adverse reaction to their vaccines have both Thrombocytopenia and a heart condition?"

Mushroom Commentary

Whilst most vets will say that lots of seven-year-old Cavaliers have heart murmurs, I do question whether so called genetic diseases can be triggered by vaccines (do vaccines create, or trigger, the genetic weaknesses in an organism?) It would be interesting to see how common these genetic weaknesses are if we were to stop vaccinating.

In fact, Merck once again jumps to the rescue, telling us that patients with T cell immunodeficiencies, characterised by heart disease, should not receive live virus vaccines. You'd have thought, wouldn't you, that the veterinary vaccine manufacturers would have latched onto this basic fact and maybe even warned that Cavaliers, with this known genetic pre-disposition, should not receive live virus vaccines.

Thrombocytopenia is a deficiency of blood clotting, haemorrhage, and bleeding into the skin, caused by various autoimmune diseases or drug-induced. Merck tells us that Immunologic Idiopathic (unknown cause) Thrombocytpenic Purpura in children is a self-limiting disorder that normally follows a viral infection, but in adults is a chronic disorder with no apparent predisposing cause. It seems to me that if a viral infection can be a cause of this blood disorder, then a vaccine could also be a cause, being as vaccines contain live viruses.

In fact, the US National Academy of Sciences IOM report concluded that the measles vaccine can cause death from measles-vaccine-strain infection, thrombocytopenia, fatal shock and arthritis. Measles and distemper are, as you know, virtually the same virus.

In discussing autoimmune disorders, Merck also says that, "the autoimmune reaction is normally held in check by the action of a population of specific suppressor T cells. Any of the above processes," (which includes, they say, a foreign antigen such as animal brain tissue in a vaccine), "can lead to or be associated with a suppressor T cell defect". It seems the scientist I met on the plane was right.

How common would these hereditary diseases be if we followed Merck's advice and stopped injecting people (dogs are people) with known autoimmune-generating triggers? The homoeopathic vet Mark Elliott has conducted some tentative research into PRA (retinal atrophy) in a litter of pups known to be genetically disposed to this hereditary disease. By waiting until the twelfth week before vaccinating, all pups were kept PRA clear. Mr Elliott concedes that this research is not conclusive, and he would welcome further research in this respect.

It is also worth stating the obvious: some of the diseases we vaccinate our dogs against - hepatitis for example - attack the liver. Others attack the heart, for example, parvovirus in the form of myocarditis. It is not beyond the realms of possibility to suggest that the vaccines fail to produce an immune response but, instead, mimic the diseases themselves.

Another thought, resulting from work conducted by the French immunologist, Jacques Benveniste - who famously contends that water has memory - places questions in my mind regarding certain methods of vaccine manufacture. Dr Benveniste has been injecting eggs into laboratory animals to produce hypersensitivity reactions in the animals' hearts. As some vaccines are cultured on eggs before being injected into our dogs, it might be that the egg protein itself could be causing the problems associated with heart murmurs or heart failure.

Just a thought.

Interestingly, Dr Benveniste's experiment involved an antibody - IgE (immunoglobin E type) - which is implicated by Jean Dodds as being the genetic 'problem' associated with some dogs' reactions to vaccines. Pedro Luis Revera DVM, in his paper entitled, 'Vaccinations and Vaccinosis', wrote: IgE mediates Type 1 hypersensitivity and is largely responsible for immunity to inhalant allergens and parasites, and the mediation of inflammatory agents acting on masT-cells or basophils. Again, do Cavaliers have T cell immuno-deficiencies (and many other breeds)? Probably certainly!

But back to Dr Benveniste, who took some human blood serum full of white cells and IgE and mixed it with a solution prepared from goats blood, which triggered the release of histamine. The solution contained an anti-IgE antibody (to represent an antigen, for example pollen).

Amazingly, the reaction took place in a test tube. Dr Benveniste diluted the anti-IgE until it eventually contained one part antibody to 10^{120} parts water (ten followed by 120 zeros) - to the point where it was `impossible' for the water to contain a single molecule of antibody. And yet the histamine reaction was set off in the test tube with the same power as before. Despite the fact that the experiment was repeated seventy times in labs in three other countries, Dr Benveniste's experiment has been repudiated by a team of scientific investigators (who included a magician) and generally discounted by the scientific community.

Of course, if Dr Benveniste is right, he poses quite a problem for, say, the vaccine manufacturers whose vaccines, cultured on, say, eggs, create allergic reactions, despite the fact that all 'extraneous proteins' have been apparently removed from the vaccine. The same fear would exist where vaccines are cultured in test tubes containing animal cells. If water has memory, it would be impossible to remove the 'memory' of those cells and rule out allergic reactions to them.

Paralysis:

Koko, Jean Garrood's miniature Poodle, seemed fine after his puppy vaccines and his first annual booster vaccine. However, within an hour of his second annual booster, Koko seemed to lose the use of his back legs and rear end. He cried when he tried to move and was very distressed. He was still very poorly the next day, so Mrs Garrood rang the vet and spoke to both partners. They assured her that it couldn't have been the vaccine but, if he was no better, he should be taken back that evening. By the afternoon Koko had begun to recover, so Mrs Garrood didn't take him to the surgery.

The following year, Koko had another booster injection. Again, within the hour, he was very distressed, crying and unable to move. He was so poorly that this time Mr and Mrs Garrood stayed downstairs with him through the night. Mrs Garrood says that, "although he was more distressed this time, he recovered quicker. He was his old self by mid morning."

Once again, Mrs Garrood took Koko for a booster the next year. "By this time my old vet had retired so we saw a new vet. I was very worried at the prospect of this year's booster and explained the situation to the new vet. He didn't appear to be surprised and accepted my story. He still advised to have the vaccination done but gave Koko a histamine tablet to ease the allergy. Nevertheless he still suffered - not being able to move easily and was distressed, but for a much shorter period this time." Mrs Garrood is now worried about giving her one-year-old puppy his booster.

Mushroom Commentary

We human beings are going to have to learn to listen to our own experiences. Why do we keep taking animals back for their boosters when the vaccine is clearly harming the animals? I know one lady who used to book three days off work at annual booster time: the first day for the booster, the second to deal with the dog's reaction, and the third day for her to recover from the ordeal.

When the same reaction occurs after the same annual stimulus, the cause is obvious to anyone with an open mind, isn't it? Or maybe we are so brainwashed by the vaccine miracle myth that we just don't trust what we see in front of our eyes. We shall, of course, be examining why some dogs react with paralysis (as opposed to organ failure, death, allergies, epilepsy, and so on), while others appear not to react at all. However, it seems clear to me that vaccines can stimulate this response. Merck has told us that vaccine-induced encephalitis can affect the brain, and also the spinal cord. Distemper, also, can induce paralysis - and as attenuated but live distemper is being injected into our dogs, it would make logical sense to say that paralysis following vaccination is vaccine-related.

Unsuccessfully attenuated vaccine:

Miss Jean Richardson had been a client of a husband and wife veterinary team - Mr and Mrs Smith (an alias used in kindness for the individuals involved) - for eleven years. As Mr Smith had developed cancer, he and his wife were practising from home. Because of Mr Smith's illness, Miss Richardson tried to give the couple loyal support by taking her 18 Labradors to the surgery.

On Wednesday, 9th October 1991, Miss Richardson took five of her seven twelve-week old puppies for their vaccine jab. Two were not vaccinated as they were to be exported to Sweden. Ten days later, one vaccinated bitch, Nel, developed green discharge from the eyes, a temperature of 104°F, running eyes, nervousness and general malaise.

On 22nd October, Miss Richardson took Nel to the vet who diagnosed distemper and gave her, in the one syringe, Pembritin and B12 Chloramphenicol. Upon arriving home, Miss Richardson noticed that a second vaccinated bitch, Meg, was unwell, so she returned to the vets, arriving at 8pm. Meg was given the same drugs.

At this time, the two puppies who had not received vaccines were blood-tested for leptospirosis before export.

By the 23rd October, Meg was very poorly: crying, whimpering, foaming at the mouth, and clenching her teeth. The first phone call to the vet was made at 8am, and Miss Richardson was advised to keep the puppy quiet. After four more phone calls, the vet told Miss Richardson to take the puppy to the surgery at 6.30 that evening - over ten hours after the first phone call.

Miss Richardson was desperate during those ten hours. She contacted C-Vet, the manufacturer of the vaccine, and spoke to a Mr Chris Taylor, Technical Services Manager. Mr Taylor was already aware of the situation as the vet had already notified him, and he told Miss Richardson that he was coming to see her the next day.

"The company had had another case at Congleton, Cheshire," says Miss Richardson, "and the dog had recovered. Mr Taylor told me it was a classical post vaccinal encephalitis, and that it was an abnormal response to a variety of unknown puppy factors to a vaccine which is normally safe. It occurs with pups injected with a modified live vaccine, but it never affects all the litter.

"I asked Mr Taylor to contact Glasgow University to speak with Dr IAP McCandlish, a lecturer in veterinary Pathology," said Miss Richardson. "She was out, so he spoke to Dr HJC Cornwell, who said the strike is uneven - one or two pups are affected and that the hyperimmune serum was a waste of time because Ian Lauder of London said it made no difference because the virus is in the brain stem, in the blood, and the hyperimmune serum won't get past the brain barrier."

On 24th October, the vet arrived at Miss Richardson's home with Chris Taylor. "Mr Taylor admitted responsibility and said he'd pay for the vet bills," Miss Richardson says. "He told me that the company's distemper vaccine was strong, and not to use C-Vet again, and to use a dead vaccine on the unvaccinated pups. The vet, Mrs Smith, said it would be difficult for her to get two dead vaccines because they came in batches, and she made no further effort to help me."

The blood samples were sent to Glasgow University. Meanwhile, the vet contacted Miss Richardson to say that the dog puppy couldn't be exported to Sweden because he had failed his blood test: his titre was very high. Miss Richardson asked the vet for a letter to go to Sweden so that the importer could claim her money back from the airline due to sudden cancellation. No letter was received.

On 25th October the vet examined the two sick puppies. Both had swollen glands. Meg was the worst - she was unable to lap or take food. Miss Richardson phoned Mr Smith on the 26th and 28th October, telling him that the pups' conditions were worsening. "I specifically said that one pup was distressed, whimpering, crying out, and unable to lap or swallow. I told him that she had been like this since the 25th October, and was told to bring the puppy in to see him at 6.30pm on the 29th - 90 hours after she had last been seen."

Miss Richardson meanwhile spoke to Professor James Armour, Vice Chancellor of Glasgow University and Chairman of the Advisory Body of the Veterinary Medicines Directorate. He told Miss Richardson to tell her vet to complete the Yellow Form MLA 252 A, Report on Suspect Adverse Reactions. The vet had not done this.

"I also phoned C-Vet on the 28th and asked whether, if the dog were put to sleep, would he want a post mortem. He never returned my call.

"Hearing the cries and the whimpering of that pup was so distressing that, by 3pm on the 29th October, I could honestly stand it no longer," says Miss Richardson. "I simply couldn't wait for 6.30pm. The previous day the vet had shown signs of irritation, as if I were a nuisance, so I phoned another veterinary surgery. I burst into tears and said I could stand it no longer and it had been 90 hours since the bitch had last been seen. The vet heard the puppy crying on the phone and told me to bring both puppies in immediately.

"She examined the bitch tenderly and with compassion and eventually told me that Meg was really suffering and should be put to sleep. She acted in the most professional way I have ever seen for a young girl. She telephoned my original vet to inform her of what was happening.

"When I arrived home the phone was ringing. It was Mrs Smith. Her phone call was most upsetting and she told me she didn't want me as a client again. She said she would send her account and demanded a cheque by return. The conversation was a one-way transmission. I spoke one sentence to ask for the return of the video of my pups. She slammed the phone down. Twenty dogs died as a result of this vaccine."

In July 1993, Miss Richardson received a letter from the Ministry of Agriculture, Fisheries and Food (MAFF). It said:

Dear Miss Richardson

As promised, I am now able to let you have a more detailed reply to your letter of 30 May. I was very sorry indeed to hear of the deaths of your dogs which, from the video, certainly seemed to live up to the claims you make for them.

I understand you have had a fair amount of correspondence with the Veterinary Medicines Directorate (VMD) who, as you know, are responsible to Ministers for the day to day licensing of veterinary medicines. You mention in your letter that the two officials concerned have been courteous, but may wish to remain impartial and avoid compromising their official position. The fact (is), however, that they are constrained by Section 118 of the Medicines Act which prohibits disclosure of any information obtained or furnished in pursuance of the Act. They are not therefore allowed to provide information on the issues you have been raising with them. Similarly with the questions you have posed to me, details of C-Vet's manufacturing processes, and their compliance with tests and other procedures are matters which I cannot disclose.

All I can do is confirm that following reports of suspected adverse reactions received at the VMD, it was decided to suspend the licences for Boostervac CPv (for canine parvovirus), Boostervac DHPi (for canine distemper, canine hepatitis and canine parainfluenza) and Boostervac CPv1 (for canine parvovirus and canine leptospirosis) marketed by C-Vet. This action was carried out on 30 April 1992, on safety grounds, under the provisions of Section 28 and 29, and in accordance with Schedule 2 of the Medicines Act 1968. The licences remain suspended.

Miss Richardson comments, "vaccinating against diseases does not positively ensure that our dogs are safe from contracting these illnesses. In trying to get a level of attenuation to produce an immunity, the balance does not always work, and certain groups of dogs can be affected. In my case, it was the strain of the virus the drug company used which was too severe."

Mushroom Commentary

It is perhaps unfortunate for C-Vet that we have the MAFF comments in writing. C-Vet is by no means unique in producing a harmful vaccine batch. In fact, it happens fairly frequently. Mistakes happen; it's part of being human, and probably inevitable in vaccine manufacture.

As an example, Rhone Merieux and Mallinckrodt Inc (Mallinckrodt's vaccines are made by Rhone Merieux), initiated a recall and discontinuation of use of all their vaccines containing distemper products. The vaccines had been associated with a higher than normally expected rate of post vaccinal central nervous system reactions, occurring 1-2 weeks after vaccination. Problems first began to be reported in January 1995, and extended to RM Canine 4, RM Canine 5, RM Canine 6, RM Canine 4+ Corona-MLV, RM Canine 6+Corona-MLV, Quantum 4, Quantum 6, Tissuvax 5, and Tissuvax 6. (JAVMA 12.1.95)

Note the phrase 'higher than normally expected', meaning some measure of post vaccinal central nervous system reactions were `expected`.

Similarly, Schering-Plough Animal Health recalled stocks of its Intrac canine bordetella bronchiseptico vaccine during 1997, after routine testing revealed that it had fallen below the product specification for live bacterial count within the shelf life of the product. The likely explanation appeared to be in the supply of Ph Eur grade bovine serum albumin and gelatin from non-UK sources - imposed as a consequence of BSE regulations. (Can bovine serum in vaccines cause BSE/CJD/FSE?)

We know from this, then, that bovine (cow) blood products are used in vaccines. We also know that vaccines can be bacterially contaminated. The Merck Manual says that serum can cause Type III hypersensitivity reactions, including a highly inflammatory skin condition involving painful local lesions leading to tissue necrosis; as well as widespread vascular injury.

Epilepsy, diarrhoea, behaviour changes, pancreas problems and death

Jenny Drastura lost a three-year-old Lhasa Apso bitch called Kanda to a fatal reaction to a corona vaccine in 1988, and has mourned her ever since. Three hours after being given a killed corona vaccine, Kanda vomited undigested food twice but seemed to feel better afterwards. Eight hours after vaccination, she became restless and was pacing, and soon went into convulsions. She was comatose ten minutes later when Jenny arrived with Kanda at the veterinary clinic. After several hours of extensive treatment, she became semi-comatose but never regained full consciousness, even after eight days in intensive care at a veterinary hospital.

Jenny's vet reported Kanda's fatal reaction to the drug manufacturer. Several months later Jenny phoned the DOA (United States Department of Agriculture), and they had a record of five fatalities, but no record of Kanda's reaction. Jenny's vet called the drug manufacturer again and there was indeed a record of her call, but the person who took the call was no longer there and no action had been taken.

Mushroom commentary

Jenny Drastura subsequently conducted her own vaccine survey in the Lhasa Apso Reporter. Of the 25 dogs surveyed, 17 reactions were reported, four of which were fatal. In her report, Jenny says that her survey was not designed to scare dog owners away from vaccinating, but to make people aware of the reaction possibilities. She urges dog owners not to leave their dogs alone after vaccination, but to be there to deal with reactions if they happen.

Jenny also advises dog owners to report any suspected reactions to the American DOA (the equivalent in England is the Veterinary Medicines Directorate). She says: "I wrote to the DOA and discovered that they researched the drug company's sterility, potency and safety tests and found them satisfactory for one and one-half years prior to my request. All they have to go on is information the drug manufacturers, veterinarians, and dog owners supply.

"According to the DOA, there is no regulation that requires that these reactions be reported once efficacy testing is completed. And there is no central database to report vaccine reactions in the US. This is a frightening thought, and all the more reason why every fatal reaction should somehow be accounted for. If everyone makes a complaint to the DOA, the DOA can't help but notice any patterns that exist.

"Second is the matter of proof. We did not let the vet school that treated our bitch do a necropsy. That was a major error on our part. We were too devastated at that point to consider it. If we only had that time over again, and if we had realised how important it was to have proof, we would certainly have done it."

The following case stories, involving firstly sickness and diarrhoea, and then skin complaints, are all aspects of the same view: vaccinosis.

Vaccinosis:

It was suggested to Janet Nolan by a homoeopath that her 21-month old Ridgeback bitch, Nelli, had suffered damage to her immune system due to a vaccine reaction. Following her first vaccination as a puppy, Nelli was violently sick and had diarrhoea lasting several days. There was a large lump around the site of the vaccination.

Mrs Nolan reports that Nelli now has dreadful skin problems, irregular seasons, and the homoeopath says that her glandular, lymphatic and urinary systems are all damaged. Now starting homoeopathic treatment, Mrs Nolan hopes that they can restore Nelli to better health.

She says, "My daughter, now aged 27, was severely damaged by vaccines - initially the whooping cough, but more seriously by the measles vaccine. She is autistic, had epilepsy, and is very disabled mentally and physically. If this can happen to humans, then it most certainly can happen to animals."

Mrs Nolan's conventional vet agreed that the lump was probably a reaction to the vaccine.

Peter Gregory, a homoeopathic vet, tells of two cases of vaccinosis in horses. The first horse had small bumps on his neck prior to vaccination, but these developed into huge swellings within a week of vaccination. The horse had warts all over his face. The owner tried conventional veterinary treatment for a year, before resorting to Peter. Peter says that his prescribing took the fact that vaccines appeared to make an existing condition worse into account, giving homoeopathic sepia. This is a constitutional remedy that also covers some vaccine reactions.

The second horse started 'head shaking' within three days of being vaccinated. "Normally," says Peter, "we usually have good success with post-vaccinal head shaking in horses. But this horse has so far failed to respond. Other homoeopaths are mentioning the same thing lately. There seems to be some sort of allergic reaction at the root of it all." Meanwhile, the horse's head shaking is so severe that he is impossible to ride.

Mrs J Rolfe has two dogs, an English Setter and a Border Collie. Mrs Rolfe has noticed that the Collie, who is nine years old, has suffered a skin irritation directly after his booster, especially during the last three years. The condition has become gradually worse each year, becoming very severe in the last recorded year. The condition lasted for three months. Mrs Rolfe says that the scratching just goes on, and becomes very distressing for him. Mrs Rolfe says she rang the surgery after his last booster, and was assured that it couldn't be the vaccine. Mrs Rolfe, however, thinks that it is.

Mr and Mrs Simon Peck's proud white Persian cat, Sasha, has changed personality since he stopped having annual boosters. "We noticed that, every year, two months after he was vaccinated, his coat started to matt. The matting was so severe - despite the fact that we dote on him and groom him regularly - that it was hurting him," says Simon. "It was so bad that we had to book him into the vets to be drugged and sedated so that they could groom him. This cost about £180 every time, and Sasha went through sheer hell." Since stopping boosters, the coat hasn't matted, and Sasha has become far happier. "He used to be a very highly strung cat," says Simon. "He wouldn't let you cuddle him. Now he's incredibly loving and lovable - the difference is unbelievable."

Mrs A Howells' dog Sunny had, for several years, suffered with a sore patch on his pad that wouldn't heal. He was provided with various 'solutions' by the vet, including a range of antibiotics. Sunny was eventually referred to a specialist at the nearest university school of veterinary studies. Sunny was left at the school and anaesthetised for biopsies. Results were inconclusive, so he was discharged with antibiotics that were double the strength of those the vet could dispense.

At this time, Mrs Howells heard about a radionics practitioner who diagnoses problems by analysing a sample of a dog's hair. The practitioner concluded that Sunny was suffering from vaccinosis (a morbid reaction to vaccines) and therefore a weakened immune system. Sunny was given a five-month course of treatment, until his ears became infected after swimming.

Meanwhile, Mrs Howells discovered that a homoeopathic vet practised nearby, and Sunny was booked in for an appointment. The vet confirmed that Sunny's eczema, ear problems and blocked anal glands were all indicators of vaccinosis, and suggested that the fact that he had all three were quite conclusive.

Mrs Howells says that they haven't looked back. Sunny is receiving a constitutional homoeopathic remedy and is much better. Sunny will not be submitted to annual boosters again.

Mushroom Commentary

In fact, there are very many reports of skin problems in animals which vets seem unable to cure and which, once treated homoeopathically for vaccinosis, do clear up.

Conclusive research was accomplished in 1983, pinning the 'blame' fairly and squarely on vaccines as a serious cause of skin diseases in dogs. Two scientists, named Frick and Brookes, assembled a group of dogs who were genetically pre-disposed to develop atopic dermatitis (atopic means inherited, dermatitis means skin disease). The dogs were divided into two groups and the first group was exposed to pollen (which is an allergen), and they were then vaccinated. None of the genetically pre-disposed dogs developed the hereditary condition.

The second group was vaccinated first, and then exposed to pollen. All developed the hereditary disease. This illustrates how vaccines sensitise an organism, setting them up for allergic reactions. The allergen could be pollen, or it could be house dust mites, or it could be fungal spores, or the petrol fumes your dog, horse or cat breathes in post-vaccination. As Merck has told us, 'children' from families with B and/or T cell immunodeficiencies (characterised by skin disease amongst other things) should not be given live virus vaccines due to the severe or fatal infections that may result. Animals or humans with atopic dermatitis should certainly not be given live virus vaccines again, because the next time, it could be encephalitis (brain damage) or death.

Frankly, my own family is so beset with B and T cell immunodeficiency related disease, that our parents should really have been sterilised at birth. I am a product of 'irresponsible breeding'! My sister Leslie has asthma; my sister Mollie has dermal sensitivities and thyroid disease; my brother Fred has hayfever; I have eczema, hayfever and cat allergies; my father has heart disease, and my mother had eczema. My great niece, Katie-Ann, reacted to her first vaccine shot and was subsequently found to be allergic to eggs. So rather than spare her the vaccine shot, the doctors decided to book her into hospital for the day so they could manage the reaction! Thankfully, Katie-Ann's parents had the good sense to read-up about the potential reactions, and realising that brain damage and death were possibilities, decided that Katie-Ann should receive homoeopathic protection instead. It's just a pity that doctors seem not to read their own medical bible.

Because the nature of a vaccine reaction varies so considerably from one individual to another, it is difficult for vets and scientists to believe that they all have the same cause. Christopher Day comments: "I believe that the variety of symptoms shown by dogs (and other species) is a function of two variables. First, the different vaccine components, methods of manufacture, etc., and secondly, the variety of constitutional responses shown by the victims. In homoeopathy, we believe that every organism has a predisposition or programmed response to disease. Put simply, one human being might have a tendency to react to the same allergen with hayfever, another might develop eczema, while another might not react at all."

The book, "Quantum Healing" by Deepak Chopra MD also provides some valuable insights into the unpredictability of the body's reactions to invaders. Simplifying Dr Chopra's explanation, he tells us that the nervous system runs down the spinal column, branching out on either side at each vertebra in the backbone; these major nerves then branch into millions of tinier pathways that communicate to every region of the body. In the 1970s, chemicals called neurotransmitters were discovered - they act in our bodies as communicator molecules and touch the life of every cell.

Dr Chopra gives an example of camels who, it was discovered, produce large quantities of a specific biochemical in the brain that allows them to tolerate high levels of pain, and this biochemical is transmitted around the body by neurotransmitters. The camels' own genetically-based intelligence' transmitted by neurotransmitters, renders the breed able to overcome an outside stimulus that would profoundly affect other species. By inference, other species and, indeed, different breeds of dogs (and even different human genetic lines) would produce their own unique 'intelligence', or chemical profile patterns: DNA.

The body also has `receptors', which are programmed to recognise certain stimuli brought to them by neurotransmitters, and react in their own specific way. The body, in fact, has a mind of its own which doesn't always follow the predictable patterns, or thus-far-observed patterns, expected when a drug or vaccine is administered. Dr Chopra says: "I realise that this makes drugs look much more dangerous than we had thought, even in an era that is obsessed with cataloguing medical disasters. We are used to a more limited idea of what a side effect is - a touch of the bitter with the sweet, like the thorn that comes with the rose or the hangover with the bottle of wine. Instead, a side effect balloons out into anything the body can think of."

Knowing as we do now that viruses and vaccines can cause encephalitis, which can involve both the brain and the central nervous system, it seems logical to suggest that both vaccines and viruses can disrupt the balance of the neurotransmitters (communicators), which proceed from the nervous system out to every part of the body. If the neurotransmitters are in a state of shock, they could be sending out confused messages.

Summary

* Vaccines appear to provoke a wide range of inflammatory diseases or, if this thesis cannot be accepted,
* A wide range of symptoms have been reported post-vaccination
* Encephalitis (brain inflammation) is an accepted vaccine reaction
* Epilepsy is an accepted sequel to encephalitis
* Autoimmune diseases are known to result from vaccination
* Allergies and skin diseases are known to result from vaccination
* Vaccines can cause the diseases they are designed to prevent
* Vaccine manufacturers and vets are suspected of under-reporting vaccine reactions
* Vaccine manufacture is subject to error and/or safety concerns
* The conventional veterinary profession seems blind to vaccine-induced disease

Chapter Three

What is the root of these diverse symptoms?

Conventional medicine, understandably, has trouble accepting that so many diverse symptoms can result from vaccination. Were the side-effects of the vaccine jab similar to the thalidomide experience, where mothers took a tablet and their children were born deformed and without limbs, it would be much easier to see that one drug or medical treatment was the cause.

A plausible answer lies in one simple paper prepared by Dr Hans Selye entitled, *"A Syndrome Produced by Diverse Nocuous Agents"*, (Selye H, 1936, Nature, July 4 138:32). This was the first important piece of work to illustrate the syndrome of non-specific responses to injury.

Selye demonstrated that living organisms have a general non-specific reaction pattern: a general defence mechanism with which they meet damage caused by a variety of potential disease-producers.

Having spent his whole life researching and defining the non-specific stress syndrome, Selye was able to report that its pathology includes enlarged adrenal cortex; intense atrophy of the thymus, the spleen and all lymphatic structures; signs of petechial bleeding (bleeding into the skin or mucous membrane) - into the lungs, thymus, pericardium and other internal organs, and intrathoracic cavity; ulceration of the lining of the stomach and duodenum; disappearance of the eosinophil cells (a type of white blood cell produced in the bone marrow) in the circulating blood; a number of chemical alterations in the constitution of body fluids and tissues; changes in the viscosity and clotting properties of the blood, and signs of derangements in body temperature control (overheating or under heating).

The clinical symptoms of Non-specific Stress Syndrome, as expressed by Selye, include general feeling of malaise, nausea, coated tongue, reflux (a back flow of liquid against its normal direction of movement), otitis media (ear infection), upper respiratory tract infections, runny nose, sticky eyes, clamminess, deranged (elevated or depressed) body temperature, rash, tenderness of the liver and spleen, diffuse pains and aches in the joints, gastro-intestinal disturbance with loss of appetite and weight, diarrhoea and/or constipation. Sounds like the effects of a good night out - but with a sliding scale of severity.

Selye recognised three stages in Non-specific Stress Syndrome:

> 1. The alarm stage, when the body is acutely affected and mobilises all of its defences and corticoid activity rises sharply;
> 2. The stage of resistance, when the body is at a maximum capacity to resist the insult, and;
> 3. The stage of exhaustion when all defences have been exhausted and the organism may succumb.

Generally, an animal or human cannot maintain a continuous state of alarm. If the organism is confronted with an insult so damaging that its normal defence mechanisms are unable to mobilise and complete a healing response, the organism will either sustain chronic damage or respond with death. If the defence mechanisms are not normal, that is, if the organism's immune system is already stressed and dealing with other challenges, chronic or acute disease will result.

How the individual responds to the stress is down to the individual. I use this analogy: imagine you have a car. Open the door, sit inside, put your key in the ignition and your foot on the accelerator. Now leave your foot there, full throttle, for half an hour. Depending on the car, the wing mirror might drop off, the engine might explode, a gasket might blow . . . wherever there's a weakness in the car, that's where you'll see signs of damage.

Christopher Day, homoeopathic veterinary surgeon, expresses it this way:

"In homoeopathy, we believe that a disease force - whether physical as in an injury, psychological, viral or bacterial - will act on the body. In health, the body is usually in equilibrium (balance). The disease force tries to disturb this state of balance but, as we know from basic scientific laws, an equilibrium system will move in such a direction as to try and maintain its equilibrium. So a disease force acts on the equilibrium and the body reacts against the disease force. This produces the symptoms.

"In a case of chronic disease, the equilibrium is shifted and a new equilibrium set up. In acute disease, three sequels are possible. One has to keep this differentiation in mind when considering disease. In acute disease, there can be a reversion to equilibrium by self-healing, there can be a continuation into chronic disease, or there can be death. I think only these three outcomes are possible from acute disease."

If you think about this in relation to your dog, cat, horse or child, a vaccine has the potential to leave him or her unscathed; or to cause a chronic disease, with symptoms depending upon the genetic pre-disposition of your friend; or to kill him. The crunch factors are your friend's general state of health, his genetic makeup, and other stresses or challenges that might be going on at the same time. In other words, his power of resistance at the time of injection - hence vaccine manufacturers' recommendations that only healthy animals and humans should be vaccinated.

Question: *please define 'healthy'.*

Knowing as we do that adult animals and humans can have vaccine reactions when they appeared not to have them as infants, it begs the following question: do vaccines cause B and T cell immunodeficiencies, which are then 'remembered' by DNA to be passed on to subsequent generations? If we can vaccinate some puppies with apparently no ill-effect, but then see reactions occur in the adult dogs, what has changed, and why? Merck seemed to indicate that T cell immunodeficiencies can be caused by a vaccine. And why is it that so many animals and children appear to have eczema, inhalant allergies, heart disease, and so on, these days?

In fact, in a paper prepared by Harold E Buttram MD and John Chriss Hoffman, entitled 'Vaccinations and Immune Malfunction', the authors state that, "The natural immunity of a healthy person is based on a series of body defences. In contrast, vaccinations inject massive amounts of antigens directly into the blood stream, thus bypassing several important defence and balancing mechanisms . . . Total immune capacity is limited, and once it becomes committed to a given antigen, it becomes incapable of responding to other antigens or challenges. . . acquired immunodeficiency syndrome-like changes occurred in T lymphocyte sub populations after the administration of routine tetanus booster vaccinations to 11 healthy adults". The paper highlights work by Sir Graham Wilson, formerly of the Public Health Laboratory Services, England and Wales. In reviewing epidemics of the past, Dr Wilson provided a number of examples in which vaccinations against one disease seemed to provoke another.

Buttram and Hoffman write that, "Considering the extreme efficiency of natural immunity, we can estimate that permanent immunity was gained to routine childhood diseases utilizing only 3 to 7 percent of the total immune capacity. In contrast, childhood vaccines are likely to commit a higher percentage of the total immune capacity, perhaps in the order of 30 to 70 percent. . . It is possible that the increasing incidence of immunologic disorders and increased susceptibility to various infections seen today are the consequences."

The very point of vaccination is that the body should mount a defence. In doing so, antibodies are said to be formed, and a degree of immunity to a specific virus is supposedly conferred to the animal or human. Vaccination is designed to plunge the body into the defence mechanism described by Selye with, hopefully, a positive outcome. But, nevertheless, every time a human or animal is vaccinated, World War III is being invoked and we're hoping the good guys win.

Exposure to stress (whether mental, emotional or physical) affects hormonal activity. The most visual example of these hormones is histamine - hay fever sufferers know exactly when too much histamine is being produced by their bodies, because they start sneezing and itching. Histamine, in sufficient quantity, is a poison. Anti-histamine drugs are given to try to combat this response. Asthmatics will react to mental, physical or emotional stress by altering their breathing patterns.

In the alarm stage of Selye's Non-specific Stress Syndrome, the cells of the adrenal cortex discharge hormone-containing granules into the blood stream. Under certain conditions, an excess production of the hormone called mineralocorticoid desoxycorticosteron (DOC) causes brain lesions. When this is coupled with vascular lesions, also characteristic of Non-specific Stress Syndrome, it may lead to the destruction of large parts of the brain.

Maybe Merck has been reading up on Selye?

What we have found, since this book was first published, is that many people don't want to believe that something they did, under recommendation from their god - a vet - could possibly have caused the horrendous condition experienced by their animal friend. And yet we already know that vaccines are recognised to be a cause of encephalitis, which is recognised to be a cause of epilepsy, which is diagnosed as epilepsy on the basis that the condition recurs, which is due to the fact that the brain isn't simply inflamed, but also damaged. There are brain lesions which, unless a congenital abnormality, first arose during the alarm stage of Selye's non-specific response to stress. And this explains why over 65% of dogs in Canine Health Concern's vaccine survey first became epileptic within three months of vaccination.

What we find, then, is that toxic assaults, such as those conveyed by injecting vaccines and other foreign substances into the body, produce a variety of responses, depending upon the person (an animal is a person) mounting the response - back to Deepak Chopra again.

Leo Kanner, the 'founder' of autism, stated in 1971 that, 'In medicine . . . any illness may appear in different degrees of severity, all the way from the so-called forme fruste to the most fulminant manifestation.'

In his book, '*Vaccination Social Violence and Criminality*', Dr Harris L Coulter builds a compelling argument to suggest that (human) learning disabilities, autism, dyslexia, aggression, hyperactivity, and sociopathic behaviour are largely rooted in vaccine damage. Coulter also noted the high incidence of allergies, seizure disorders, appetite disorders, a lack of control of bowel and urinary functions, breathing problems, and nervous disorders in autistics and minimally brain damaged children. He traces all of these conditions back to neurological damage, or encephalitis (brain inflammation). Coulter contends that the most common cause of this encephalitis in modern day America, where childhood vaccination is mandatory, is vaccination itself.

Could it be that a vaccine doesn't produce either encephalitis or allergies - but both in varying degrees? Couldn't encephalitis simply be one aspect of a wide-ranging condition characterised by inflammation and disruption of parts or the whole of a body?

Mr Taylor of C-Vet was quoted earlier as saying a dog had experienced a 'classic post-vaccinal encephalitis'. Encephalitis is described in the Concise Oxford Veterinary Dictionary as, 'inflammation of the substance of the brain. If the inflammation also involves the membranes enclosing the brain, the condition is termed meningencephalitis (see meningitis). Many encephalitides extend to involve the spinal cord. Infection is invariably the cause. Viral encephalitis may be caused by the viruses of rabies, . . . canine distemper . . . (and others).' How about the vaccines relating to these viruses? Merck seems to think this possible in humans.

It is my contention, and the contention of many, more learned, individuals, that the 'cure' - vaccines - can and do cause the conditions they are trying to prevent, in addition to creating new acute and chronic diseases.

Indeed, encephalitis could be a *symptom* of a larger, more wide-ranging disease which homoeopaths call vaccinosis - the disease that vaccine manufacturers would prefer to describe as a 'myth'. Epilepsy can similarly be a *symptom* of vaccinosis, as can allergies, skin diseases, and other inflammatory conditions . . . the 'itis' diseases (cystitis, pancreatitis, dermatitis, etc.). The overriding consideration must be . . . when did the condition develop in relation to vaccination? As there is no adequate reporting system to answer that question, this thesis cannot be discounted.

Demyelination is another factor within the thesis, and demyelination is capable of being induced by a vaccine. The Merck Manual states: "The myelin sheaths of many nerve fibres promote transmission of the neural impulse along the axon. Many congenital metabolic disorders affect the developing myelin sheath. Unless the innate biochemical defect can be corrected or compensated for, permanent, often widespread, neurologic deficits result.

"In acute disseminated encephalomyelitis (post infectious encephalitis), demyelination can occur spontaneously, but usually follows a viral infection or *inoculation* (or, very rarely, a *bacterial vaccine*), suggesting an immunologic cause. The 'neuroparalytic accidents and peripheral neuropathies that can follow rabies vaccination with brain tissue preparations . . . are similar demyelinating disorders with the same presumed immunopathogenesis."

Microscopical examination of tissues were made of pups who contracted distemper after their mother was vaccinated (*Distemper encephalitis in pups after vaccination of the dam*, AIP McCandlish, et al, *Veterinary Record*, 1992). These post mortem examinations revealed a wide range of effects. Pups one and two revealed depletion of lymphoid tissue in the thymus and spleen, and encephalitis characterised by acute neuronal acidophilia or by neuronal degeneration. Post mortem examination of pup three showed marked wasting of the right foreleg, and a small thymus. In the brain, there were severe encephalitis, with mid- and hindbrains severely affected. Small areas of Demyelination were present in the hindbrain and in the grey matter of the spinal cord. No virus could be isolated from the brain, but "the results obtained strongly suggest that the vaccinal rather than a field virus was responsible for the syndrome observed".

Merck talks only of encephalitis following rabies vaccination, but we also know now that measles itself can cause encephalitis, so why not the live vaccine? We know from research illustrated previously that distemper vaccination can also cause encephalitis and demyelination. In my view, it seems that they've only been able to 'prove' various conditions arising from individual vaccine components - but that doesn't mean that the process itself, irrespective of the virus or bacterin contained in the vaccine, couldn't cause vaccinosis.

Harris Coulter and Barbara L Fisher, in their book, '*DPT: A Shot in the Dark*', explain that the process of myelination and its interruption is key to vaccine damage. They write, "Myelin is the tough, white, fatty, waterproof substance that coats the nerves like insulation on an electric wire, and has the same function."

Coulter and Fisher explain that myelin develops in children after birth; in some nerves it doesn't start forming until the child is eight months old or later, and in others it continues to form until the person is aged 45. Coulter contends that vaccines can cause inflammatory reactions in the nervous system and interrupt that myelination. The result in many cases is encephalitis - inflammation of the brain, plus allergic reactions, hypersensitivity, enteritis, autism, dyslexia, and other conditions.

Jean Dodds DVM has, in many papers, drawn her readers' attention to the dangers of vaccinating young dogs while their systems are still immature. She also explains that the larger breeds mature more slowly than the smaller breeds, which might indicate that larger breeds are immunologically less mature than smaller breeds at the same age; it would be interesting to compare the vaccine regimes and illnesses experienced by large and small breeds and, indeed, between large horses and small cats. The contention here is that, by interrupting the myelination process and stimulating inflammation, vaccines render dogs and other species 'sensitised'. This sensitivity could feasibly extend throughout the entire organism: mind, body and spirit.

Many of the people I have spoken with say that their dog who was apparently damaged by vaccines was a 'one in a million dog': the best dog, best friend, the person has ever shared their life with. I wonder whether some of this might be connected to the vaccine 'sensitising' the animal? An alternative thought is that dogs bred for their sensitive (kind, empathetic, obedient) temperaments might be physically as well as mentally sensitive and unsuited to the violent assault of vaccination.

I mentioned in the introduction that Samson had autoimmune disease and subsequently fell victim to vaccine-induced death. Samson was the most sensitive dog in every respect. He had, for example, been helping Dr Rupert Sheldrake test his theory of morphic resonance, a theory suggesting that we are all connected by thoughts. Samson always knew when we were coming home - to the extent that he knew the exact time of the departure of our plane home from Greece, and demonstrated his knowledge by running to the door and waiting for us.

Samson was sensitive in other ways. He knew when I was tired, taking my arm in his mouth and marching me upstairs to bed. He knew when Gwinnie had managed to find a way out of the garden to go chasing rabbits - even if he was lying down inside asleep, he would wake up and tell me Gwinnie had gone. He knew if I was thinking of nipping up to the shops - he'd tell me he knew by placing his huge paws on my lap and asking to go, too; even though I was still sitting at my computer typing away, and hadn't done anything to indicate 'walkies'. And he knew if something had upset me, even if I wasn't aware of it!

On the physical level, Samson was allergic to certain foods, and his digestive system suffered if there was any upset in the house.

Could it be that vaccines sensitise the entire mind, body, spirit? I think that this is possible, although I would not welcome laboratory trials to 'prove' it.

Certainly, if brain damage is involved, vaccines are rendering people and animals less than they were meant to be. I have such great pity for the parents of 'naughty' children. Others are so quick to criticise and suggest that the parenting is at fault. But could it be that their disruptive children are vaccine damaged? Andy Wakefield at the Royal

Free Hospital has been treating autistic children with steroids and achieving remarkable results. Steroids, of course, are anti-inflammatories, and encephalitis is an inflammatory condition . . . and vaccines are known to cause encephalitis. It seems strange to me, then, that Dr Wakefield's vaccine-autism link has been so violently opposed by both the government and the medical establishment.

Many dogs these days are allergic to wheat and milk products (known in the human field as celiac disease). As Roger Mugford has shown, canine aggression can be minimised by placing the dog on a strict white meat and rice diet, thereby avoiding the foods that the dog is allergic to. One must ask why dogs are suddenly allergic to foods they have eaten for millions of years? Is this down to 'irresponsible breeding', or, rather, are vaccinated dogs more allergic than non-vaccinated dogs? Human children, too, are manifesting more and more inflammatory conditions, with inhalant allergies such as asthma being particularly prevalent - is the breeding at fault here, or are we over-vaccinating?

If people who do not vaccinate their dogs came forward in greater numbers, Canine Health Concern would be able to answer this question - for animals and humans.

Dr Harris Coulter draws comparison between autism and allergies: "four fifths of autistic children and adults have severe allergies. In its most severe form this becomes celiac disease. . . Hyperactive and minimally brain-damaged children also manifest a high incidence of allergic manifestations." (Remember, Coulter contends that autism and hyperactivity are consequences of vaccines.)

Coulter quotes Doris Rapp, a paediatric allergist practising in Buffalo, who said: "I have repeatedly noted in the history of many of the small children whom I treat for allergies that they get a DPT (diphtheria, pertussis, tetanus shot), and then within a month or two they begin to regress. . .

The parents keep giving me this history and they ask, 'is it related?'".

Indeed, encephalitis and allergies are totally related. Anaphylaxis is another word for allergies; anaphylaxis means 'sensitisation', and it is a word used by vaccine manufacturers to describe a possible consequence of vaccination, the most severe form of which is called anaphylactic shock, which can result in death.

The prominent American scientist, Thomas Rivers, produced brain inflammation in monkeys merely by injecting them repeatedly with extracts of sterile normal rabbit brain and spinal cord material (not a nice thing to do). As a result, encephalitis was seen to be an allergic phenomenon, and this explains the association of allergies and autoimmune states with a previous case of encephalitis: encephalitis which can be caused by vaccines.

As a non-scientist and an animal lover, it is highly frustrating to have to cite these experiments upon animals, when our collective experience of companion animals makes it quite clear that encephalitis is an allergic phenomenon. This is one of the reasons why troublesome dogs who are changed from processed pet food, full of chemicals and additives, onto real food, often calm down. They are simply unable to cope with the aggravations of chemicals in their food, and this is exacerbated by a shortage of nutrients in the food.

But, it seems clear from talking to dog owners, that they can survive fairly well into old age on low quality pet foods IF they aren't vaccinated every year. Put them on real food, though, and they are doing more than simply surviving - they're thriving. (Canine Health Concern's diet survey revealed an 85% drop in visits to the vet once dogs were put on natural food.)

We ordinary people are going to have to learn to trust our own observations. Christopher Day, for example, through observation, has been able to note that epileptic dogs also suffer from a wide range of allergies. What science needs, desperately, is a cataloguing of data from the field, rather than proprietary information amassed in laboratories and kept away from the public unless commercially helpful.

Indeed, many vets have made similar observations about dogs, unconnected to the laboratory-based research, but moving from their own observations in practice. Pedro Rivera, DVM, was quoted in Wolf Clan magazine as saying: "In our practice, we have seen hypothyroidism, chronic yeast ear infections, immune-mediated diseases and worsening of them, joint maladies, and behavioural problems as secondary reactions to over-vaccination."

In the same magazine, Pat Bradley DVM claims that behaviour problems such as fearlessness or aggression often begin shortly after vaccination. Stephen R Blake DVM says, "There are a lot of chronic conditions that develop some time after vaccinating. Some of these conditions that I see are digestive problems, seizures, skin problems, and behavioural problems."

For some 15 years, Great Dane breeders in America have been questioning possible adverse effects following the aggressive use of vaccines on immature dogs' immune systems. Subsequently (probably because it's not true until a man in a white coat says it's true), Great Dane people conceptualised a study which was carried out by a team at Purdue University under the direction of Larry Glickman, VDM, DrPh, and Dr Harm HogenEsch.

Unable to house a controlled group of Great Danes, the team chose Beagles for their study. Although genetically distinct from Great Danes, the Beagle trial produced some dramatic results simply by following vaccine manufacturers' recommendations.

The study was funded by the Hayward Foundation. Its Trustee, Dr William R La Rosa, MD, appealed for further funds whilst writing of a paper presented to the International Veterinary Vaccines and Diagnostics Conference, 1997, and subsequently published in 'Advances in Veterinary Science and Comparative Medicine'.

The team studied the effects of routinely used vaccination protocol on the immune and endocrine system of Beagles. One control group was not vaccinated and the other group was vaccinated with a commercial multivalent vaccine at 8, 10, 12, 16 and 20 weeks of age, and with a rabies vaccine at 16 weeks of age.

The vaccinated group developed significant levels of autoantibodies against fibronectin, laminin, DNA, albumin, Cytochrome C, transferring, cardiolipin, and collagen. "The responses varied among individual animals, probably reflecting genetic differences," wrote Dr La Rosa. "The clinical significance of those autoantibodies remains to be determined, but speculation must be that something in the vaccine is one of the etiologies (in the genetically susceptible dog) of such diseases as Cardiomyopathy, Lupus, Erythematosus, Glomerulonephritis, etc.."

Naturally, the call is for further studies. This makes me cross. How many more dogs have to suffer or die in order to prove what we already know? Have we all gone soft in the head? And talking of the head . . .

Autism - which has its root in encephalitis - is fundamentally a neurological disease: involved with the brain. It was first diagnosed and named by the child psychologist Leo Kanner in 1943. Autism is distinguished by the person's aloneness, detachment, inaccessibility, refusal to smile, inability to look others in the eye, and extreme fear and anxiety - usually, but not always, accompanied by mental retardation. For the first ten years of the disease's study, psychiatrists put parents through the ring, particularly the mothers, suggesting that autism was caused by the behaviour of the parents. The term 'refrigerator mother' was coined.

I can't help drawing parallels between the mothers of autistic children and dog owners who take themselves and their conceivably vaccine-damaged dogs off to animal behaviourists hoping that, if they, the humans, change their behaviour, the dog will stop biting the children, or stop running off, or become more obedient. And remember Barbara Woodhouse's counsel that 'there are no bad dogs, just bad owners'? Would she concede that there are brain-damaged dogs? In fact she did: she called it schizophrenia - a condition which, again, bears many neurologic parallels with autism.

Autistic children suffer from a large range of cranial nerve disorders. Cranial nerves run from the eyes, ears, nose, vocal cords, mouth and muscles of the face, over the skull to the brainstem, which is at the back of the neck between the spinal cord and the brain. Some twenty to thirty per cent of autistics are now known to have a seizure disorder: convulsions, fits, clonic spasms, temporal lobe epilepsy, psychomotor epilepsy, staring spells, and others - all neurologically based complaints.

The salivary glands are regulated by derivatives of the cranial nerves and are affected by the same cranial palsies. The tendency of autistics to salivate, drool, and spit indicates damage to these nerves.

Gwinnie, our youngest Golden Retriever, who has been treated by a homoeopathic vet for vaccinosis, is the first Golden Retriever I have personally met who drools. Similarly, Gwinnie could be described as hyperactive. Like autistics, Gwinnie doesn't like looking people in the eye (Christopher Day, who has treated many Golden Retrievers for vaccinosis noted that this was a common symptom of Golden vaccine-damaged dogs). Like autistics, Gwinnie cannot be trusted to stay close when out on walks or if the gate is left open.

For those people whose dogs are fussy eaters, Coulter unearthed a clue, reporting that Christopher Gilbert, a leading Swedish researcher, found a link between autism and anorexia nervosa in 1985. Similarly, autistic children have been noted as having a tendency to bulimia, 'being indiscriminate about what they eat'. Food, once eaten, is digested with difficulty. Autistics suffer frequently from colic and other gastrointestinal pains. Once again, I remind you that science has linked these conditions with neurological disorders or damage, and these conditions are extremely common in today's dog population.

Coulter quoted Hetzler and Griffin, writing in 1981 that, "The extremely heterogeneous autistic population may represent a variety of central nervous system dysfunctions resulting in overlapping overt behavioural manifestations". And didn't Merck tell us that encephalitis can be caused by vaccines, and that central nervous system damage can be part of the picture?

Sudden uncontrolled, seemingly unprovoked aggression is another hallmark of autism. Has anyone ever wondered why the Dangerous Dogs Act should be thought to be necessary in modern day England? Have dogs become more violent, or do we humans only perceive them to be more violent? I personally know of at least two dogs who are lovely most of the time, but fly into strange violent rages without provocation. And other dogs, in loving homes, who cannot be trusted not to wander off. Are these dogs suffering from post-vaccinal encephalitis?

I have had Gwinnie to see a behaviourist; I have asked a friend who is an experienced dog trainer try to train Gwinnie not to run away. I have had Gwinnie treated by a homoeopath, and I have tried everything I can think of myself. And she eats an entirely natural, wholesome diet (none of that pet food muck for my dogs.) But still . . . Gwinnie cannot be trusted off the lead. Is it me? Have I failed? And, in which case, why do my other dogs not have the same problem? Personally, I believe we have a brain-damaged, vaccine-damaged dog here, adorable though she is.

One of Leo Kanner's earliest findings, whilst studying the first cases of autism, was that the parents were generally of above average intelligence (another observation that ties in with parents of schizophrenics). Of Kanner's first 100 cases, 96 of the fathers were college graduates, and 92 of the mothers were high school graduates. Kanner noted: "Many of the fathers and most of the mothers are perfectionists . . . The mothers felt duty-bound to carry-out to the letter the rules and regulations which they were given by their obstetricians and paediatricians". Just like me, who would trot off to the vet every year to have my dearly beloved canine 'children' vaccinated.

This, in my limited experience, ties in shockingly with the observation that it's always the dogs who are given every care, who are bought the 'best' food (for 'best', 'most expensive' might be exchanged), who are taken to the vet regularly, and who are vaccinated each year, who develop skin complaints, allergies, aggressive behaviour, autoimmune haemolytic anaemia, and so on. The dogs who are kept in the barn, get thrown the odd bone and table scraps, and never have their annual vaccination, always seem to be the ones who live the longest and remain the healthiest. Further research needs to be conducted in this respect.

On the subject of minimally brain damaged children, where cranial nerve palsies are also thought to be involved, Coulter notes that these children have difficulty in understanding abstract concepts. Whilst the ability to use abstracts develops with age, the MBD child never moves out of the literal or concrete: 'In school he has an easier time with

101

precise factual subjects such as history or geography but serious trouble with literature, poetry or mathematics'.

One thought is that animal behaviourists might well have success with vaccine-damaged dogs because they teach the owners to give clear, concrete, signals at all times: signals that the neurologically damaged can get to grips with. How much more successful would the behaviourists be if they worked alongside homoeopaths to treat vaccine damage?

Animal behaviourists should also consider the typical autistic child's fear of separation, which might explain why so many of today's dogs cannot be left alone without extreme anxiety in the dog, which may lead to destruction of the dog's surroundings. I'd like to know how many of these fearful dogs had any observable vaccine reaction.

Coulter quotes of autistic children: "The essential feature is . . . excessive anxiety on separation from major attachment figures or from home or other familiar surroundings. When separation occurs, the child may experience anxiety to the point of panic."

Borrowing from Coulter once more, one of the most important observations of his book, 'Vaccination, Social Violence and Criminality', is the parallel he draws between studies of outbreaks of viral encephalitis after World War I, and post-vaccinal encephalitis. Known now as the swine flu virus, the viral epidemic appeared first in China, then spread to Romania, France, Germany and Austria. Outbreaks were later found in most countries of the world. Between 1919 and 1928, more than 500,000 deaths and a million cases of severe neurologic impairment were attributed to epidemic encephalitis.

"A remarkable feature of encephalitis," says Coulter, "whether of epidemic origin or due to an infectious disease, traumatic injury or vaccination, is the multifarious diversity of its physical, neurologic, mental, and emotional symptoms." Coulter quotes HH Merritt, emeritus professor of neurology at Columbia University: "Since any portion of the nervous system may be affected, variable clinical syndromes may occur . . . meningeal, encephalitic, brain-stem, spinal cord, and neuritic."

Diarrhoea, vomiting, flatulence, gastroenteritis, stomach aches, headaches, enuresis, constipation, loss of sphincter control (a ring of muscles that surround an orifice), breathing difficulties, hyperactivity, obsessiveness, inattentiveness, mental retardation, seizures, paralysis, aggression, and other conditions were known to be sequelae arising from viral encephalitis.

These are the same symptoms which arise in some children and animals after they have received a vaccine shot.

Most interestingly, and providing the most compelling argument against vaccination - for animals and children - is that there doesn't necessarily need to be a severe acute reaction for damage to ensue. Although Coulter suggests further research is needed in the case of vaccine-induced encephalitis, he states that encephalitis from all other causes is known to produce severe neurologic damage in the absence of an acute reaction. He asks why encephalitis from vaccination should be an exception.

When a child, dog, or other animal reacts to a vaccine with drowsiness, a slight fever, or appears off his food, there is every reason to fear that this is a hypersensitivity reaction, which can cause inflammation, which can cause encephalitis, which is capable of producing quite severe neurologic consequences. Further, the symptoms need not manifest themselves immediately.

Dr JA Morris, leading US infectious disease expert declared: "We only hear about the encephalitis and the deaths, but there is an entire spectrum between fever and death, and it's all those things in between that never get reported." Of course, the spectrum in between does get reported in the dog population: it gets reported by the owners who wonder why they are forever at the vets. Unfortunately, the connection between vaccination and chronic illness is rarely noticed or acknowledged by the vet.

Dr R Mendelsohn said: "There now exists a growing theoretical concern which links immunisation to the huge increase, in recent decades, of auto-immune diseases, e.g., rheumatoid arthritis, multiple sclerosis, lymphoma and leukaemia." Dr Jean Dodds has done tremendous work to show us that these conditions in our dogs are also vaccine-related.

A report in the Revue de Pathologie et de Physiologie Clinique stated, "The vaccine modifies the terrain of the vaccinated, driving it towards alkaline and oxidised terrain; the terrain of cancer, the fact can no longer be ignored.' Well, actually, yes - it was ignored. They're still vaccinating anyway.

Professor R Simpson of the American Cancer Society said that vaccines may cause rheumatoid arthritis, multiple sclerosis, systemic lupus erythematosus, Parkinson's disease, and cancer.

Dr G Buchwald, a German medical director, conducted extensive studies of the effects of smallpox vaccination leading to encephalitis. His studies were eventually determinant in the German government's decision to abolish smallpox vaccination altogether. Dr Buchwald expressed his suspicion that multiple sclerosis could also be a belated consequence of smallpox vaccination. Indeed, Dr Viera Scheibner tells us that people routinely develop multiple sclerosis within four weeks of vaccination (Miller, H., Cendrowski, W., and Shapira, K., 1967. *Multiple sclerosis and vaccination. British Medical Journal*; 22 April: 210-213).

The French magazine, *'Vie et Action'* (Mar/April 1966) commented: "In Great Britain, smallpox vaccination hasn't been compulsory since 1898, and yet five times fewer people have died of smallpox in Great Britain than in France, where this vaccination is compulsory."

Jean Dodds DVM, states in her paper, *'Vaccine Safety and Efficacy Revisited'*, " . . . (MLV vaccines) can overwhelm the immunocompromised or even a healthy host that is continually bombarded with other environmental stimuli. This scenario may have a significant effect on the recently weaned young puppy or kitten who is placed in a new environment. Furthermore, while the frequency of vaccinations is usually spaced two to three weeks apart, some veterinarians have advocated vaccination once a week in stressful situations. This practice makes no sense from a scientific or medical perspective. While puppies exposed this frequently to vaccine antigens may not demonstrate overt adverse effects, it is clear that their immune systems may still be immature. Consequences in later life may be an increased frequency of chronic debilitating diseases. Many veterinarians trace the present problems with allergic and immunologic diseases to the introduction of MLV (multiple live virus) vaccines some twenty years ago."

Pat Bradley DVM, once again in Wolf Clan magazine, says: "The bodies of most animals have a tremendous capacity to detoxify poisons, but they do have a limit. I think we often exceed that limit and overwhelm the body's immune system function with toxins from vaccines, poor quality foods, insecticides, environmental toxins, etc. This is why we've seen such a dramatic increase in allergies, organ failures, and behaviour problems."

Christina Chambreau DVM says, "Routine vaccinations are probably the worst thing that we do for our animals. They cause all types of illnesses but not directly to where we would relate them definitely to be caused by the vaccine."

Coulter and Fisher contended in their book, *'DPT, A Shot in the Dark'*, that a minimum of one thousand (human) babies die from the DPT vaccine every year in the USA, while 12,000 are permanently damaged. His figures were never challenged by the medical establishment. Indeed, one vaccine manufacturer later announced publicly that it was putting a substantial portion of its profits aside to pay vaccine damage compensation claims.

Dr Viera Scheibner goes further in her book, *'Vaccination, 100 Years of Orthodox Research'*. She says: "These figures are much higher. Cot death researchers published evidence in 1967 to show that cot deaths were between 15,000 and 25,000 children per year in the US. The majority of these deaths are caused by vaccination."

In an article by Yvonne Roberts in the *Sunday Times* colour supplement of December 17th, 1995, Dr Reed P Warren at Utah State University was quoted. He and his colleagues have discovered that the measles virus (for measles read distemper, as they are from the same family of viruses) tricks the immune system into attacking the body's own myelin instead of battling with the virus. If myelin is damaged, the Utah team suggest, this could be the cause of hearing and learning difficulties as well as autism.

Similarly, the Inflammatory Bowel Disease Study Group at the Royal Free Hospital School of Medicine, led by senior lecturer Andy Wakefield, believes it has found a connection between inflammatory bowel disease and the measles vaccine. Indeed, the group believes that vaccinated children appear three times more likely to suffer from inflammatory bowel disease than unvaccinated children (linking with the colitis experienced by vaccinated dogs).

A *Sunday Times* article provides a harrowing example of a child who became epileptic following vaccination (remember epilepsy is a brain disorder). It says, "In 1988, Hannah was the youngest of Carol and Tony Buxton's four children. At 18 months old, she was among the first children in the country to have the MMR (measles, mumps, rubella) vaccine. A week later she developed a high temperature. That evening she had a convulsion. Three weeks later she had a fit.

"Over the next 17 months, Hannah continued to have fits. The Buxtons eventually decided to apply to the Vaccine Damage Payments Unit. A month before her third birthday, Hannah died in the night during an epileptic fit. A week later, the VDPU wrote to say that as the child was deceased, the case was closed. The Buxtons decided to appeal, because by now their suspicion that the vaccine was the cause had become a certainty. Parts of Hannah's brain were sent for analysis, and months later the Buxtons were told it had been agreed that Hannah had developed epilepsy as a result of the MMR."

In the UK, the Vaccine Damage Payments Unit offers up to £30,000 to parents whose children's lives have been ruined or prematurely terminated by vaccines. **In America, the Vaccine Injury Trust Fund paid out $465 million in three years.** Officially, it is rarely admitted that vaccines are the cause.

Anti-vaccinators are labelled as irresponsible and alarmist, but, repeatedly, pro-vaccinators seek to hide or minimise the evidence.

But what of your dog? Every dog has a price on his head: of between £5 and £500, depending upon his bloodline. So if you manage to extract an admission of responsibility from the vaccine manufacturer, you may be able to buy a replacement - although I have personally never heard of a vaccine manufacturer doing anything beyond paying vet bills, and this in rare circumstances. Financial compensation would be fine, though, if dogs were things that could be replaced, as opposed to people with their own personalities. Money would in no way make up for the suffering that has been caused.

But the root problem still needs to be addressed: vaccine manufacturers and vets tell us that vaccines create more good than harm. They treat us as though we were mushrooms, deciding not to tell us about the possible adverse reactions because they have taken it upon their own shoulders to make the decisions for us. In effect, they take the authority but reject the responsibility. We animal guardians and parents are the ones who shoulder that responsibility: we are the ones who must sit with our loved-ones as they die, and we are the ones who generally pay the price, both financially and emotionally.

The onus is therefore on the guardians to become as knowledgeable as vets. Personally, I think that the evidence points towards a need for us to become more knowledgeable about vaccination than vets. So let's take a look at what vets know, and also at what they don't know - before we submit our friends to their annual booster jab.

Summary

* Organisms often have a non-specific response to stress, which can affect every system in the body
* The ability to respond positively to that stress relies on a variety of factors: the severity of the stress, other concurrent challenges, and the ability of the animal or human to counteract the stress
* Vaccines are injected directly into the bloodstream, bypassing many natural immune responses but demanding a greater effort by the immune system than would naturally-occurring disease
* Encephalitis, as illustrated by the swine flu virus, provokes a wide diversity of physical, neurologic, mental, and emotional symptoms
* An increasing number of vets and scientists link encephalitis and other inflammatory conditions with vaccines
* The official line minimises suggestions of vaccine-related illness

Chapter Four

What vets should know about vaccines.

The vaccine manufacturers state, in their own literature: in the veterinary data sheets, that vaccination is not without risks. The following information is made available to vets, but vets rarely warn dog owners of the risks of vaccination. Maybe this is because they believe adverse reactions occur in only a tiny minority of cases. This, in turn, could be because vets are blissfully unaware of the range of reactions we have been examining. An anonymous vet tells me that they just aren't taught about adverse reactions to vaccines.

The following information is taken from the *Compendium of Data Sheets for Veterinary Products 1994-1995*. All trademarks are acknowledged.

C-VET (Veterinary Products) writes in the Compendium:

Contra-indications: Only healthy dogs should be vaccinated. Dogs under treatment with immuno-suppressive drugs should not be vaccinated. Following primary vaccination, dogs or puppies should not be exposed to infection for at least 7 days. A small number of animals in any population may fail to respond to vaccination as a result of immunological incompetence or for some other reason. Hypersensitivity reactions occur very rarely. They should be treated by the paranteral administration of an antihistamine, corticosteroid or adrenaline as appropriate.

Intervet UK Limited, again in the Compendium, writes:

Contra-indications: Only healthy dogs should be vaccinated. Following initial vaccination dogs should not be exposed to infection for at least 14 days. Generalised hypersensitivity reactions following administration may occasionally occur. In this event administration of Adrenaline Injection BP by the subcutaneous route may be indicated.

Under 'further information', Intervet adds, "A good immune response is reliant on the reaction of an immunogenic agent and a fully competent immune system. Immunogenecity of the vaccine antigen will be reduced by poor storage or inappropriate administration. Immunocompetence of the animal may be compromised by a variety of factors, including poor health, nutritional status, genetic factors, concurrent drug therapy and stress.

SmithKline Beecham Animal Health writes (again in the Compendium):

Contra-indications: Do not vaccinate unhealthy or pregnant animals. Side-effects are extremely rare and no specific treatment is recommended if they occur. If an allergic reaction occurs for any reason, administer adrenaline. The use of hyperimmune serum or immunosuppressant drugs is contra-indicated within one month of vaccination. In any animal population a small number of individuals may fail to respond to vaccination.

Please note that all of the vaccine manufacturers understand and **know that only healthy dogs should be vaccinated**, and a dog who is being given 'immune suppressant' drugs - such as steroids - should not be vaccinated.

Christopher Day comments: "It is customary for a manufacturer to state that one should only vaccinate healthy dogs. This is rarely heeded in the real world, in that a great many unwell dogs, even those under constant long-term treatment from their vets, are still boosted annually." And this despite the warnings against it.

All of the above vaccine manufacturers concede that hypersensitivity or allergic reactions may occur following vaccination. They stop short of stipulating what these reactions might be. Pitman-Moore Ltd, another vaccine manufacturer, gives us a clue. They say, in the Compendium:

"Adverse Reactions: Any vaccine may very occasionally stimulate an anaphylactic reaction. In such cases appropriate treatment such as adrenaline, antihistamines or corticosteroids should be administered without delay."

So going back to the veterinary dictionary to look up the word 'anaphylactic', we find:

"anaphylaxis 1. Hypersensitivity. 2. A particular form of Type I hypersensitivity in which generalised damaging changes are induced by the release of histamine. Anaphylactic shock is an extreme and generalised allergic reaction in which widespread histamine release causes bronchial constriction (and hence respiratory distress), dilation of the veins, circulatory collapse, and possibly death."

The Concise Oxford Veterinary Dictionary says that four types of hypersensitivity reactions are recognised, namely:

1. Type I reactions are brought about by an antigen reacting with tissue masT cells bearing specific antibodies on their membranes. This releases substances which cause inflammation. The signs of Type I hypersensitivity vary with the species affected, but can include bronchial constriction, diarrhoea, vomiting, salivation, abdominal pain, and cyanosis.

'Cyanosis' is a bluish discolouration of the skin and mucous membranes due to lack of oxygen in the blood. It occurs in certain conditions affecting the heart and circulatory system. It is therefore possible that vaccines can cause heart failure.

It should also be noted that we expect our dogs to be sick and have diarrhoea after vaccination. This isn't them feeling slightly ill - it's a Type I hypersensitivity reaction, an allergic reaction to the vaccine.

In a paper prepared by R Brooks of the Commonwealth Serum Laboratories Limited for the Australian Veterinary Journal (October 1991), entitled 'Adverse reactions to canine and feline vaccines', systemic reactions to vaccines are described.

Under Type I hypersensitivity, the paper shows that clinical signs in dogs include an initial restlessness, vomiting, diarrhoea and dyspnoea (difficult breathing). R Brooks tells us that some cases can progress to collapse and death.

2. Type II reactions are a form of cell damage induced by antibody (antibody is produced by the body in response to the presence of antigens; antigens are substances, such as toxins and invading organisms, that are recognised as foreign, e.g., vaccines). Tissue may be injured, but blood cells are particularly susceptible. The dictionary suggests we look at 'autoimmune disease', which is described as any disorder involving inflammation or destruction of tissue by the body's own immune system.

The dictionary says, "Specific autoimmune diseases in the dog are well studied and include canine autoimmune haemolytic anaemia, systemic lupus erythematosus, autoimmune thyroiditis, a number of skin inflammations, and possibly rheumatoid arthritis". For those whose dog died of kidney failure shortly after vaccination, Glomerulonephritis is also listed as an autoimmune disease (which can be caused by the body reacting to antigens like vaccines), the effects of which are acute renal (kidney) failure.

Similarly, hepatitis, an inflammatory condition of the liver, is questionably autoimmune mediated. Viral hepatitis can occur in, amongst other things, canine parvovirus infection. Chronic active hepatitis is queried as an autoimmune-mediated disease in the Concise Veterinary Dictionary. Where dogs have died of liver failure after vaccination, is it unreasonable to suspect that the vaccine may have caused that failure? A vaccine is, after all, a dose of a disease injected straight into the body.

3. Little is said of Type III hypersensitivity in the dictionary. Reactions are caused, we are told, by antigen-antibody complexes.

However, R Brooks of the Commonwealth Serum Laboratories Ltd tells us that it is possible that in young, small puppies with maternal antibody, antigen-antibody complexes activate the complement system and cause the release of lymphokines, and this could be part of the pathogenesis of the lethargy sometimes seen after vaccination. Anxiety, stress and car sickness could also be involved in some cases.

Blue-eye in dogs is a type III hypersensitivity reaction after immunisation with living canine adenovirus I or natural infection with this virus. However, as canine adenovirus 2 is now used in all live hepatitis vaccines, blue-eye is said to be no longer a problem.

4. Type IV reaction is thought to be essentially protective rather than damaging, although the dictionary says that a number of diseases seem to occur as a result of uncontrolled Type IV processes, including contact hypersensitivity (presumably skin or dermal), autoimmune thyroiditis, and a number of granulomatous conditions - a granuloma is a chronic inflammatory lesion produced in response to a variety of stimuli, such as bacterial or protozoal (single cell organism) invasion, or a foreign body (a vaccine could be described as the introduction of a foreign body).

In short, all these autoimmune diseases are caused by the introduction of a foreign body which the immune system copes with by going crazy.

The word, 'autoimmune' keeps coming into the picture. What does it mean again? 'Any disorder involving inflammation or destruction of tissues by the body's own immune system'.

Going back to Merck's Veterinary Manual, published in 1991, it states: "In the last decade, the frequency of diagnosis of immune-mediated haematological diseases and autoimmune thyroid disease in man and dog has increased." The author postulates that one explanation might be viral infection of the marrow and/or suppression or destruction of stem cells. Another thought is that genetic predisposition - in man and dogs - may have increased.

Autoimmune haemolytic anaemia (AIHA) is a disease where autoantibodies (an antibody formed by the body in response to its own tissue) attack red blood cells (erythrocytes). Affected animals have clinical signs that directly relate to anaemia. These include pallor, weakness, lethargy accompanied by fever, jaundice, and other signs associated with destruction of the liver. Other clinical signs include an increase in heart rate (tachycardia), a complete loss of appetite, vomiting, or diarrhoea. The outcome is usually death. Swift death. Painful death.

Tizard's Veterinary Immunology, 4th edition, states that the cause of autoimmune haemolytic anaemia is unknown, although some cases may result from the alterations on the surface properties of erythrocytes (red blood cells), perhaps induced by drugs or viruses. *There is evidence, they say, for a genetic predisposition to the disease in some animals. However, "its onset may be associated with obvious stress such as vaccination using modified live virus, virus disease, or hormonal imbalances such as pregnancy or pyometra."*

Just to complicate matters, what Tizard doesn't mention is that the drugs used to prevent a bitch coming into season can cause pyometra, and drugs used to treat pyometra might also be implicated in the production of autoimmune disease.

In fact, as many as 30 or more drugs are now suspected in an apparently increasing number of immune mediated haematology (blood) reactions. Among those associated with such reactions are the sulphonamides and nonsteroidal anti-inflammatory agents (Merck Veterinary Manual).

Sulphonamides are used to treat bacterial infections, such as respiratory conditions, foot rot, enteritis, skin infections, mastitis, and urinary tract infections. They are used in cattle, poultry, and small animals, and are thought to be short-lived. This means that animals treated with sulphonamides are not thought to be dangerous to eat.

It also means that dogs being treated for skin infections, enteritis, respiratory conditions and so on, are not healthy dogs. Not only will their immune systems be depressed through ill health, but they may also be receiving drugs which render vaccines harmful by rendering the immune system unable to combat the vaccine antigen challenge.

In our attempt to protect our dogs from disease, we inject them with vaccines which have the potential to create the imbalances which cause skin infections, enteritis, respiratory conditions, and other autoimmune diseases. Then, in an attempt to alleviate these conditions, we administer drugs that suppress the immune system and have the potential to cause imbalances in the blood, leading perhaps to autoimmune diseases and blood-mediated cancers. Sure, all of these drugs have their place - but they should not, I contend, be used as a first resort every time a dog is taken to the vets. They are violent measures used best where violence is the only thing that will make the dog live.

Vets are warned, by the vaccine manufacturers, not to vaccinate sick dogs (more usually expressed as 'only healthy dogs should be vaccinated'). Herein lies one of the major dangers of vaccinating animals - because they cannot always tell us how they feel. Is a dog who had a (coincidental?) epileptic fit the last time he was vaccinated a sick dog, and should he be vaccinated again? Is a dog who feels slightly queasy a sick dog? Is a dog who has been sitting in a hot car for 14 minutes a sick dog? When you feel unwell, can a doctor examine you and always discover why - in the space of a five-minute appointment? How many people are accused of malingering when they say they don't feel well but look perfectly normal?

In a paper appearing in DVM magazine, Dr Ian Tizard, professor and head of the Department of Veterinary Microbiology and Parasitology at Texas A&M University, stated: "In making modified live vaccine you make it for an animal that you assume is immunologically normal. Essentially, you're doing a balancing act: taking an agent and attenuating it (making it less harmful) so that in the immunologically competent host (the normal animal), it will not cause disease. The trouble is, you cannot assume that every animal you vaccinate is functioning immunologically normal. There will be a proportion of any population that is not immunologically 100 per cent. This can immediately tilt an animal towards disease susceptibility. In addition, a vaccine may not cause frank disease itself. It may cause mild immunosuppression."

We have also heard that vets are warned not to vaccinate dogs who are taking immunosuppressant drugs (corticosteroids, for example, suppress the immune system, yet these are recommended when dogs experience hypersensitivity reactions to vaccines). What if the dog has eaten a tin of dog food that contains animals who were injected with corticosteroids before they were slaughtered? Do pet food manufacturers test for these drugs in their food? No. Do these drugs degrade in the cooking process? Some, but not all of them. Some become more toxic.

One does wonder whether the food our dogs eat might contain traces of sulphonamides and/or anti-inflammatory drugs and these, combined with multiple live virus vaccines (not to mention pesticides), might give rise to a 'cocktail effect' that pushes a dog over the edge? Why else might you be able to get away with vaccinating a puppy, and then see them react at the age of four or eight?

Some of the vaccine manufacturers, and much of the research, points to a genetic factor relating to hypersensitivity reactions following vaccination (as The Merck Manual has done). Does your vet ask you whether your dog's mother, father or brothers and sisters have ever had epilepsy, skin conditions, heart or liver failure, allergies, autoimmune disease, or any other of the conditions that are so very common in the modern dog? And if a genetic predisposition is suspected by the vaccine manufacturers, why do vets continue to inject dogs who have already had epileptic fits, skin conditions, arthritis, heart murmurs, and so on? Researchers have found a common thread of allergies running through human families whose members have suffered vaccine reactions. Why can't we use our common sense and accept that animals might also require the same considered thought?

The point - surely - is that the dogs/people with genetic predispositions would never have succumbed to the life-threatening diseases had they not been vaccinated. It is not too far-fetched to draw a parallel example: if dogs, who are (genetically) predisposed not to respect fast cars didn't play in the roads, they wouldn't get run over. We don't have to let them!

Why does the Merck Manual for humans stipulate unequivocally that live virus vaccines should not be administered to certain classes of humans, whilst no-one says this about animal vaccines? Is this because we can always go out and buy a new dog or cat? Do their lives matter less because they're a commodity?

As nearly a quarter of all dogs die of cancer (rising to 46% of those over the age of ten), and as most dog owners know - only too well - that their dogs are prone to arthritis, allergies, skin conditions, thyroid problems, infertility, behaviour problems, and so on, it is not too far fetched to suggest that the vaccine regime must be seriously questioned.

The vaccine manufacturers state that immunocompetence of the animal may be compromised by a variety of factors including nutritional status. Do vets ask whether dogs are fed properly? Do vets know what constitutes a good diet for a dog? How much time do vets spend, at college and after college, studying canine nutrition? (Answer: about two days, if that, and often on a course organised by a pet food manufacturer.) And how much effort do the vaccine manufacturers put in to educating dog owners and dog guardians about dog food? Or do they leave it all to chance? One vaccine manufacturer, at least, does not. Intervet markets a product called SA37, a dietary supplement.

How many of us give our dogs water straight from the tap? How many of us know that fluoride, added to drinking water, has an adverse effect on the thyroid? And that a dog with a diseased thyroid, when vaccinated, can be triggered to develop an autoimmune disease?

The vaccine companies also mention stress as a factor that might 'compromise immunocompetence'. Is a puppy likely to be stressed when he is taken from his mother and litter mates, introduced to a new family in a strange environment, and taken to the vet's for its first or second vaccine shot? And has the vet ever asked you whether you had a row with your husband/wife on the morning of a dog's vaccination, or whether the dog had any physically stressful walks that day, or has just returned from its agility class? Come to think of it, isn't extremely warm weather stressful to a dog, and should we vaccinate a hot dog?

Importantly, is 'immunocompetence may be compromised' sales-speak for "your dog might die" . . . ? Probably: if the dog is unable to mount an effective immune response because his diet is wrong, or his genes are wrong, or he's under stress, or he's just been playing in a field recently sprayed with organophosphates, or he's taking steroids to cure an existing physical problem, your dog could well die after he's vaccinated.

So many questions . . . so few answers. And too many assumptions. If we don't know whether our dogs are genetically susceptible; if we don't know whether their diet is adequate; if we don't know whether they are feeling unwell; and if the vet doesn't realise your dog shouldn't be vaccinated because he's been given immune-suppressing drugs . . . aren't we rather playing Russian roulette with our dogs' lives when we vaccinate them?

By comparing experiences, we are able to see that some dogs appear to react fatally or severely to vaccines. We are also able to see that, by dipping into a few sources of information available to us, that vaccines are known to present risks to those being vaccinated. Yet most vets, like Steve Dean, tell us that vaccines are perfectly safe except for a tiny minority who are genetically defective; and that vaccines pass rigorous safety procedures and therefore they're fine, don't worry your little self about it. I've never visited a vet to have any of my dogs vaccinated where the vet actually warned me that there were risks involved.

What percentage of the dog population is never vaccinated or boosted? Where is the long-term research to tell us how these unprotected dogs fare? And where is the long-term research to show us how vaccinated dogs fare in comparison? Dr Schultz, when questioned, stated that when his un-revaccinated Golden Retrievers died in their teens, they still had antibodies to diseases vaccinated for years previously.

Dr Schultz also reveals in the *Journal of the American Veterinary Medical Association*, that: "There are . . . . . families of dogs, notably in the Doberman and Rottweiler breed, but probably in every breed, that do not respond to vaccination." (Although this statement was, admittedly, denied by David Sutton of Intervet in a letter to a worried animal guardian.)

So what has happened to these Doberman and Rottweiler families, and families in probably every breed, who do not respond to vaccination? If vaccination is so important, why haven't these families been overrun with viral disease and simply died out?

We also hear, in the same article, that the parvovirus vaccine is highly unreliable. Dr Schultz tells us: "At the Infectious Gastroenteritis Symposium of the North American Veterinary Conference, we reported on a study where we evaluated 6 parvovirus vaccines that were administered 2 times, 3 weeks apart. We found that only 2 vaccines provided 100% protection against challenge with CPV-2a and -2b. One vaccine provided partial protection, and 3 did not protect at all."

So if three out of six vaccines chosen, presumably at random, failed to protect the dogs from disease, why don't 50% of all vaccinated dogs die of parvovirus? If only half a population has been successfully immunised, how can anybody claim that it's only thanks to vaccines that our dogs aren't all dying of the disease? Why are we being frightened into injecting our dogs every year when the vaccines themselves not only present the risk of inducing death and disease, but cannot offer more than a 50% guarantee of immunising?

Cynics might say that this has something to do with the fact that vaccines are the number one earner for veterinary practices, which is a fact. But I have spoken to vets who genuinely believe that vaccines are efficacious. One, who I trust implicitly, told me, "we just don't see these type of reactions in our practices, and if we do see what appears to be a vaccine reaction, we generally find that there was another cause when we investigate the matter." I have to say, though, that this particular vet has since admitted to me that it is not politic for him to think about vaccine damage, considering vets make so much money out of vaccines.

But what about the homoeopathic vets who diagnose 'vaccinosis', treat the animal for vaccinosis, and the dog responds? Doesn't successful treatment indicate that diagnosis was correct? Especially those dogs whose owners exhausted conventional treatment - steroids, creams, antibiotics - before moving to a homoeopath for a successful cure.

But don't panic. Read on. Because no-one is advising you to expose your dog to potentially deadly viruses without protection. There are answers.

One so far unanswered question is: "how likely is it that your dog will contract parvovirus, distemper, leptospirosis, hepatitis or kennel cough if you leave him unvaccinated?

I told a sincere pro-vaccinating vet that I don't vaccinate my dogs any more. He said, "That's all right. No problem. These diseases hardly exist any more. It's highly unlikely that they will come into contact with the virus." Steve Dean may have been right in one respect: the diseases aren't lurking round every street corner waiting to get your dog and, ergo, even water will work!

But, not taking one man's word for it, or even two, I telephoned the National Office of Animal Health (NOAH). This is a trade association whose members include most, if not all, the companies that manufacture vaccines for animals in the UK. NOAH doesn't keep these statistics. They suggested I telephone the Kennel Club. The Kennel Club doesn't know how common these diseases are.

The Kennel Club suggested I telephone the Royal College of Veterinary Surgeons (which is a sort of trade association for vets). The RCVS told me that they don't keep these statistics, either. They said maybe I should telephone the Royal Veterinary College who, unable to help, suggested I telephone the RVC Animal Hospital. Drawing a blank once again, it was suggested I telephone the British Veterinary

Association who suggested I telephone the British Small Animal Veterinary Association. No-one could help.

So, as a last resort, I wondered if the Ministry of Agriculture Fisheries and Food might know how prevalent these diseases are. I had a lovely chat with a man who suggested that the manufacturers of the vaccines might know, but he said they were hardly likely to tell me, so he gave me a direct line to the Animal Section of the Ministry dealing with all aspects regarding animals.

The very nice lady I spoke with explained that they keep statistics concerning rabies, which is a notifiable disease, but not the others. She suggested that the drug companies might know but, she said, they wouldn't tell me unless the diseases were very common, giving themselves a nice sales plug. She suggested that, perhaps, local environmental health officers might have a clue. I wondered whether individual vets might be the solution - ask them whether they ever saw these diseases these days (except in vaccinated animals). But then, I thought, they would immediately become suspicious if I asked, and I'd draw a blank once again. Later, at a seminar, I met a vet who was surprised that so many dogs in our survey (see chapter eleven) had come down with distemper, parvo, lepto, etc., within three months of being vaccinated. "I don't know where you got these dogs from," he said, "because I haven't seen any of these diseases for years."

So I decided to write to some of the vaccine manufacturers, rather than phone, so I had a record of the dialogue. None of them replied. A case of silence speaking volumes? Does it seem right to you that we should be expected to buy products from people who refuse to answer our questions, refuse to address our fears, and refuse to release 'proprietary' information that might influence whether we buy their products or not?

Veterinary immunologists such as Ron Schultz are talking about newer, safer, vaccines coming onto the market soon. I am tempted to tell the vaccine manufacturers where to shove them. So now I'm supposed to trust you?

It seems that the vaccines we loving, caring, responsible dog owners pump into our animals every year are to thwart the onset of unquantified diseases - no-one seems to know the level of the risk we are running from. But we do know - now - some of the risks associated with the vaccines.

In 1968, Professor Rene Dubos wrote in 'Man, Medicine and Environment', "Smallpox vaccine does produce serious encephalitis in a few persons even when administered with the utmost care. The chance of contracting smallpox is now so slight that the risk of accidents originating from the vaccine is much greater than the chance of contracting the disease itself."

So, ditto, with the lives of our dogs. Who is quantifying the risk of viral infection versus vaccination? And - most importantly - are there safer ways of protecting our dogs? I think there are . . . so read on.

Summary

* Vaccine manufacturers admit that adverse reactions can occur post-vaccination, but claim the reactions are extremely rare
* Allergic reactions can manifest as diarrhoea, difficult breathing, pain, autoimmune diseases, organ failure, skin disease, thyroid disease, and death
* Vaccines are made for immunologically normal animals, but not for immunologically compromised animals
* Animals with genetic faults should not be vaccinated, but vets assume most if not all animals are genetically fine, or they don't understand that genetically compromised animals should not be given live vaccines
* Various environmental factors render vaccines harmful, including stress and poor diet
* Vaccines have been shown not to guarantee immunity

Your notes

Chapter Five

The diseases themselves

So let's see what these 'deadly' diseases are that require our dogs to be vaccinated every year.

Canine parvovirus

Canine parvovirus is closely related to feline viral enteritis virus. The sudden widespread appearance of the disease in 1979 has led to the suggestion that it originated from an attenuated feline enteritis vaccine strain (source: *Concise Oxford Veterinary Dictionary*). Read that sentence again: it is thought that a vaccine caused parvovirus.

In fact, the parvovirus vaccine and the feline enteritis vaccine are the same for all intents and purposes. A theory about vaccines in general, supported by the fact that parvo didn't exist before we started vaccinating cats for enteritis, is that vaccine antigens are shed in the environment (in faeces and urine), and these are picked up by other species and spread throughout the ecosystem. In short, vaccines keep viruses going when they might otherwise die out.

The puppy Daniel, who was infected with parvovirus from the vaccine is one such example. Having been injected with parvovirus, Daniel passed the disease on to Sebastian, his litter mate.

Another theory for the sudden appearance of the disease is that it was brought into the country after dingoes in Australia were deliberately infected with the virus as a culling measure. An Australian vet told me that, in his opinion, this rumour is unfounded.

Another rumour is that an RAF chap brought an infected animal into the UK from Germany where the disease was prevalent. And yet another rumour is that a woman importing monkeys into the UK is responsible, because the monkeys were carrying the virus. The monkey rumour might be particularly significant, especially when we view the origins of AIDS later.

In fact, rumours aside, a *Sunday Times* article quoted scientists as saying that **parvovirus was created by vaccine manufacturers** who cultivated the distemper vaccine on cats' kidneys that were infected with feline enteritis. In other words, parvovirus is a cross-species, vaccine-induced disease. It's ironic that parvo is always mentioned by vets who defend vaccines: "We were jolly glad of vaccines when parvo appeared; people were queueing at our doors to have their dogs vaccinated". I guess the vets weren't to know - the vaccine manufacturer seems not to have owned up too vociferously.

The *Sunday Times* article came with the colourful heading: "New killer viruses are emerging every year, unleashed by the very medical and technological advances that promised to control our environment."

The article states, "there is no doubt that new medical developments, such as vaccines grown in animals cells or animal-to-human transplants, might easily contribute to an epidemic. In nature, viruses generally have to persist before they find a way into new species."

According to the *Concise Oxford Veterinary Dictionary*, in puppies below the age of eight weeks of age, and occasionally in older dogs, parvovirus causes damage to the heart muscle. A high percentage of affected puppies under the age of eight weeks die of heart failure. Only 10% of young dogs over the age of eight weeks will die of the disease. Death is rare in older dogs, and enteritis is the main consequence of infection.

However, puppies may, or may not, be protected by maternal antibody until they are 16 weeks of age.

So, from this we can conclude that puppies below 16 weeks of age are probably protected without vaccination. Evidence, put forward by Dr Viera Scheibner, suggests that vaccinated mothers fail to pass on effective antibody to their puppies/children - so by vaccinating the mother, we might be putting the progeny at risk.

When, however, we vaccinate puppies who still possess maternal antibody, what we are doing is rendering the puppy unprotected against infection. This is because the vaccine and the maternal antibody cancel one-another out. (As stipulated in the manufacturers' data sheets.) A tiny number of vets will therefore run blood tests on puppies to see whether maternal antibody is still present. If it is, vaccination is postponed.

Please pay particular attention to the statement that parvovirus is rarely life-threatening in older dogs. In fact, they only tend to get the trots. So if we can't guarantee protection for puppies from the vaccine, and adult dogs aren't at great risk, why vaccinate? I suppose it means we are at least trying to do *something*.

Vaccine company recommendations:

C-VET (Veterinary Products) markets a range of canine vaccines. Citadel 12 CPV is a freeze-dried live virus vaccine for parvovirus. Despite the fact that maternal antibodies may be present in puppies until they are sixteen weeks of age, C-VET advises that puppies be vaccinated with Citadel 12 CPV at between 6 and 9 weeks of age, with a second given when the puppy reaches twelve weeks of age. C-VET's literature carried in the NOAH Compendium of Data Sheets for Veterinary Products 1994-95, states: "In puppies under 12 weeks of age, high levels of maternally derived antibody may interfere with the development of active immunity to canine parvovirus."

Intervet UK Limited also manufactures a range of vaccines for dogs, including NOBI-VAC PARVO-C, a live attenuated strain grown in cell-line tissue culture. Intervet states, in the Veterinary Data Sheet Compendium, "The preferred age for vaccination of puppies with Nobi-Vac

Parvo-C is the earliest time at which residual maternal antibody will have waned to levels unlikely to interfere with the immune response . . . Where the antibody status of a pup is unknown or where it is known to be of low order, vaccination at 6, 9 and 12 weeks is recommended."

With regard to booster vaccinations, Intervet recommends that "dogs 'which' are exposed to field infection should be vaccinated annually. Where no such exposure is believed to have occurred the owner should be advised to consult his veterinary surgeon as to whether revaccination should be carried out earlier."

SmithKline Beecham Animal Health provided, in the Compendium, details of a product called Vanguard* CPV, a live canine parvovirus. *The Guardian* newspaper, however, reported that SmithKline Beecham was selling its animal health division to a rival US pharmaceutical group for $1.45 billion (£920 million). SmithKline Animal Health, which specialised in vaccines, made profits of $104 million on sales of $614 million in 1993. During the first nine months of 1994, its operating profits were $72 million, up 17 per cent.

SmithKline claimed that Vanguard CPV was capable of stimulating active immunity in the presence of significant levels of maternally-derived antibody. Their Data Sheet says that puppies should be given their first injection at six weeks of age, then nine weeks, then 12. Annual booster vaccination is recommended.

Websters Animal Health (UK) Limited markets Protech* Parvo. Once again, the company advises that the vaccine should be administered to pups at between 6 and 9 weeks of age, and a second when the puppy reaches twelve weeks. Websters agrees with its competitors, stating that "in puppies under 12 weeks of age, high levels of maternally derived antibody may interfere with the development of active immunity to parvovirus."

Websters also advises that only healthy dogs should be vaccinated, dogs under treatment with immuno-suppressive drugs should not be vaccinated; a small number of animals may fail to respond to vaccination; and hypersensitivity reactions occur 'very rarely'. Finally, all dogs should be vaccinated against parvovirus each year.

But the manufacturers' recommendations don't take into account one fact: parvovirus in the adult dog is rarely fatal. Further, parvovirus in unvaccinated dogs causes enteritis (chronic or acute inflammation of the mucosa of any part of the small intestines). As we have seen that dogs who have been given the parvovirus vaccine are also prone to enteritis, one must question whether we should run the risk of the dog picking the virus up naturally, or whether we should run the risk of injecting him with it year after year - especially when no-one seems to know how common the disease is in the first place.

Are dogs not the most unhygienic creatures on the planet? Don't they stick their noses into just about everything, and eat just about anything? Ask an elderly person whether dogs used to be chronically unhealthy before vaccinations started. Which dogs were the ones with distemper? Which dogs are the ones with viral disease today?

The inner city dogs, the crowded kennel dogs, the dogs under stress - separated from their special person, under-nourished, neglected, are the ones who tend to contract distemper. Dogs with appropriate food, exercise, caring attention and a relatively stress-free environment very rarely manifest the disease - although it is sometimes caused by the vaccine itself.

Some people believe that dogs in boarding and rescue kennels need to be vaccinated because these are the places where epidemics are prevalent. But couldn't it be that these diseases are prevalent because dogs with weakened immune systems are injected with the live virus, and epidemics are thus created?

Importantly, in relation to parvovirus vaccination, in the *Journal of the American Veterinary Medical Association, Vet Med Today*, it is stated: "It is known that some vaccines provoke short-lived immunity and should be given annually to dogs at risk. These include canine parainfluenza, Bordetella, and leptospirosis vaccines. Questions arise about the need for annual boosters of almost all other vaccines."

Dr Leland Carmichael, professor of virology at Cornell University's Baker Institute for Animal Health, added: "I kept a litter of dogs in isolation for over 5 years, and they still had antibody to parvovirus and distemper after being vaccinated as pups."

On the subject of maternal antibody, Phillips and Schultz write in the 1992 edition of '*Current Veterinary Therapy*': "The most successful and cost-effective approach to immunising animals with unknown amounts of maternal antibody is based on multiple vaccinations, with the last immunisation occurring at approximately 22 weeks of age for a puppy and approximately 16 weeks of age for a kitten.

"It is important to note that many of the previous puppy immunisation schedules recommend that the last immunisation in the series occur at 12 to 16 weeks of age. New information (as of 1992) on maternal antibody to canine parvovirus demonstrates the need to extend the last immunisation in the series to 20 to 22 weeks of age. As many as 20% of dogs at 18 weeks of age have enough maternal antibody to prevent successful canine parvovirus immunisation."

Dr Scheibner adds: "It is shown by human researchers that vaccines are destroying maternal immunity, which is essential for the protection of babies during the first two years of their lives."

But we still need to remember Dr Schultz's research which shows that three out of six brands of parvo vaccines were totally ineffective. I would take this fact a little further and postulate a theory (only a theory, not a fact): vaccination is a highly unpredictable procedure. Some vaccines immunise, some don't. Some are successfully attenuated, some aren't. Some are given to healthy dogs, some aren't. Some cause chronic illness, some cause death. Some side effects are acknowledged and understood, some are totally overlooked. Who was it that called vaccination a shot in the dark?

Distemper

Distemper is a serious contagious, viral, disease of dogs, foxes, ferrets, and mink (according to the *Concise Oxford Veterinary Dictionary*). Distemper is characterised by fever, gastroenteritis, bronchopneumonia, and nervous signs. Symptoms include diarrhoea, vomiting, pneumonia, and, in pregnant bitches, abortion, together with incoordination and loss of appetite. Some strains of the virus also cause thickening of the skin of the nose and pads, causing the condition known as hardpad. About half of affected dogs may die and those that recover frequently show persistent involuntary limb jerks or nervous tics.

Infection is usually by the inhalation of virus-contaminated breath from an infected animal. Puppies born to infected bitches may also develop distemper. Maternal antibody can, according to some sources, protect puppies for up to twelve weeks. Once again, vaccines can interfere with maternal immunity for distemper, and one may cancel the other out.

Makes you wonder why all these six-week-old vaccinated - unprotected - puppies don't drop dead with distemper all the time. Maybe the virus isn't the all-pervasive, lurking-round-the-corner-waiting-to-get-you, scary monster we think it is. Or maybe puppies, and adult dogs, don't come into too much contact with the breath of infected animals.

These remarks which, whilst no doubt appearing flippant and irresponsible to the pro-vaccinators, are made in the light of the knowledge that vaccine reactions can be just as deadly as the chance contraction of the actual disease. The unanswered question is this: given that serious side-effects, and even death, can ensue from vaccination, how do we measure the risk of disease against the risk of vaccination, especially as the disease is apparently unquantified? Elsewhere in this book we shall be exploring how we can protect our dogs against viral disease without the use of vaccines.

Black's Veterinary Dictionary tells us that an attenuated measles virus vaccine was developed for use in the dog to give protection against distemper - so measles and distemper vaccine/virus are related. The significance of this fact will become clear when we examine human vaccine reactions.

Dr Larry Swango, associate professor of virology in the Department of Pathobiology, College of Veterinary Medicine, Auburn University, stated in the DVM vaccine roundtable, December 1988: "Probably some of our least attenuated canine distemper vaccines, when used in a very young animal that does not have a fully developed immune system, are where some of our greatest risks lie. We have some very good distemper vaccines, (which) when used in the animal at an age for which they were developed and intended to be used, are relatively safe. But when used in a younger animal in which the immune system has not developed to the point of being able to respond and contain the modified live virus antigen, then we do get vaccine-induced disease." Could Dr Swango be referring to the effects of myelin interruption? The allergies, skin problems, fits, brain damage . . . or does he mean that vaccines can cause the diseases they're designed to prevent?

Dr Tizard, in the same paper, says that the production of vaccines is an evolutionary process. While, he says, we have to give credit to modified live veterinary vaccines for having a tremendous impact in controlling disease, "they do represent a fairly basic technology that can be improved upon."

Dr Swango adds that animals under 4 weeks of age, but extending to 6 to 8 weeks of age in some instances (might be at risk). "Now this may be a function of genetics of that breed or that bloodline, but we have some indication that even in 6 to 8 week old puppies the distemper vaccine may occasionally induce disease."

Finally, I will remind you that Dr Ronald D Schultz, professor and chair of the department of pathobiological sciences at the university of Wisconsin, was quoted in the *Journal of the American Veterinary Medical Association*, August 15th, 1995. Dr Schultz says: *"Canine distemper and adenovirus-2 vaccines both provide lifelong immunity. These need not be given annually. One disadvantage to over-vaccinating is the cost. The client is paying for something with no effect or with the potential for an adverse reaction. I believe that adverse effects are increasing, because we are putting more and more components into these animals."* But we also know that not all vaccines confer immunity.

Interestingly, a paper appearing in 'Neurology', 1995, by Rohowsky-Kochan, et al, postulates that a high titer of canine distemper virus antibodies is significantly associated with multiple scleroris in humans. As vaccines produce antibodies, and as the virus itself can shed . . . and as distemper itself is now very rare, one must assume it possible that the humans who vaccinate their dogs with the distemper virus run the risk of developing MS. The paper doesn't link the Measles, Mumps, Rubella vaccine with MS, even though distemper and measles are virtually the same virus.

Leptospirosis

Leptospirosis is a disease caused by bacterial infection. It can affect humans, cattle, pigs, sheep and goats, and rarely cats. There are two types of lepto in the dog, which can cause fever, jaundice, vomiting, loss of appetite, depression, and pain in the region of the kidneys (one form attacks only the kidneys, the other attacks the liver and kidneys). The dictionary doesn't mention death, but this might just be an oversight or omission.

Leptospirosis can be contracted through contact with an infected animal's urine. Alarmingly, there are around 150 strains of the leptospirosis bacterin, and only maybe three of these strains are contained in the vaccine. So if your pet comes into contact with a form that isn't in the vaccine, he probably isn't protected at all.

Intervet doesn't caution vets against vaccinating unhealthy animals with their Nobi-Vac* L leptospirosis vaccine, but says that occasional hypersensitivity reactions may occur, usually of the uticarial type (uticaria is a raised, itchy, reddened area on the skin). Annual vaccination is recommended.

SmithKline Beecham, on the other hand, in the data sheets accompanying their Vanguard* Lepto ci vaccine, says:

"Contra-indications, warnings, etc. Do not vaccinate dogs for at least one month following cessation of treatment with hyperimmune serum or immunosuppressant drugs. Side-effects are extremely rare and no specific treatment is indicated if they occur. If an allergic response occurs administer adrenaline." Annual vaccination is recommended.

(I'd just like to make a comment here: the vaccine manufacturers keep telling us that side-effects are extremely rare. But as our case stories seem to indicate, side-effects are extremely rarely acknowledged. There is a difference.)

Pitman-Moore's data sheets stipulate (for their Quantum* Dog L vaccine for leptospirosis):

"Do not vaccinate unhealthy dogs. Do not vaccinate dogs under 6 weeks of age. Do not vaccinate dogs that have been treated with immuno-suppressive drugs within the last month.

"Adverse Reactions: Any vaccine may occasionally stimulate an anaphylactic reaction. In such cases appropriate treatment such as adrenaline, antihistamines or corticosteroids should be administered without delay." Annual vaccination is recommended.

Dr Jean Dodds tells me that it is "widely recognised and accepted that the lepto serums tend only to be effective for a few months. In fact, I and others have explained the fact that the bacterin vaccines against leptospirosis typically induce short-lived antibody titres (3-6 months duration) and so boosters should be given two to three times a year if one wants to assure protection in endemic, high-risk exposure areas."

However, Dr Dodds adds: "Clinical leptospirosis is a RARE disease in pet animals today. And the strains causing disease are often NOT the same as those that the existing commercial bacterins protect against."

In other words, your annually vaccinated dog may be unprotected against leptospirosis for nine months between shots. Indeed, he may not be protected at all if the strain of lepto he is exposed to doesn't match the strain in the needle. Once again, why aren't our dogs all dying of this disease during the unprotected slot if vaccines are so absolutely necessary that dire consequences will follow if we stop vaccinating?

Jean Dodds goes further. At a seminar, Dr Dodds also added that, in her opinion, "totally unnecessary vaccines include those for Lyme disease, corona virus, canine hepatitis, leptospirosis, Bordetella, parainfluenza, FelV, FIP, ringworm, and rota virus infection". (Cat lovers please note.)

Finally, Phillips and Schultz inform us that: "On rare occasions, anaphylaxis (type I hypersensitivity) may occur after immunisations. Anaphylaxis usually develops within an hour after immunisation, presenting as weakness, dyspnea, vomiting, mucous membrane pallor, collapse or death. The vaccine component that is most commonly associated with this reaction is the leptospirosis bacterin, although any component of the vaccine can cause anaphylaxis."

Canine viral hepatitis

This is a contagious disease of dogs and foxes transmitted through contact with animals with infected urine, or through contact with equipment and pathways/fields contaminated with infected urine. The principal causes of hepatitis are canine viral hepatitis (adenovirus), the herpes viruses and the parvovirus. Hepatitis in cats is caused by the coronavirus.

The effects of viral hepatitis vary according to the age of the animal or the virus strain, ranging from mild and invisible, to enlargement of the lymph glands and tonsils, severe abdominal pain, and death.

Hepatitis is considered strictly an inflammatory condition of the liver. In fact, most cases of Hepatitis B in humans present clinically as laryngitis and do not go on to affect the liver. Hepatitis can be caused by a virus, bacterial infection, toxic agents, or drugs, as well as dietary deficiencies or imbalances. Canine chronic active hepatitis, thought possibly to be an autoimmune disease, may also have a genetic predisposition.

In its data sheet relating to the combined Nobi-Vac* DHP vaccine (distemper, hepatitis and parvovirus), Intervet states that dogs should be vaccinated against distemper every two years, parvovirus every year, and that dogs over 12 weeks of age should acquire permanent immunity to contagious hepatitis. Intervet tells us that maternal antibodies are conferred against canine hepatitis until a pup is up to 12 weeks old.

Solvay Duphar Veterinary, another vaccine manufacturer, states that its inactivated liquid canine hepatitis and leptospirosis vaccine should be used for primary and booster vaccination of healthy susceptible, immune competent dogs. They further state that the vaccine may not be effective in dogs incubating the disease at the time of vaccination.

(I think we have got the general idea: vaccines shouldn't be used on sick dogs; vaccines may not work in certain circumstances; some dogs react to vaccines, and these reactions include allergies, liver and kidney failure, heart failure, circulatory distress, and death. Some vaccines confer permanent immunity, so do not need annual boosting. I think it is safe to say that the facts as they see them are now well established.)

Despite the fact that some vaccines are said to convey permanent immunity, it's almost impossible to get separate vaccines, which means it's almost impossible to vaccinate against some diseases, say, every two or three years, and others every year. Is this a commercial decision, or a medical decision?

Dr Fred W Scott, professor of virology and director of the Cornell Feline Health Centre says, "I believe that immunity to herpes virus (one of the causes of hepatitis) is also long-lived, but antibody titres don't correlate with immunity . . ." Please note this point: the scientific literature tells us that there's no point measuring antibody titres to see whether your dog needs vaccinating. Titres and immunity are not the same thing.

Dr Schultz, of course, believes that vaccination (once) confers lifelong immunity to the herpes virus.

And you mustn't forget that, if the vaccine chances to protect against the strain of viral hepatitis your dog picks up, he is still unprotected against hepatitis caused by parasites, bacteria, fungus, chemicals, drugs, or dietary deficiencies or imbalances.

Rabies

Unfortunately, if your dog lives in a country where rabies is present, you don't seem to have a choice. Rabies vaccination is apparently mandatory. But for the concerned animal guardian, there is one important exemption. All vaccines, including rabies vaccines, are legally and medically approved in healthy animals only. So if your dog is suffering from a chronic or acute disease, he should not, and legally need not, be vaccinated. Good luck if you're going to fight this one.

At time of writing, we await the decision of a committee appointed by the British government to see whether we must vaccinate our pets against rabies in the UK. By the time the book is published, the decision will have been made. Just a word of warning: if anyone tells me that, by law, I must vaccinate my dogs again, I shall seek to change that law. I will not be forced into potentially killing my dogs because someone else tells me I must, or a vaccine company welcomes the opportunity of increasing its turnover. After I wrote to my MP, the committee wrote to Canine Health Concern asking for evidence that vaccines can cause harm, and the first edition of this book was swiftly despatched. I don't know about you, but I think we have some evidence of harm in these pages. Whether they choose to take note is another matter. (Stop press: it is rumoured that mandatory rabies vaccination will not be imposed.)

In the UK at present, where rabies in dogs is unheard of, it is against the law to vaccinate dogs against rabies unless the dog is being taken abroad or going through quarantine. In

Australia, where no rabies has been recorded, the authorities began to request that dogs be vaccinated against rabies. Why?

Time for a little healthy questioning here: why is it currently against the law to vaccinate a British dog against rabies? Could it be because the vaccine might shed in the environment and cause an epidemic? Once again, we shall quote our experts who tell us that MLV vaccines can cause disease; and that inactivated virus strains contained in vaccines can mutate and shed in the environment. In most cases, the mutants die out, but in some cases, they become virulent (harmful). Dr Tizard gives an example of poultry vaccinated in the Northeast of America and moved to the Southwest where they were kept with non-vaccinated birds: "These vaccinated birds are a source of infection for the naive (unvaccinated) flocks and cause clinical laryngotracheitis".

Dr Swango gave the example of Dr Max Appel at Cornell who showed that, "within a population of virus particles of a modified live distemper vaccine, there was a certain small percentage of that population that was still virulent." Dr Swango talks of the possibility of transmission to other animals, perhaps not causing an acute distemper, but maybe the chronic infection within the species. So one can guess that the same thing might happen with the rabies vaccine.

Similarly, if rabies vaccines are as effective as they are claimed to be, why must imported vaccinated dogs currently be kept in quarantine for six months? We know, of course, that rabies has a long incubation period and that there is no way of telling whether an organism is incubating rabies unless the animal is killed and his brain examined. But might it also be because the vaccine has a chance of causing the disease in the vaccinated dog, or shedding in the environment, or failing to protect the dog against the disease?

Because rabies can be passed to humans, you can be sure that work has gone in to try to ensure that the rabies vaccine is the safest of all vaccines. Despite this, Merck and others talk

143

of brain damage caused by rabies vaccines cultivated on brain tissue.

But we have already examined evidence to say that vaccines can shed, mutate, and cause disease in non-vaccinated animals. We already have evidence that vaccines are not 100% effective in vaccinated animals. And, quoting Dr Ted Rude, founder of Veterinary Consulting Services, a consulting firm for the veterinary biologic and pharmaceutical industry, we can assume that it is at least possible that a vaccine, of any virus, can cause the disease it is designed to prevent, if not in acute, then in chronic form.

Dr Rude asks: "There have been reports in the literature about chronic canine distemper and old dog encephalitis. Chronic canine distemper is usually seen in young dogs 2 to 3 years old, whereas old dog encephalitis may be seen in dogs 5 years of age or older. Many of these dogs have been vaccinated as puppies with modified live virus canine distemper vaccines." He asks: "Do you believe there may be a connection between old dog encephalitis or chronic distemper and the use of these vaccines?"

Dr Rude is answered by Dr Swango, who explains that it is difficult to produce chronic infections in a laboratory, but . . . "I'm not sure". Dr Tizard helps Dr Swango out, suggesting that you "cannot assume that every animal you vaccinate is functioning immunologically normal. . . This can tilt an animal towards disease susceptibility. In addition, a vaccine may not cause frank disease itself. It may cause mild immunosuppression."

Anyway, we all know that rabies is a serious disease: we've all seen the horror films. It is, we are led to believe, usually fatal. In the furious form of rabies, the infected animal becomes very aggressive, salivates, and bites indiscriminately at other animals or inanimate objects. Convulsions, coma and death usually follow. In the dumb form, more typically seen in herbivores, a change in voice is first noticed, followed by a paralysed lower jaw, difficulty in swallowing, and drooling.

Hans Ruesch, in his book, '*Slaughter of the Innocent*', throws some interesting light on rabies. He tells us that fewer than one in a hundred people bitten by a rabid dog are likely to catch the infection. It was Pasteur who developed the first rabies vaccine. Ruesch says: "*To be safe, everybody who has been bitten by an animal suspected to be rabid gets the special treatment developed originally by Pasteur. But sometimes the vaccinated person dies anyway. In that case the death is attributed to a defective vaccine. But often it has been demonstrated that the vaccine and not the bite caused the infection - for instance when the animal later turned out to be healthy.*"

Ruesch wrote: "*In his best-selling 'Microbe Hunters' (Harcourt, Brace, 1926/1953), Paul de Kruif gave a highly fanciful account of 19 Russian peasants who, bitten by an allegedly rabid wolf, travelled to Paris in order to receive the newly announced Pasteur treatment from the old master himself. According to de Kruif, 16 of these Russian patients were 'saved' by Pasteur's shots, and `only three' died. Three deaths out of 19 makes over 15 per cent casualties. But knowing, as we know today, that not one in a hundred people bitten by a rabid dog is likely to catch the infection, we must infer that at least some and probably all three of those Russian peasants died because of Pasteur's vaccine, as did uncounted people later on.*"

Ruesch cites statistics quoted by the US Public Health Service in its Morbidity and Mortality Annual Supplement for 1970. Exactly two out of 205,000,000 people were reported as having rabies, compared with 148 cases of tetanus, 22,096 of salmonellosis, 56,797 of infectious hepatitis, and 433,405 of streptococcal infections and scarlet fever.

Ruesch further quotes a World Health Organisation technical report, WHO Expert Committee on Rabies, Sixth Report, 1973. The report announced that evidence is accumulating (to say) that paranteral injection of antirabies vaccine causes human deaths under certain conditions, and states, 'The Committee recommends that production of Fermi-type vaccines, since they contain residual living virus, should be discontinued.'

Ruesch tells us that 'residual living virus' simply means that probably the very rare cases of humans who died of what had been diagnosed as rabies have not died from something received from a dog but from a doctor.

Interestingly, the WHO recommends in its report that the most valuable procedure in post-exposure rabies treatment is the local treatment of wounds. This, they say, should be done by washing with soap and water. Hippocrates, it seems, was right all along: the best protection against infection is cleanliness!

Just recently, a biologist named Roger Burrows from Exeter University contacted me. Roger has been studying five packs of rare wild dogs in Africa. He told me: "It was decided that the dogs should be vaccinated against rabies. Within a year they were all dead." Two explanations come to mind. The first is that they may have been nutritionally compromised. The second is that they had all been exposed to the rabies virus and mounting an effective response. The vaccine could have tipped them over the edge.

Finally, let us look at the parainfluenza virus, which is related to the kennel cough range of viruses.

The Concise Oxford Veterinary Dictionary doesn't say very much at all about parainfluenza virus, apart from the fact that its members cause disease (meaning there is more than one type. In fact, as we know in the human field, flu viruses mutate all the time, so vaccine manufacturers are chasing a moving target).

The dictionary explains that kennel cough is a highly contagious condition characterised by a hacking cough. It's called kennel cough because the disease spreads rapidly in places where dogs are in close contact with one-another, such as kennels. Clinical signs are usually mild. Mild cases of the disease will clear if the dog is kept quiet and given throat-soothing agents such as honey. More severe cases may require antibiotics. The dictionary tells us that whilst vaccines are available to protect against kennel cough caused by adenovirus, parainfluenza virus, and bordetella bronchiseptica infection, they do not offer complete protection.

It's worth mentioning the **adenovirus**, as many of the vaccine companies market adenovirus vaccines. Basically, adenovirus is a family of viruses that infect most animal species, usually causing relatively mild respiratory signs, although one member of the family causes canine viral hepatitis.

Summary

* Notable immunologists tells us that immunity to a virus persists for years, or for life, and annual vaccination is not necessary
* Leptospirosis is a bacterial disease, so permanent immunity is not conferred by a vaccine. However, current vaccines are short-lived, providing limited protection
* Vaccine manufacturers stipulate, in their data sheets, that only healthy animals should be vaccinated
* Vaccines pose a risk of cross-species infection, and the creation of new diseases

Chapter Six

Vaccines do not immunise

So far, we have described the possible horrendous consequences of viral disease, and of vaccination. The next question is how effective are vaccines, anyway? Already, we have seen cases where dogs have gone down with the diseases they are supposed to be protected against. Pro-vaccinators explain this by saying that a puppy may have had maternal antibodies present, which cancelled out the vaccine; alternatively, they say that the dog/person was probably incubating the disease at the time of vaccination. Occasionally, they admit that the vaccine itself was from a 'bad batch'. Another theory, not suggested by the pro-vaccinators, is that vaccines might not actually protect against disease at all. I know some people have a hard time with this theory, but I am unable to discount it entirely myself.

Pro-vaccinators argue that diseases like smallpox in humans, and distemper and parvovirus in dogs, have died out thanks to vaccines. But the plague, cholera, the bubonic plague, yellow fever and other epidemics have also almost, if not entirely, disappeared - without vaccination. Could this have anything to do with soap, water, better hygiene, isolation, or healthier eating habits?

And could not smallpox, distemper and parvo have died out themselves were it not for vaccines keeping them in the ecosystem?

Dr Viera Scheibner, a retired senior research scientist living in Australia, has done a great deal of work in the field of vaccination. Her work began by accident. She was involved in a project that measured childhood breathing patterns, where a monitor was designed to emit an alarm if the children's breathing patterns changed. However, something disturbing started happening: the machines were alarming at an alarming rate! The initial reaction of many doctors was to tell the parents to switch the alarm off (Dr Scheibner says that the advice was tantamount to advising nurses to switch heart monitors off in intensive care wards if they alarmed.)

Dr Scheibner couldn't understand why the alarms should sound so frequently; she began to look deeper. Pretty soon it became apparent that babies' breathing patterns were changing after vaccination. Indeed, the sixteenth day after vaccination was critical, although larger babies tended to take longer to react to their vaccines than smaller babies. Dr Scheibner now calls cot death 'a convenient waste basket in which to put vaccine damaged babies'.

Many years later, and having studied some 60,000 research papers on the subject of vaccination, Dr Scheibner has concluded that vaccines do not actually protect people (and by inference, dogs and other animals), from the diseases they are supposed to prevent. For those who like to see detailed facts for themselves, I recommend Dr Scheibner's book, *'Vaccination - 100 Years of Orthodox Research shows that Vaccines Represent a Medical Assault on the Immune System'*.

Meanwhile, a pot pouri of facts from Dr Scheibner's book will give you an idea:

In 1977, an epidemic of whooping cough occurred in a rural practice in Shetland, Scotland, containing 144 children under 16. Before 1 July 1974 all children were immunised against pertussis (whooping cough), but after that date immunisation stopped. The incidence of infection was similar in those who had and who had not been immunised, and in those born before and after 1974. Ditchburn (1979) described the epidemic in detail. The first child affected by the pertussis epidemic was a 15 year-old girl who was fully immunised as a child. The first eight of the case children were fully immunised. Overall, whooping cough occurred in 46 (49%) of 93 immunised children and in 18 (44%) of 41 unimmunised children.

Ditchburn (1979) considered it interesting that the outbreak started among the older children, the immunisation rate of whom was 94%. If the immunisation had been effective, this high rate should have produced herd immunity sufficient to have prevented the epidemic. It did not and almost half of the children under 16 years and some adults were affected. The illness was relatively mild. No child suffered permanent damage and there were no hospital admissions, though the disease was unpleasant and prolonged. One child who started having convulsions on the night of his second triple antigen injection in 1969, who required anti-epileptic treatment until 1976, developed whooping cough in the 1977 outbreak. Ditchburn concluded that there was no evidence to support routine immunisation against pertussis in rural Shetland.

On the subject of measles vaccines, Dr Scheibner reports Barraff and Ablon (Baraff, L., Ablon, W., and Weiss, P, 1983, Pediatr Infect Dis; 2:7), who 'investigated an outbreak of measles in Florida from December 1968 to February 1969 and found there was little difference in the incidence of measles in vaccinated and unvaccinated children. However, while 43% of unimmunised children developed a rash, only 12% of those vaccinated developed a proper rash.'

Dr Scheibner gives many similar examples, including: 'In April 1993, the Ministry of Health and Welfare in Japan decided to discontinue the use of measles, mumps and rubella vaccine (Sawada et al 1993; Lancet; 342, 7 August: 371). This decision was prompted by published reports of vaccinated children and their (unvaccinated) contacts contracting mumps from the MMR vaccine, and reports of one in 1044 vaccinees developing encephalitis.'

Dr Scheibner reports upon a paper prepared by Chaiken et al (1987) that showed that 'while the number of people vaccinated against mumps was low, the incidence of mumps was low. As the compliance increased, mainly due to enforced vaccination, quite substantial outbreaks of mumps started occurring.'

On the subject of rubella (German measles), Dr Scheibner says, 'A very important study on rubella vaccine was performed and published by Dr Beverly Allan in Australia. In 1973 she published her report on two trials of the Cendevax rubella vaccine in army recruits selected because of their lack of immunity as determined by a blood test.

'The men produced antibodies to rubella after being given Cendevax (an attenuated rubella virus). They were then sent to a camp which usually had an outbreak of rubella. Three to four months after vaccination, 80% of the men became ill with rubella. A further trial, performed shortly after the army trial, on institutionalised retarded people, resulted in a similar failure of vaccine to protect against rubella disease.'

The above case is interesting in that it demonstrates that circulating antibodies (titres) do not equate to immunity. It's also interesting in that it illustrates how people who can't answer back - such as institutionalised retarded people - are used as guinea pigs. God help your animals.

Many scientists support vaccine programmes because they believe that epidemics have been eradicated by vaccination. However, Dr Scheibner, using data from the 60,000 research papers she has collected over the years (the vast majority of which were written by pro-vaccinators), contends that a natural herd immunity ensues once 67% of a population has been exposed to a virus, and epidemics thereby naturally die out. Dr Scheibner adds that outbreaks of infectious disease occur every three to four years, whether you vaccinate or not. If there are any vets or scientists reading this book, please suspend your judgement until you, too, have examined the raw data provided by the scientists who claim that vaccines work.

Interestingly, it is possible to stumble across evidence to support Dr Scheibner's claims in the most innocent of places. The *Readers Digest Book of the Road*, for example, tells us about a village called Eyam in Derbyshire. During the great plague of 1665/66, Eyam received cloth from London which brought plague to the village. The 350 villagers placed themselves in quarantine for 13 months to stop its spread; 257 died. In fact, this is a survival rate of about a third, roughly supporting the 67% herd immunity threshold.

Viral agents are often found in people (and animals) who are well. For some reason, viral infection does not automatically kill or render everyone ill. Why? Personally, I think this is a far more interesting question than how we can render vaccines safer. Surely we should be asking what makes some organisms more able to combat disease, rather than trying to stimulate millions of immune systems, all of which are capable (or incapable) in varying degrees of mounting a response.

It could even be argued that the dogs who become ill or die as a result of vaccination, would equally become ill or die as a result of the natural infection. Similarly, dogs who seem to remain healthy after vaccination probably have immune systems that are strong enough to fight off natural infection.

Viera Scheibner has demonstrated that viral epidemics naturally die out of their own accord. *She is able to show that vaccine programmes have invariably been introduced after herd immunity has been established, and after the massive numbers of people had stopped showing symptoms of the disease. It could therefore be argued that the vaccine manufacturers and their supporters have claimed the credit for a natural occurrence.* In reality, they could well be responsible for keeping disease in the ecosystem through the process of shedding and mutation described by our learned experts, and by causing the disease itself in immunologically susceptible hosts, ready to be passed on to others. Also, as was noted earlier, vaccine manufacturers could be (are) responsible for introducing new cross-species disease.

However, Dr Salk believes that if you immunise a fraction of a population, the rest of the population will be protected (through shedding). (Question: why can't this be equally true for the natural virus if measures are taken, such as a good diet, to ensure a healthy immune system?)

Evidence to support Dr Scheibner's claims - that vaccines do not immunise but sensitise - is not hard to come by. According to the British Sunday Times: in Sweden, when concerns about the pertussis vaccine ended its use, deaths and hospital admissions continued to drop. In Japan, when the diphtheria, pertussis and tetanus vaccination was, for a long period of 13 years, not given to babies under two, cot deaths practically disappeared.

Moving back to dogs, there are many vets and scientists who believe that vaccination fails to prevent disease. Dr JER McDonagh, FRCS, bacteriologist, wrote in *'The Nature of Disease'* Vol 1, "Immunisation with an attenuated virus cannot prevent distemper. The author has treated many dogs, which have developed distemper despite two or three injections of the preventative agent. He is of the opinion that fits, chorea hysteria, etc., in dogs have become more frequent since the use of the distemper vaccine. Successful prevention will never be achieved by inoculation." I actually wonder if the dogs developed distemper *because* they received two or three injections of the so-called preventative agent?

In the *Journal of the Veterinary Medical Association*, August 15, 1995, an article appeared entitled, "Are we vaccinating too much?" In it, Dr Ronald D Schultz, professor and chairman of the Department of Pathobiological Sciences at the University of Wisconsin, Madison school of Veterinary Medicine, and holder of joint appointments in the Medical School and the Department of Veterinary Science, College of Agricultural and Life Sciences, and whose undergraduate and graduate training in bacteriology, biochemistry, immunology and pathology were done at Pennsylvania State University, commented on the fact that canine parvovirus continues to take its toll despite vaccination. The problem, the article said, may be that of vaccine failure, interference by maternal antibody, or overwhelming exposure from which no vaccine could protect.

Dr Schultz said: "Weekly vaccination is unnecessary and could be harmful (some people were resorting to weekly vaccination in an attempt to counteract vaccine failure). The antibody half life is more than one week, so it will tie up any antigen presented by repeated vaccination and there won't be an adequate immune response. Also, if you ever want to experimentally reproduce hypersensitivity, all you have to do is give multiple small doses over a short period, and give a challenge dose later."

Effectiveness of vaccines is measured by the level of antibody titres found in the animal's blood. Indeed, vaccine manufacturers look for these titres to demonstrate their brand's superiority. However, antibody titres, the very measure adopted to assess a vaccine's efficacy, do not in fact demonstrate immunity. It's a total red herring.

Dr Schultz tells us that the veterinary community is 'having problems' when it considers antibody responses to mean protective immunity. He tells us that whilst some of the titres are higher than ever seen before, "the vaccines are no more efficacious against challenge with the disease organism than were the older non-infectious products that didn't induce, or induced a just detectable antibody response. . . If veterinary biologic companies will keep that in mind and will stop using antibody titres as a marketing ploy which they have used for years to the veterinary practitioner, most of whom feel antibody titres are synonymous with protective immunity, we might better serve our clients and their animals".

In summing up, Dr Scott, also quoted in the article, says, "We (vets) have to change our focus from a yearly vaccination to that of a yearly physical... Another option is to perform an annual physical examination and antibody titre screen to determine which vaccines need be administered. However, we need better tests for this to be feasible." (The need for better tests is further demonstrated by human studies which show that people with high levels of antibody titre can still contract the diseases.)

Finally, Dr Schultz added that, *"I don't think there is a need to vaccinate adult dogs, since early vaccination will be sufficient to stimulate memory cells. . . There are also families in dogs, notably in the Doberman and Rottweiler breed, but probably in every breed, that do not respond to vaccination."*

To honour the balanced view, I have to contend that Dr Schultz is in favour of vaccination, but he does state that, **"there is no scientific justification for annual revaccination."** He also states, "I see no justification for the use of canine coronavirus (the coronavirus family cause respiratory and intestinal disease in dogs, pigs and cattle), or Lyme disease vaccines. . . We are about to see a new vaccine launched for canine rotavirus. I don't even know the disease it's supposed to prevent."

(The rotavirus is, in fact, a genus of the reovirus family. It includes viruses that can cause gastrointestinal disease in cattle and horses. The reovirus family contains, in addition to the rotavirus, orbiviruses; orbivuruses can infect dogs. But if Dr Schultz hasn't seen it, it's unlikely to be a huge risk.)

The natural question, then, is whether the vaccine manufacturers are anticipating that dogs will start to pick up these viruses from cattle or horses? Are they expecting their vaccine antigens to shed from the cattle and horses, mutate, and cross species? Dr Swango, in DVM, gives us one example where this has been known to happen. "We have evidence of this type of phenomenon when distemper vaccine was used in a different species. A single passage of a modified live virus canine distemper vaccine through a grey fox, in which it was virulent, resulted in reversion of virulence for the dog. The virus isolated back from the grey fox was no longer attenuated (harmless) for the dog."

But getting back to the question in question, statistics abound to show us that vaccines do not always (if ever) immunise. Over a period of four years in the UK, 66% of all measles cases were in vaccinated children. In a 1986 outbreak of measles in Corpus Christi, Texas, 100% of the children had been vaccinated. Trials on the rubella vaccine in the USA and Australia show a failure rate of between 80% and 93%.

In the face of statistics of this type, one has to ask whether vaccines prevent disease at all. In fact, I could go on almost for ever giving you research findings of this nature. Is there something else in the body that prevents its owner from contracting viral disease?

In 1920s England, only two towns - Leicester and Dewsbury - rejected smallpox inoculation in the face of a national epidemic. They relied instead upon hygiene and sanitation. Consequently, these two towns had the lowest death rates from smallpox in the country. Similarly, in 1990s England, where the poor and underprivileged have been economically deserted by the government, TB is on the increase. Mental stress, poor hygiene and poor food are providing the earth in which the TB seed can flourish.

In September 1991, The *Lancet* reported an outbreak of paralytic poliomyelitis in Oman among fully vaccinated children. The authorities decided that dose rates and frequencies should thereafter be increased (!).

In April 1995, The *Lancet* reported on diphtheria immunity in UK blood donors. The report read:

"Individuals in the 30-39 age group would have been vaccinated during 1955-64. Up until 1955, many children were immunised with aluminium-containing diphtheria toxoids, however, after a suggestion that exposure to toxoids linked to aluminium or combined with pertussis or tetanus might provoke paralysis due to poliomyelitis, it was recommended that diphtheria immunisation might be carried out in future with single-antigen preparations of formal diphtheria toxoid or toxoid antitoxin floccules. Unfortunately, formal toxoid was later shown to be much less immunogenic than aluminium toxoids. Policy was revised in 1961 . . . . This history may account for why only 28.8% of individuals in this age group were fully protected."

The paper then goes on to tell us that in a current epidemic of diphtheria in the former USSR, "diphtheria is generally deemed to be a disease of childhood that occurs rarely in adults. In the Russian epidemic, diphtheria has been predominantly an adult disease occurring in both the immunised and un-immunised." (Peter A Maple, et al)

The previous two examples of vaccines failing to stimulate immunity were very interesting to me as I came across them at random, by chance. I just happened to have a copy of The *Lancet* on my desk to look into a report concerning the fear that environmental chemicals cause infertility (which also affects our dogs). As two vaccine studies were contained in the contents listing, I decided to have a look. Without even trying, I had chanced upon yet more evidence that vaccines don't immunise. Come on scientists, don't damn what I'm saying - have a look at those research papers. To quote the fashion doyen Vivienne Westwood, "If you think that something is right just because everyone believes it, then you are not thinking". Could it be that, because scientists are told with such certainty that vaccines immunise, they don't question whether they do or not?

According to Beddow Bayly, in 1936, cases of aseptic meningitis were more often reported as a separate disease from polio, 'but such cases were counted as polio before the vaccine was introduced'. Similarly, Viera Scheibner has noted that polio vaccinated children are diagnosed as having viral or aseptic meningitis, whereas non-vaccinated children have the same disease but it's called polio.

In the *South Yorkshire Times*, in March 1938, the medical officers for health at Wath-on-Dearne, were reported as saying, "Where they have done the most immunising (against diphtheria), they are getting the most diphtheria".

The *International Vaccine Newsletter* reported that in England and Wales, deaths of children under 15 years attributed to scarlet fever, diphtheria, whooping cough and measles had already declined by 90 per cent before the introduction of antibiotics and immunisation.

Perhaps the most damning statement comes from Dr Jonas Salk (of Salk vaccine fame) who, in 1976 testified that the live virus vaccine, used almost exclusively in the United States since the early 1960s, was "the principle if not the sole cause" of all reported cases of polio in the United States since 1961.

In February 1992, the Federal Centers for Disease Control (USA) admitted that the live virus vaccine has become the dominant cause of polio in the United States today. According to their figures, 85% of all cases of polio between 1973 and 1983 were caused by the vaccine. More recently, from 1980 through 1989, every case of polio in the US was caused by the vaccine. During this same period, three of the five people that caught polio during foreign travel were previously vaccinated against the disease.

Quoting the homoeopathic vet, Dr Richard Pitcairn, according to a study conducted by the World Health Organisation, chances are 14 times greater that measles will be contracted by those vaccinated against the disease than those who are left alone.

The second part of the hypothesis - that vaccines do no immunise, they sensitise - is explained by the Veterinary Data Sheets which all agree that hypersensitivity reactions may occur. Knowing, as we do, that we don't need to see a severe immediate reaction for encephalitis to occur, one has to ask the question: "how many humans/dogs have been physically, spiritually and/or mentally changed from their original state by vaccines?"

Would I have hayfever had I not been vaccinated? Would your dog be allergic to red meat had he not been vaccinated? Would your dog be less hyperactive had she not been vaccinated? We will never know. But we could know, if we dog owners compared experience, whether vaccinated dogs suffer from post-encephalitis-type conditions more, less or equally, to/than unvaccinated dogs. See interim results - chapter eleven.

Patrick Rattigan ND says in his booklet, '*Vaccine Legacy, the Modern Plague*': 'Criminality, juvenile delinquency, social disorder, asthma, glue-ear, epilepsy, cot death, dyslexia, multiple sclerosis, autism, cancer, leukaemia, AIDS, encephalitis, cerebral palsy, arthritis, and meningitis can result from the vaccine programme.' He further states that, 'the symptoms of post-vaccinal encephalitis are identical to the symptoms of encephalitis arising from any other cause. Since any segment of the nervous system may be affected, every possible physical, intellectual and personality deviation and combinations of them are possible'.

Professor Gordon Stewart of Glasgow University has shown that vaccine damage from the whooping cough vaccine is widespread, and that the protection conferred by the vaccine is slight. Vaccinated children are as likely to catch and transmit whooping cough as the un-vaccinated, though their symptoms may be less severe. (*Lancet*, 29 January 1977).

According to Professor Stewart, adverse reactions to whooping cough (vaccine) could be predicted but the warnings are ignored. In a group of vaccine-damaged children, 65 per cent showed contra-indications to vaccination before the first injection. A further 20 per cent reacted adversely to their first exposure to the vaccine although they had shown no initial contra-indications, and they were given a second dose despite their reaction to the first. Further, 95 per cent of children who reacted adversely to one injection had similar or more severe reactions to subsequent exposures. In all but a few of the children in Stewart's study, the adverse reaction was followed by arrest or loss of mental development and physical handicap ranging from spasticity to complete paralysis of all but the vital reflexes. (Source: *Cured to Death* by Arabella Melville and Colin Johnson: The *Lancet*).

Surely the veterinary profession needs to take these observations on board? Or do we, the guardians of the animals, need to place our hands in the fire ourselves, and feel the pain, before the lessons are learned?

The logical extrapolation of this information about humans, is that 'genetically susceptible' dogs, who show contra-indications - such as fits, allergies, skin problems, arthritis, and other immune-mediated diseases - should certainly not be vaccinated. And if the cause (as Steve Dean suggests) is genetic, no dog should be vaccinated if any of his relatives have the same problems.

In the human field, nurses are supposed to routinely ask parents whether any family members suffer from these conditions, and if so, vaccination is cancelled. If a dog comes from a family whose relatives are prone to these reactions, vaccination should therefore be avoided. I would go further: from what I know of my own breed, Golden Retrievers, I would suggest that no Golden be vaccinated. The breed was manufactured from a small gene pool, and so predisposing 'defects' are bound to exist in most, if not all, of the dogs. But this comment only stands if it is proven that faulty genes can be blamed for canine vaccine reactions. If the vaccine itself is at fault, which is my view, then no breed should be vaccinated.

Perhaps most worrying of all, is the fact that many homoeopaths believe that vaccine damage can be passed-on genetically to offspring. Vaccine damage goes into genetic memory!! If this is true, then successive generations will, indeed, as Dr Schultz acknowledges, manifest more and more adverse effects to the vaccine programme.

In fact we know now that it is true. The Salk polio vaccine, for example, administered to thousands of children in the UK during the 1950s and '60s has been shown to have been contaminated with SV40, a monkey retrovirus. Although the British government was warned of the problem at the time, it was decided to go ahead and vaccinate anyway. Since then, SV40 has been turning up at human cancer sites and - alarmingly - at the cancer sites of the children of the people who received the contaminated vaccine. Scientists explain that SV40 switches off the part of DNA that protects from cancer. So now we have vaccine-induced, inheritable cancer. Overseas readers should note that when the British government eventually decided that the vaccine posed too great a risk to its citizens, they granted a license to a vaccine manufacturer to sell it overseas. Waste not, want not.

Finally, Hans Ruesch in 'Naked Empress' writes that in the course of a vaccination trial that took place in France in October 1981, Professor Mercie, former director of the Pasteur Institute was asked why the Institute kept producing and selling its anti-flu vaccine that was recognised as worthless. Professor Mercie replied: `Because it helps financing the Institute's research'.

I might add that mushrooms are a cash crop.

Summary

* Vaccines do not confer guaranteed protection
* The effectiveness of vaccination can legitimately be questioned
* In areas where vaccines were not used, diseases naturally died out
* In areas where vaccines were used, large percentages of the population still contracted the disease
* Vaccines are capable of introducing inheritable genetic defects
* Vaccines can introduce cross-species disease
* Vaccines from one species can shed and mutate and cause disease in other species
* Antibody titers are no measure of immunity

Chapter Seven

Vaccines are deadly poisons

The first, obvious, observation is that when you vaccinate an animal or a child, you are deliberately injecting a virus, or several viruses and maybe a bacterin or two, into a dog or child's bloodstream. If the disease were contracted naturally, it almost certainly wouldn't be contracted through the bloodstream.

Many of the vaccine manufacturers talk about attenuated virus vaccines. Attenuation, you will remember, is the reduction in virulence of a previously pathogenic organism - the term often refers to the laboratory manipulation of a virulent organism to render it safe for use in a live vaccine. But we have seen that attenuation isn't always successful.

Dr Joanna Cleeton, a Wrexham GP, is against immunisation because, she explained in a *Sunday Times* article, "the immune system has to be taught how to operate. Catching measles gives it a good kick-start. The measles virus is picked up naturally through the nose and mouth and mobilises the whole system. A vaccination, in contrast, moves directly into the bloodstream and bypasses most of the immune system's mechanisms, usually at a time when it is still developing."

A separate *Sunday Times* article quotes Frank Ryan, a consultant physician from Sheffield and the author of *Virus X*. Mr Ryan sets out a theory called aggressive symbiosis, which proposes that viruses are actually helpful agents in the animal in which they normally reside. His theory is that viruses are part of our evolutionary ammunition, defending us against other predators.

The view that vaccines bypass most of the immune system's mechanisms is confirmed by a paper appearing in the November 1996 issue of *Veterinary Times*. Sue Stephens BVetMed, MRCVS explains that equine influenza vaccines containing whole killed influenza virus have aimed to protect horses against flu by the stimulation of circulating antibodies alone. The upshot is that the vaccinated horse is unprotected from clinical disease once antibody levels drop below a certain figure (Mumford and Wood, 1992), hence the need for frequent boosters.

In contrast, Sue Stephens explains, after natural flu infection, although serum antibody levels fall below the certain figure, the animals remain protected from disease for at least 62 weeks (Hannant et all, 1988). This protection has been shown to be the result of cell mediated immune mechanisms, and in particular long-term T-cell memory.

Sue Stephens' paper was written to explain ISCOM technology, which was developed in Sweden to find more efficient ways of presenting antigens in vaccines, and to stimulate other immune mechanisms in addition to the circulating antibody. Ms Stephens tells us that conventional vaccines (adjuvants) are thought to produce effects due to the fact that antigens collect at the injection site. ISCOMs, however, are rapidly transported to the lymph node or spleen where they remain for a significantly long period of time and stimulate the immune response.

So although 'technology' is moving forward, the experts acknowledge that conventional vaccines generally bypass important mechanisms in the immune system. As Dr Tizzard was previously quoted as saying: "Vaccines represent fairly basic technology which can be improved upon." On this basis, we have to accept that vaccines are poisons which are unnaturally injected into an organism - but maybe the natural method of developing immunity is best. The only truly effective way of developing lifelong immunity is to get a disease and survive it.

Richard Moskowitz MD, in an article entitled, 'The Case Against Immunisation', points out that the creation of circulating antibodies, "is only one and by no means the most important" of the mechanisms by which the body handles a viral attack. In fact, he says that by vaccinating, we short-circuit very important primary responses to disease and have, "accomplished what the entire immune system seems to have evolved in order to prevent: we have placed the virus directly into the blood, and given it free and immediate access to the major immune organs and tissues, without any obvious way of getting rid of it". (*Tiger Tribe* Sept/Oct 1992)

The vet James L Newns described it to me in another way: "If the invaders are outside the castle wall, you can at least see them coming and mount a defence. If they're catapulted inside the castle, as they are with vaccines, you have very little chance of even witnessing the attack before they've overwhelmed you."

Dr Donna Starita Mehan, a vet, voices a similar view: "Not surprisingly," she says, "most of the problems (resulting from vaccines) involve the immune system. The body may overreact to normally harmless substances (allergies, especially flea allergies and other skin problems), or even produce antibodies to itself (autoimmune disease). At the same time, the body may be sluggish in responding to those things that it should reject, such as common viruses, bacteria, fungi, and parasites. This can result in increased susceptibility to acute infections (such as ear infections in dogs, bladder infections in cats), chronic tapeworm problems or, in more degenerative cases, cancer."

Mike Kohn DVM expresses the problem in yet another way: "Unfortunately our society is in the grasp of a health panacea and this panacea is fuelled by the biomedical and pharmaceutical industries. Vaccinations have become the modern day equivalent of leeching. First of all, introducing foreign material via subcutaneous or intramuscular injection is extremely upsetting to the body's defence system. In response to this violation, there have been increased autoimmune diseases (allergies being one component), epilepsy, neoplasia, as well as behaviourial problems in small animals.

167

"Even though man and animals have been around for thousands of years, formal vaccines were introduced within the last century. Interestingly, the increase in cancer, respiratory disorders (most air quality standards are higher today than in decades past) and autoimmune problems have likewise escalated alarmingly during the previous decade. Vaccines are not the only culprit for these increases; however, I feel they are one of the primary offenders."

So what goes into vaccines?

Deadly poisons . . . the pertussis (whooping cough) vaccine, for example, is used in animal experiments to produce anaphylactic shock, and to cause an acute auto-immune Encephalomyelitis. If that ain't a poison, I don't know what is.

Vaccinia is an infectious disease affecting a wide range of mammals, including humans. It is characterised by the formation of pustules. The vaccinia virus was used to protect humans against infection with smallpox. The virus, however, occurs in domestic and wild animal populations. According to the Concise Oxford Veterinary Dictionary, the vaccinia virus spread into domestic and wild animal populations, causing the development of small swellings which eventually become pustules which then rupture and become scabs. The vaccinia virus has been genetically engineered to include segments of the genetic material of other viruses. As with the feline enteritis vaccine, vaccines are able to mutate in the environment and actually create disease. If that ain't a poison, a global poison, I don't know what is.

The smallpox vaccine, Vaccinia, is/was produced by shaving the bellies of live calves and making long slashes in the skin, into which are dripped and rubbed cowpox/smallpox cultures. Fever sets in and the wounds fester, pustulate, and form a scab over a reservoir of poison as the increasingly sick animal, immobilised in a stock, is prevented from its natural attempt to lick the wound and ease the intense suffering. After six days the calf is bound and strapped to an operating table; the vesicles are clamped and the mixture of skin, flesh, pus, hair and blood is scraped off. This is then mixed, sieved, and transferred to containers.

However, as one of our case studies illustrated, there is no law that makes it mandatory for vaccine manufacturers to tell us how their vaccines are made. Indeed, it seems there are laws to prevent civil servants from telling us. In other words, the consumer has no right to know what he is buying. If the manufacturers wanted us to know, they would proudly advertise it.

Dr Viera Scheibner tells me that canine vaccines are often cultured on dog kidneys, monkey kidneys, (keep this in mind for debate about AIDS later), and chick embryos. According to information supplied in the Rabdomun rabies vaccine box, canine vaccines are also of brain origin.

Vaccines also contain serum, often bovine serum, which conceivably poses a BSE threat in addition to serum reactions.

On the 9th December, 1995, the *Washington Post* reported a Swiss discovery. Swiss scientists have found an enzyme, reverse transcriptase, in the live measles and mumps vaccine. This was traced back to chickens whose cells are used to create vaccines. Reverse Transcriptase (RT), which copies RNA into DNA, has also been reportedly detected in yellow fever and some influenza vaccines prepared in chicken embryo cells.

Reverse Transcriptase activity is associated with the presence of retroviruses, a class of viruses which can permanently alter human (and canine) genes, a report from *'Leading edge vaccination news and discoveries'* tells us. Scientists at Merck, the manufacturer of MMR vaccine in the United States, are reportedly trying to find out where the RT came from. One possibility is that the RT activity in MMR vaccine signals the presence of an avarian leukosis virus, a retrovirus that infects some birds and can cause a leukaemia-like illness. Do avian (chicken) viruses belong inside human and canine bodies? And I have to ask, is this where Pru's leukaemia came from? So we know, now that both cancer (from SV40) and leukaemia can be caused not only by the vaccine disrupting the immune system, but also from cross-species viruses in the vaccines.

Debate currently surrounds the use of animal parts in human organ transplant. This is called by some, xeno transplantation, and by others genetic pollution. Using baboon hearts and pig hearts, scientists believe they can extend human life. However, Jonathan Allen, an eminent American virologist, (and many others) warns of the risk of placing foreign animal viruses into humans. He tells us, for example, that 40 per cent of baboons carry a cancer virus, and adds, "There is a virtual guarantee that you will be transferring viruses to humans." Some viruses have long latency periods; they will take years to manifest.

Consider also that you're not just risking the life of the person who receives the animal organ. OK, that person is taking a chance in order to have a chance to live. But what if the transplantee then infects other people with the virus?

So what else comes, as an added extra, in a vaccine mix?

The typhoid vaccine is made from the excrement of infected people. We wouldn't put it in our mouths, but we allow the scientists to inject it into our bodies.

Rabbit tissue was listed as an ingredient of the rabies vaccine in 1983. Hamsters are also used. Before that, until at least 1947, Millicent Morden MD, told us that to make the rabies vaccine:

> 1. A rabbit, dog or goat is strapped and its head held.
> 2. With no anaesthetic, a cut is made through the skin on top of the head.
> 3. The skin is separated from the skull.
> 4. A circular saw removes some bone.

5. A piece of the brain of the so-called rabid dog is inserted and the skin sewn up; the animal is placed in a cage to die.

6. Within between 13 to 27 days death occurs from inflammation of the brain. At death, the brain and spinal cord are removed, dried, and mashed in a distilled water and salt solution, to which carbolic acid or chloroform is added.

7. After straining, it is ready for animal or human use.

As the Rabdomun information tells us, brains are still used to culture vaccines. ("Because Rabdomun is produced on an established cell line, it has safety advantages over inactivated brain-origin rabies vaccines. Tissue-origin vaccines contain extraneous protein in addition to rabies antigen that can lead to autoimmune disease.")

As a person who recognises the ability to suffer and the inherent goodness of all animals, I would like to know if they still do this to living creatures? (No-one wrote to answer that question after the publication of the first edition of this book. In fact, no vaccine company has approached me to confirm or deny anything here, although I know for a fact that some of them have read it.) So if they do still cultivate vaccines on living creatures, there's even more reason not to buy these products.

So let's look at the hard facts:

Monkey kidney tissue was, and for all we know still is, used as a culture medium in vaccine production. Professor J Clausen of the Institute of Preventative Medicine, Odense, Denmark, stated: "It is possible that it will take up to 20 years or more before the eventual harmful effects of this virus (monkey simian virus) will be manifest."

Dr Viera Scheibner tells us that around 70 per cent of African Green monkeys, the species used to produce the polio vaccine, had Simian Immunodeficiency Virus (SIV), very similar to the Human Immunodeficiency Virus (HIV). The virus, which occurs naturally in these monkeys, does not cause disease in this species but kills Rhesus macaques, which were used in American laboratories to produce polio vaccine until the early '60s. Macaques used in American laboratories died of SIV infection which they contracted from Green monkeys in captivity.

Dr Salk, in DVM magazine, tells us that "the last thing in the world that one would want to do now is to make vaccines out of the tissues of monkeys that come from the jungle". Presumably, monkeys that don't come from the jungle are still OK?

Dr Scheibner tells us that polio vaccines proved to be contaminated with a great number of animal (simian) retroviruses, called SV1 to SV40. She contends that in the 1970s in the United States, homosexual men were exposed to both SIV and SV40 through unauthorised use of polio vaccine administered at weekly intervals in an attempt to treat genital herpes (Kyle 1992).

Kyle published an article in The *Lancet* in 1992 proposing a link between contaminated polio vaccines in the treatment of herpes, coinciding with the simultaneous outbreak of AIDS in American homosexual men.

Louis Pascal, described by Dr Scheibner as the epitome of the independent scholar, published a working paper for the University of Wollongong in 1991. In this paper, Pascal demonstrated that AIDS originated in the Belgian Congo as a direct result of mass oral polio vaccination while the vaccine was contaminated with a simian immunodeficiency virus (SIV).

Let me spell this out for you: it looks as though AIDs was created by vaccines.

Once more, we refer back to the Rabdomun data sheet inserted within the box carrying a killed rabies vaccine. The manufacturers state: "Tissue-origin vaccines contain extraneous protein in addition to rabies antigen that can lead to autoimmune disease." And to Merck's Veterinary Manual which states that: "Some viruses induce immunological deficiencies, usually via effects on the bone marrow. Examples are human immunodeficiency virus (the cause of AIDs in man), simian (monkey) immunodeficiency virus, feline immunodeficiency virus, and human and canine parvoviruses. Bone marrow suppression . . . have been associated with . . . both retroviral and parvoviral infections in man and other species. Also, *modified live parvovirus vaccines in dogs, and killed feline leukaemia virus vaccine are suspects as causes (in genetically susceptible animals)."*

And so . . . even if they use dog brains or dog kidneys to produce canine vaccines, there is quite a chance that the parvovirus, which can cause hepatitis, which is involved in AIDs, which is the collapse of the immune system, can be present in the dog whose body is being used as a culture site to produce vaccines, which then go in to your dog's body. And so are AIDs and other cross-species diseases, born and spread far and wide.

Jean Dodds writes, in her paper, *'Current issues on vaccine safety and efficacy'*:

> *"Immune-mediated haematologic disease and transient bone marrow failure are increasingly recognised sequelae of viral disease and recent vaccination with single or combination modified live virus vaccines, especially those containing parvovirus.*

> *"Immune dysregulation mediated by viruses of the retrovirus, parvovirus, and herpes virus classes occurs in man and animals. The immunosuppression and leukaemia's-lymphomas produced by the HTLV and HIV agents in man, SIV in primates, and FeLV and FIV (formerly called FTLV or feline lentivirus) in cats, to name but a few of the pathogenic retroviruses, have had profound clinical and epidemiological significance over the last decade. It is likely, therefore, that one or more canine retrovirus agents exist and contribute to the immunosuppression and leukaemias-lymphomas in dogs.*

> *"These vaccine-associated reactions usually occur 1-3 days or 10-21 days after vaccination. Typical signs are fever, stiffness, sore joints and abdominal tenderness, collapse with autoagglutinated red blood cells and icterus (jaundice), and/or generalised petechiae (bleeding in the skin) and ecchymotic haemorrhages (similar to purple bruises). Liver enzymes may be markedly elevated and liver and/or kidney failure may go along with bone marrow suppression."*

I've just had a thought: when Prudence was dying, she made a point of sitting outside a neighbour's house where cats lived and staring inside. She never did this before she was ill. Could Pru have been trying to tell me that her leukaemia came from a cat vaccine, shed into the drive? Yes, I know, scientists will squirm to read this. But I should imagine they've learnt a few things they didn't know about vaccines here, too. I think that science will discover a lot about animals and their abilities in the coming years.

Does the rise in modern diseases such as asthma, cancer, leukaemia, other autoimmune diseases, AIDS, parvovirus, and so on, share a root cause in the vaccination programme? And is that root cause the use of contaminated animal tissue used in vaccine manufacture or, indeed, the very presence of foreign animal tissue setting up a crazy immune response?

Dr Len Horowitz takes us a stage further. He claims that AIDs and other new diseases are 'designer' diseases - deliberately created by scientists in the lab to deal with world over-population. Dr Horowitz names names and possesses what he claims are contracts from the American government, giving scientists the task of creating diseases such as AIDs. Interested readers should obtain the book called, '*Emerging Viruses*' by Horowitz. It's only frightening if you let them at you with a needle.

Christopher Day comments: "I have long believed that asthma in humans is vaccine related. One study, recently reported in the television programme, "Trust Me I'm A Doctor" stated that asthma in East German cities, where there is terrific pollution, is at a much lower level than in West Germany where they have cleaner air.

"The researchers felt that the asthma may be related to vaccine policies. The reason they put forward is that vaccines reduce childhood diseases, which would have helped the immune system to develop. My view is that the damage done to the immune system by the vaccines causes asthma, rather than the lack of development of the young immune system."

Whether or not they - AIDs, canine autoimmune haemolytic anaemia and feline leukaemia - share their roots in the vaccine programme, we can once again draw upon the expert discussion carried in DVM to illustrate that vaccine contamination is a real problem.

"A second common example of an adventitious agent is another group of viruses of concern to the veterinary community, the parvoviruses, particularly the porcine parvovirus which gets into tissue culture from contaminated trypsin. So, yes, we must be ever aware of vaccine contaminants. We must also be aware of mycoplasma contamination and every other contaminant that can end up in cell culture that have products like fetal bovine serum and trypsin used on them." (Dr Schultz) Trypsin, by the way, is an enzyme found in the intestine.

Talking about cows, bovine autoimmune haemolytic anaemia is a disorder in newborn calves in which the red blood cells are destroyed. The veterinary dictionary tells us that the disease 'may be accidentally induced by the use of vaccines derived from blood'.

What are the vaccines our dogs and cats are injected with made from? It's a trade secret, protected by government. So you, dear customer, have no right to know what you are asking the vet to inject into your dogs and cats. You have to trust the manufacturers, whose secrets are protected by law. (I have recently learnt that the phrase, 'trust me' is the veterinary term for 'screw you'. We are taught that we should trust people who have been to college, but I think we should trust people who show themselves worthy of our trust. And vets can hump and bump as much as they like at that statement.)

Other vaccine-induced problems: Rabies and FeLV (feline leukaemia virus) vaccines have been associated with the development of fibro sarcomas and other tumours in cats. "I estimate that there are about 22,000 cases of vaccine-associated tumours per year," said Dr Dennis W Macy. (Source: *Journal of the American Veterinary Medical Association.*)

Vaccines have been associated with Gulf War Syndrome, where soldiers in the Gulf were either ill themselves, or produced seriously ill children. Dr Howard Urnovitz, a microbiologist from Berkeley, California (a specialist in the field of immune-system reactions) presented his findings to the Presidential Advisory Committee on Gulf War Veterans' Illness. He believes that environmental exposure factors provided a trigger mechanism affecting the immune systems of many Gulf War veterans. These triggers acted as immune system suppressants or, as he calls it, 'immune paralysis'. Dr Urnovitz contended that the precipitating factor was multiple vaccines.

Of course, other theories have been put forward, such as the pill soldiers took to protect them against chemical warfare, and the bombing of the Iraqi chemical weapons plants. More recently, it was admitted that our troops sprayed Iraqi PoWs with organophosphates (arguably the most deadly group of chemicals ever invented by man). We heard it on the news, but I haven't since heard anyone acknowledging that spraying captives with deadly chemicals was a shameful thing to do; neither have I heard anyone protesting that their government shouldn't be doing these things. We just let the experts get on with it.

It could be, then, that Selye's non-specific stress syndrome can be caused by any violent challenge to the system, of which vaccines are just one. This could be called 'the cocktail effect' or 'the threshold'.

But back to the known effects of poisonous vaccines. Drs Aleksandrowicks and Halileokowski, Medical Academy of Cracow, Poland, were reported in the *Lancet* in May 1967. They said: "Smallpox vaccination has been followed by violent local and general reactions and by leukaemia."

Dr R Brooks (Commonwealth Serum Labs), when writing about canine and feline vaccines, tells us that pain can be caused by vaccination due to a number of components of the vaccine. These can include stabilisers, various salts and formaldehyde. Formaldehyde is a known carcinogen; it is used to embalm corpses.

In fact, vaccines are made of a cross-section of animal-derived proteins, viruses, mucus, pus, blood, faeces and urine, carbolic acid, formaldehyde and mercury - scientifically prepared to be 'safe' and injected into your child's, dog's, and cat's system.

Brooks further states that vaccines can become ineffective for a number of reasons: "Stress in general, including pregnancy, extremes of cold and heat (Webster 1975), fatigue or malnutrition, can inhibit the normal immune response, probably because of increased steroid production (Tizard 1982)." By 'ineffective', Brooks probably means 'dangerous'. If the normal immune response is inhibited, your child, dog, cat, horse, or rabbit could die if you subject him to a vaccine challenge. Further, as the vaccine manufacturers tell us, the way your vet stores and handles the vaccine will have a bearing on whether or not the vaccine is safe and/or effective.

Dr Robert Mendelson, a Paediatrician and Professor of Preventative Medicine at the University of Illinois, says, "There now exists a growing concern which links immunisation to the huge increase, in recent decades, of autoimmune disease, e.g., rheumatoid arthritis, multiple sclerosis, lymphoma and leukaemia."

Merck agrees.

Got the picture?

Summary

* Vaccines can contain a mixture of viruses, aluminium, mercury, formaldehyde, salts, blood products, pus, faeces, urine, acid, contaminated trypsin, mycoplasma, etc.
* Vaccines have been implicated in the creation of new diseases, including AIDS, leukaemia, cancer and parvovirus
* Vaccines are typically cultivated on monkey, dog, and cat brains and kidneys, chick embryos, hamsters, etc. This allows viruses to enter vaccines and create cross-species disease
* Vaccine safety procedures are fallible
* Vaccines bypass many immune system defence mechanisms
* By vaccinating, we may be preventing the immune system from learning how to function

Chapter Eight

Vaccines can cause the disease they are designed to prevent

We have already heard that the polio vaccine has been proven to cause polio: parents can catch the disease from their vaccinated children, simply by changing their nappies. Indeed, we have seen quite a lot of evidence to suggest that many if not all vaccines can cause the disease they are designed to prevent - certainly, many of our case stories indicate that this is possible.

In DVM magazine, Dr Jonas Salk, founding director and professor in international health sciences at the Salk Institute for Biological Studies in San Diego, California, whose lifelong biologic research has involved, especially, polio, was asked: "Does shedding of modified live virus vaccine viruses from vaccinated animals have the potential to cause disease in non-vaccinated contact animals of the same species and/or different species?"

Dr Salk's answer was: "Well, it's self-evident that this is what happens with polio. . . In the US, vaccine virus is the principal cause of continuing polio."

In another paper prepared by Dr Schultz and a colleague, Tom R Phillips (*Current Veterinary Therapy XI*, 1992), the gentlemen state: "Incomplete vaccine attenuation or vaccination of an immunosuppressed host can result in modified live vaccines causing the disease they are designed to prevent. Examples of this problem are feline respiratory vaccines causing a mild upper respiratory tract disease after immunisation and the development of post vaccinal encephalitis subsequent to canine distemper vaccination. An even more alarming example is vaccine induction of clinical rabies. The reasons why vaccines become virulent are not always known. (!!!!)

"However, it is important that veterinarians be familiar with these possible outcomes of immunisation and give modified live vaccines only to approved animals that are in good general health and have no indication of immunosuppression."

As an aside, the immune system is itself a defence mechanism that the body develops against bacterial and viral infections. Cells responsible are in the thymus gland, spleen and lymphatic system. The immune system is impaired by malnutrition and certain vitamin and mineral deficiencies, particularly vitamins A, E and C, beta-carotene, and the minerals selenium, iron and zinc. The same nutrients, plus certain enzymes, are believed to be essential in quenching harmful free radicals, protecting against cell and tissue degeneration, and reducing the harmful effects of irradiation and pollution.

This means that an apparently healthy dog who relies upon one so-called complete and balanced processed food for his nourishment, might well be malnourished to the extent that he is lacking one or more of the essential nutrients - despite the fact that 'science' believes, for example, that extra vitamin C is unnecessary for the dog. These nutritional deficiencies could then lead to immunosuppression, causing the vaccine to induce the disease itself. As with vaccines, there is no legal requirement for a pet food manufacturer to tell you what is in its food, except for vague descriptions such as 'animal derivatives' and 'ash'. Only vitamins that have been added after manufacture need be stipulated.

But let's have a look at the possibility that vaccines can cause chronic disease, as postulated by a number of our experts.

The homoeopathic vet Richard Pitcairn, in the 1993 proceedings of the American Holistic Veterinary Medical Association, put forward the view that vaccines produce chronic rather than acute disease (although our case stories have also shown us evidence of acute disease in the form of death). (Chronic means long-standing; acute describes a disease of rapid onset, severe signs, and brief duration.) Dr Pitcairn says:

"The vaccination, having created a chronic disease ahead of time, can predispose the patient to a more serious natural illness which combines with the established vaccinosis. We can expand our definition to say that vaccinosis is the establishment of, instead of the acute natural disease, a chronic condition which now has the time to develop a multitude of manifestations not ordinarily seen. Another way of saying this is that the process of laboratory modification of a viral disease to make a vaccination strain is the conversion of the disease from acute to chronic."

Describing the acute form of distemper, Dr Pitcairn then compares it with the chronic, vaccine-induced form of distemper. He explains:

"A dog with distemper would have watery discharge of eyes and nose; a dog with chronic vaccine-induced distemper would have a tendency for watery fluid to drip from the nose. Similarly, the dog with distemper induced conjunctivitis would have, instead, vaccine-induced chronic conjunctivitis, eye discharge, and entropion (malformation of the eyelid and eyelashes, which turn onto the eyeball inflicting pain, inflammation, and ulceration). "

The Concise Oxford Veterinary Dictionary claims that entropion eyelids are hereditary in many breeds of dog. This begs the question whether the genes of the dog dispose him to react to vaccination with entropion, or whether the genes cause entropion of their own accord. Or whether the vaccine causes entropion. Personally, I'd like to see statistics showing how many unvaccinated dogs contract the so-called hereditary entropion. Pitcairn continues:

"Where the distemper-challenged dog would have vomiting, diarrhoea, and loss of appetite, the chronic vaccine-effected dog would have chronic gastritis, hepatitis, pancreatitis, and appetite disorders.

"Where the dog with distemper would have watery faeces, mixed with mucous, offensive and often bloody faeces; intense malaise, loss of weight, and death; the chronic form would produce parvovirus, recurrent diarrhoea, and sensitivity to foods with resultant diarrhoea.

"Where the dog with distemper would have spasms, fits, epileptiform seizures, and paralysis, the chronic condition would produce epilepsy, rear leg paralysis, and spondylitis (degeneration of the spinal discs, with outgrowths).

"In the distemper case we would see eruption around the mouth where hair meets the naked skin of the lips; the chronic form would show lip fold dermatitis and allergies.

"Swelling of the feet and red footpads would be exchanged for the habit of licking the feet; eruptions between the toes, inflammation and swelling of the toes and bottoms of the feet; interdigital dermatitis, and allergies.

"Instead of pneumonia, the chronic form of distemper would produce kennel cough and chronic bronchitis. Rather than eruptions on the skin of pustules, on the abdomen, inside the thighs, and elsewhere, the chronic form would produce chronic skin eruptions involving the abdomen, inside of thighs, and the lower half of the body, plus allergies."

Pitcairn contends that the many ramifications of chronic vaccine-induced distemper lead to it being given new names from the mistaken idea that they are different and distinct diseases.

Two unanswered questions:

Researchers have been finding that, where human mothers have been vaccinated against disease known to cause problems with unborn foetuses, their babies have developed childhood diseases much earlier than they otherwise would. Measles, for example, is occurring in significantly younger babies, at an age where they are less able to mount a defence. The inference, therefore, is that vaccines damage maternal antibody. It would be interesting to see whether this is an issue for dogs. It probably is.

Finally, there is some evidence to suggest that cancers and leukaemias are higher in vaccinated children than they are in un-vaccinated children. For example, children who develop the full measles rash, as opposed to the distinct measles rash that occurs in vaccinated children, are statistically less likely to suffer from cancer or leukaemia in later years.

The question is: do these naturally-occurring viruses confer immunity to more serious disease in later life? We already know that cancer cells are often found around vaccine sites, and that vaccines can cause cancer and leukaemia. It might also be possible that the vaccines themselves harm the immune system and render it more susceptible to diseases in which the host attacks itself.

But surely there is a safer way? How can we protect our dogs, cats and children without running these unquantified risks?

In a *Lancet* report in 1909 (March 20), it was stated: "Many organisms which are considered to be causal are frequently found in healthy persons. The organisms of enteric fever, of cholera, and of diphtheria may be cited as examples of this". The key, therefore, it to find out why some people (and animals) are able to withstand the ravishing effects of disease, while others aren't.

In fact, the vaccine manufacturers themselves point towards a safer way in their own contra-indications. The root of vaccine safety, and, ironically, the root of good health, grows in an absence from stress (or an ability to rise above the stress), nourishing food, good breeding, and absence from toxic assault (from chemicals and drugs).

Once you have your puppy, there's nothing you can do to change his genetic status - but breeders, theoretically, can. At least, they will be able to just as soon as the scientists are able to isolate the genetic markers which predispose progeny to disease. It wasn't more than three years ago, for example, that the Animal Health Trust announced a breakthrough: they had been able to isolate the gene that caused retinal atrophy in Irish Setters. And besides which, if vaccines are introducing genetic disease, what's the point of keeping on looking for the responsible genes? We're just going to keep them occurring unless we stop vaccinating.

Obviously, there are a lot of genes to that are yet to be isolated.

Shall we all whistle amongst ourselves (quietly in the dark like good little mushrooms with the manure landing on our heads) until the scientists are able to provide all the answers? Or are we commoners to exhibit a little common sense?

Interestingly, Dr Jean Dodds contends that underlying thyroid disease should be pinpointed, and dogs with this condition should be removed from the breeding programme. Thyroid disease, you will remember, is an inheritable condition which pre-disposes dogs to autoimmune disease. MLV vaccines are a major trigger. Dr Dodds has developed a range of blood tests which are (currently) rarely given outside her practice: she is able to show that the T4 test for thyroid disease is inadequate and often lets thyroid-diseased dogs slip through the net. Dr Dodds' address is listed at the back of this book.

So until the scientists know a little more, breeders need to make informed choices about breeding stock based upon parental health. But, however conscientious breeders are, they are no less mushrooms than the rest of us - ordinary human beings can only see through a glass darkly. Everyone does their best. (Scientists, incidentally, are mostly human beings. This rule - the mushroom rule - applies to them, too.)

It should also be noted that vaccines, by introducing genetic defects (as we have seen with cancer and SV40), make it incredibly difficult as time goes by to FIND dogs without genetic defects. If we continue vaccinating them to death, there will be none at all. Our survey, for example, does not link thyroid disease with vaccines. Is this because thyroid disease is not caused by vaccines (despite other scientific evidence to the contrary), or is it because we have vaccinated generation after generation of dogs, and thyroid disease has thereby become congenital?

It's difficult to know what you can do to minimise the stress in your puppy or adult dog's life. You can, at least, refrain from having your dog vaccinated in hot weather or after active play or sport. Similarly, you can try not to get upset when you receive a letter from the mortgage company threatening to evict you from your home (or other such stressful event in your life which is bound to be sensed by your dog) before he is vaccinated - if you must vaccinate at all.

I sincerely believe that stress plays a central role in our dogs' ill health and, in this modern world, stress is endemic. Many of us are beginning to recognise that our dogs are our teachers: their ill health can lead us towards our own personal growth.

On the subject of modern pharmaceuticals, I believe we dog lovers really need to read up about drug contra-indications if we intend to continue vaccinating our dogs. As our case stories indicate, it may be necessary to warn your vet not to vaccinate your dog if he's on steroids or other immune-suppressant drugs. Better still, work towards inherent health so that synthetic drugs are unnecessary.

But of equal importance - and one of only two factors you have real control over - is that you can ensure your dog's diet is the optimum diet. And now for the good news: a dog who is fed properly has an immune system that is more able to fight viral disease. Conversely, a dog who is not fed properly is more likely to succumb to the adverse effects of vaccination.

As an example, in one experiment, puppies who were deliberately starved of vitamin B5 were injected with vaccines, and they died. Vitamin B5 can be destroyed when cooked or frozen - and most dogs are given (cooked) processed and/or frozen food. The minerals selenium and vitamin A are vital for healthy thyroid function - pet food additives ethoxyquin, BHA and BHT are proven to destroy both selenium and vitamin A. As stated earlier, underlying thyroid disease pre-disposes dogs to autoimmune disease, triggered by vaccines.

At this point I strongly recommend all dog lovers to read up on canine diet. There are many good books around - see the back for a few suggestions. The key is to look for real food, not the dead stuff that is designed to sit around on supermarket shelves for months or years at a time and make lots of money for its manufacturers.

Dogs thrive on raw meaty bones (such as chicken, lamb, rabbit), lightly steamed or mashed raw vegetables, raw meat, liver, kidney, tripe, cottage cheese, fish, pasta, and fruit. If you have one dog, then good quality table scraps (i.e. unprocessed food) will be infinitely better than pet food. Please feel free to contact Canine Health Concern for further information.

But that's another story . . .

The fear that our much loved companions might die of diseases like distemper without vaccines is a real one and cannot be ignored. However, no-one knows how real the threat is: how common these diseases are at any one time. Similarly, the risk of adverse reactions to vaccines is itself not satisfactorily quantified.

Part of the answer must surely be that quality of life is important, as well as quantity. There is, as has already been stated, a vast spectrum of disease - from a mild fever all the way through to epilepsy, chronic enteritis, diabetes, paralysis and death - associated with vaccines. Would a dog prefer not to die of distemper but instead suffer for years with an horrendous skin condition or arthritis? Even then, if vaccines were known to be a hundred per cent effective, chronic disease might be a price we were prepared to pay on our dogs' behalf. We might even accept that the odd dog would die as a result of vaccines 'for the greater good'. But the fact is, some vaccines might work, some definitely don't.

And there's a safer alternative!

Summary

Vaccination is a risky business. Providing you know your dog's genetic, dietary, stress, and drug status . . . and providing you're sure you trust the safety standards of the particular vaccine your vet has on his shelves . . . go ahead and administer the needle.

There are around thirteen factors which render vaccines a risk to your dog, namely:

1. Your dog's (unknown) genetic status
2. Your dog's state of health
3. The food you feed your dog
4. The level of stress in your dog's life
5. Your dog's hormonal status
6. Whether or not your dog has been exposed to other infectious agents
7. Poor storage of the vaccine by your vet
8. Inappropriate administration of the vaccine by your vet
9. Other drugs your dog might be taking
10. Unsuccessful attenuation by the vaccine manufacturer
11. The presence of extraneous proteins in the vaccine
12. The presence of other challenges such as chemicals and pollutants: your dog needs a healthy immune system to survive vaccination
13. The presence of cross-species viruses in the vaccine.

Your notes

Chapter Nine

People who believe their pets were damaged by vaccines - some more case stories

Miss C Hughes says that her nine-year-old Cavalier King Charles Spaniel was very ill on the same day as his annual booster vaccination. He was panting very heavily, was very restless, had noisy breathing, and didn't want food or water. He was taken to the vets and Miss Hughes was told that maybe it was a reaction to `something'. He was overheating to a dangerous level, and the inside of his throat had swollen so that it was nearly impossible to breathe. The vet kept the dog in overnight, and told Miss Hughes that she would give him something to try to combat the reaction and douse him with water to keep the temperature down.

The next day the vet said that she thought the dog might die as he was so ill. Miss Hughes says, "He is a member of our family, and we were all devastated." However, the vet allowed the dog to go home, so long as the family made sure he stayed cool. The summer was spent soaking the dog in water and worrying that he might die.

After a few months the dog seemed much better. In hindsight, Miss Hughes feels it must have been the vaccination, as the dog had never been affected by the heat before, and the effects started about ten minutes after the booster.

Mrs D Wiltshire took her Beagle for his annual booster in September 1995. Within fifteen minutes he had collapsed unconscious. He was rushed back to the vet, who advised that the dog was in shock. An injection was given and the dog slowly recovered (the vet didn't tell Mrs Wiltshire what the injection was). Mrs Wiltshire says, "Our vet did all he could to contact the vaccine company. Eventually he was advised that this reaction is very rare. To be fair, in fifty years of keeping dogs of various breeds, this has never happened before."

Mrs J Heath took her three miniature long-haired Dachshunds for their annual booster jab. The older dog was fine, but the two youngest, aged four, suffered reactions, one more severe than the other. Mrs Heath says, "They were vaccinated at about 5 o'clock, came home and ate dinner as usual at 6 o'clock, and about an hour later, one walked as if drunk and became very inert, although continued to breathe normally and could be roused especially outside in the cold air. The other was similarly affected but less severely. The whole episode lasted for about six hours.

"I took them back to the vet the next day as this was the worst reaction they had so far. He told me to weigh up the risk of a fatal disease against this reaction. I obviously think the risk of fatal disease is worse, but am worried as the reaction seems worse each time and I don't know if this could be fatal."

Mrs V Davies' Beagle puppy was vaccinated at twelve weeks of age. Three days later he lost his appetite; five days later he had stopped eating altogether. He was salivating copiously and swallowing, and he was very listless. Antibiotics were prescribed by the vet, but no improvements were evident; in fact, he appeared worse. The dog was hospitalised, sedated, and was given painkillers and antibiotics, and was fed intravenously. The vet suspected a blocked bowel, which was checked with a laparoscope and, later, surgically. The bowel was so inflamed that it was blocking itself.

Several days later, the Beagle puppy was taking liquids and later changed to solids. Although he was allowed home, he was still salivating. Mrs Davies says, "The vet claimed not to know what the cause of the illness was and I mentioned distemper. He agreed it could be a possibility. The pup is now well but prone to stomach upsets." (Vaccines are suspected to be the cause of Crohn's disease in humans.)

Ms E Hayden-Prince has a Labrador cross bitch called Cromwell who came home at seven weeks of age from Woodgreen Animal Shelter. She was returned to the Centre for her first vaccination in July 1989. Two hours after the injection Cromwell was in serious distress. Her breathing was rapid, her nose dry, and her eyes and whole face were swelling. Ms Hayden-Prince says that the dog didn't know what to do with herself. Because the Centre was so far away, and the weather so hot, Ms Hayden-Prince decided to take Cromwell to the local vet, who injected steroids. The Woodgreen Animal Shelter told Ms Hayden-Prince that vaccine reaction was such a rare occurrence that they don't warn people so as not to cause them unnecessary worry.

The vet said that Cromwell would need to start her vaccine course again, and they gave her three days' of antihistamine with the vaccination, and she was fine.

The next year, at annual booster time, Ms Hayden-Prince explained the previous year's problem and asked for some antihistamine. She was told that reactions would be dealt with as and when they occurred. Not happy with this attitude, she went to another vet who rang Woodgreen to discuss the problem. It was decided to vaccinate Cromwell without the antihistamine as she may have grown out of the problem. Ms Hayden-Prince says that she hadn't, of course, but being older and larger she coped with less distress. "The size of the sac of fluid that collected at her chest was grotesque," she says. "The problem has subsided over the years, but I shall never forget the panic I felt on seeing such a poor little scrap suffering so much for something I had subjected her to."

Ms Hayden-Prince said she believes in the principle of vaccinations, but would have preferred to have been aware of the possible side-effects and solutions before they actually occurred.

RA Butler's Whippet bitch was `a perfectly normal puppy' before she was taken for her first vaccination at ten weeks of age. The vet gave the puppy a thorough examination before vaccinating and was pronounced `fine'. The journey home lasted for thirty minutes, at the end of which Mrs Butler put the puppy on her rug. She crawled to the fire and lay there shivering. Although she seemed to recover the next day, the reaction seemed to worsen after the second injection.

"She just went from bad to worse," says Mrs Butler. "At one stage we thought we would lose her, she was so ill. The weight dropped off her because she wasn't eating, and she had no life. We had her tested for autoimmune disease, but this was negative. My vet wrote to the vaccine company asking them if it was possible that she'd had a bad batch of vaccine but they denied this."

Mrs Butler's Whippet is fine now, and protected homoeopathically.

Julie Treneer's mother had three cats, two of whom died within a short time of each other. After discussions with the vet, a third cat and two kittens (who had been in contact with the two cats who died) were blood tested to see if they had caught `Cat Flu' or leukaemia. They were clear. Each cat was vaccinated.

When they were around 18 months old, the young cats were taken back to the vet, along with the older cat. Because one of the young cats had a sore eye, he wasn't vaccinated but the other two were.

During the evening all seemed fine, but the young female cat was found dead the next morning. "The vet was horrified," says Julie Treneer. "She was so full of beans the day before."

The vet conducted a post mortem at the vaccine manufacturer's expense and told Julie that she found nothing out of the ordinary. Samples were sent to the vaccine company for further tests. The company's report stated that there was no obvious reason for the death, apart from `shock' from the vaccination.

J White's puppy had her last vaccine injection on January 14th 1993. The next morning she was unable to walk and was very drowsy, and by the afternoon she was having convulsions. Mrs White took the puppy to the PDSA.

"They told me she had parvovirus," says Mrs White, "and that it was a reaction to the injection she had been given. It took well over a month for her to get better. I was up all night nursing her. I even had to get a doggie sitter in if I went out. She wasn't allowed out while she was ill and, when she was well again I let her into the garden. She was so excited that she crashed straight into some bricks I had hidden in a corner of the garden and broke her leg. So by the time she recovered from that, it was March before I could take her on her first proper walk. Today she's a really happy dog with a tail that's always wagging."

JB Wakefield's six-year-old German Shepherd bitch was vaccinated, and a few days later she had her first fit. Other fits followed. The vet administered Phenobarbitone which she now takes every day. This has controlled the fits. Mrs Wakefield says that the vet told her he had heard other vets say that they knew dogs who had fits after vaccination, but the vaccine manufacturer denied the connection. Meanwhile, Mrs Wakefield is convinced that the vaccine started the fits.

Mary Zannettou took her Lhasa Apso, Millie, for her booster shot. Two weeks later Millie had a severe fit which caused her neck to twist so severely that it resulted in high cervical vertebrae spinal dislocation causing respiratory failure.

Mrs Zannettou says, "despite heroic attempts by the vet to resuscitate her, Millie died. I have another little dog named Zoe now. She is due for her booster soon and I am at a loss as to what to do next. I haven't talked to my vet as I don't want him to think I blame anyone."

Mrs Pauline Khourie took a Japanese Chin bitch called Squeek for her first vaccine when she was six months old. Because Japanese Chins are so small, and because four of Pauline's dogs had previously experienced vaccine reactions, Pauline took the decision to delay vaccination until the puppy was older and larger.

Squeek was vaccinated on the 28th December 1996. By January 1st, Pauline discovered that Squeek had vomited bile and was walking in a disorientated manner. By 2pm on January 4th, Squeek was having massive fits which continued more or less non-stop.

Pauline Khourie is full of praise for her vet, saying that she came out and spent two hours with the puppy. Valium was prescribed, starting with an intravenous injection, followed by an injection into the puppy's muscle, and then Valium tablets were given by Pauline every four hours. The fits, however, continued. The vet suggested that the puppy should be put down but Pauline wanted to fight for her, and blood tests were taken, with samples going to the vaccine manufacturer and Glasgow University.

"A friend then suggested I contact John Saxton, a homoeopathic vet," says Pauline. "He gave Squeek some nosodes and another homoeopathic remedy. After the first nosode she walked out of her crate. I couldn't believe it. She had eaten nothing for five days and I couldn't get her to drink, but I had managed to syringe some glucose solution into her. She took her first drink after the nosodes, too."

Squeek stayed on the nosodes for five days and seemed to recover, but when they were withdrawn she started to fit again. New nosodes were sent in the post and Squeek rallied round once again. "She's not had any nosodes for four days now," said Pauline, "and she's pottering around and the fits have stopped. Her temperament is back to normal, too. At one point I couldn't pick her up without using a towel, she had turned really nasty and was biting out. I'd hate to think how the owner of a large dog would cope with this reaction. I would imagine the dog would have to be destroyed."

Pauline's vet dealt with the vaccine manufacturer; Pauline says that the vet told her the drug company would pay the vet bills.

"The last thing I want to do is hurt my vet," says Pauline. "She's a wonderful person. But I can't go along with these vaccines any more. I'll take my dogs for check ups and support my vet, but never - as long as I live - will I give a dog a vaccine again. I was so angry at one point that I wanted to tommy gun the agents who sell those vaccines. They act as though you don't matter. No-one has written to apologise, or anything. I will never again pay to have this lethal stuff injected into a dog."

Mr and Mrs Paul Ridd's six-year-old mongrel suddenly started having epileptic fits within a week of his annual booster vaccine. They were sporadic, but nonetheless frightening, occurring initially once daily and then more frequently. After a week they stopped, only to return with a vengeance a few days later. The couple contacted the vet who could find nothing wrong with the dog and, when the apparent connection with the vaccine was mentioned, the vet `rather wrote the idea off'.

Around two weeks after the fits started, they began to get more frequent - three times a day - and the vet advised a powerful drug to control the fits. Mrs Ridd knew that this was likely to change his entire well-being and character, so they waited a few days to see whether the fits would stop. Thankfully they did. "I struggled with the decision at the time," says Mrs Ridd, "watching him so distressed when he came out of each fit, but I am very glad that I decided not to give him the drugs. I haven't heard of any apparent connection between vaccines and epilepsy, but (despite my being a biology teacher and therefore naturally sceptical) it is very hard to avoid the conclusion that Thompson's epileptic fits were the direct result of the vaccine."

Mrs Beryl Stirling's five-year-old Springer Spaniel, Briar, had his first epileptic fit the day after his vaccine booster.

Mrs Carole Sandler believes that it is possible that her Dalmatian puppy had a bad reaction from her second vaccination at the age of twelve weeks. She felt that it could have been a mild dose of distemper. The puppy began to have fits every two hours, exactly ten days after her final jab. Until this point, Mrs Sandler says that she was a healthy puppy, and none of her litter mates were affected.

The Dalmatian has been tested for all possible causes by Mrs Sandler's vet and the breeder's vet, and one vet did suggest contacting the vaccine company to see if they would be interested or able to help solve the problem. Neither vet was able to determine the cause of the fits.

By the time she was five months old, the puppy had not had a fit for three weeks. She was gradually being weaned off her daily dose of Phenobarbitone, with the fear that she might start fitting again.

Mrs E Rouston has owned and bred Boxers since 1953. In 1989, a six year old Boxer bitch had her annual vaccine; nine days later she had her first fit. Several minor fits followed during the year and, in 1990, she had another annual booster. Once again, the bitch had a violent fit nine days later. Mrs Rouston mentioned this to her vet, who suggested that the distemper part of the vaccine might be responsible. The bitch continued to have fits until eventually she went into status epilepticus and couldn't be brought out of the fits. She was put to sleep in November 1990 at the age of nine.

The bitch had had a litter of puppies when she was two, before any signs of epilepsy. Mrs Rouston kept a dog from this litter. He was apparently perfectly well until 1992 when, after a spell in boarding kennels, he came out with kennel cough. He had an injection and had his first fit several days later. (You may notice that owners' accounts often fail to tell us what an injection contained, or which tablets were given to a pet. Maybe we should be asking our vets questions.)

About three months after this, the dog had the nasal inoculation against kennel cough before going into kennels. He had his second fit the day after returning home. He started fitting again some six or seven days after his next annual booster. The fits gradually worsened until he, too, had to be put down owing to status epilepticus.

When Mrs Rouston discussed the fits and the vaccines with the vet, she says he denied any knowledge of his suggestion referring to the distemper vaccine. "The drug companies, of course, deny that there is any connection," Mrs Rouston says, "their attitude being `prove it', which of course is difficult."

Mrs IP Howard took her four-year-old British Bull Dog for his vaccination one Monday morning. He had his first fit on the Wednesday, and these gradually worsened. Although treated by his vet and later at the Liverpool Veterinary Hospital, the dog died six months after the jab.

Mr and Mrs Howard told their vet and the consultant at the hospital that they thought the vaccine had caused the fits, but both denied that there could be a link.

Mrs Lambelle's puppy Hollie, a King Charles Spaniel, was vaccinated at eight weeks of age. Twenty-four hours later she started having fits, and she has been epileptic ever since.

Mrs M Beresford took her Pomeranian bitch to the vet for her first vaccine and exactly ten hours later she started to take a fit. Mrs Beresford contacted the vet who told her that it was definitely not caused by the vaccine, even though she had never had fits before.

After two weeks elapsed and the bitch was due for her second injection, Mrs Beresford informed the vet that she wasn't going to take the puppy for the rest of them.

"By this time," says Mrs Beresford, "the vet had attended a seminar and had been informed that, yes, it probably was the vaccine as there was a bad batch out at that particular time, and this was probably the reason for the fits." The bitch continued to have fits throughout her life, particularly if she had eaten something that didn't agree with her.

Mrs R Etherington took her Maltese Toy Terrier for her annual booster vaccination during April 1995. The vet told her that he had included the Parainfluenza (Pi) vaccine. Mrs Etherington said it wouldn't be necessary, as her dogs don't go into kennels. However, the vet told her that they were being urged to incorporate this as kennel cough was becoming very widespread. Within less than two hours, the previously healthy, happy, dog was in a terrible state, with diarrhoea, vomiting and restlessness. "She then ran around the kitchen bashing her head continually and purposely against the furniture. Her eyes were unfocussed and wide, and she did not respond to my voice or touch."

Mrs Etherington rang the vet and asked whether the dog could be having a bad reaction to the vaccine, but was told that it must be a virus she had picked up. "I phoned the vet later," Mrs Etherington says, "and told him she was no better. I arranged to meet him at his surgery. He gave her another injection and said that if she had had a reaction to the vaccine, she would have some head or facial discomfort. This information cost me a £46 call out fee plus injection fee and a £15 taxi fare. The vet wouldn't admit that there was a problem, so I tried to find some answers for myself. But I met with a blank wall with the veterinary schools and hospitals I rang for advice."

Mrs Etherington says that it took almost three months before her beloved little dog was back to her normal self. "She couldn't see properly and lost all co-ordination. She couldn't even jump up and down the step into the garden. I have felt so alone and helpless about what happened."

Mrs V Smith took her Yorkshire Terrier puppy for booster injections and a check up. She mentioned to the vet that the puppy was very small - he was about 13 weeks old and just fitted into Mrs Smith's hand. The vet confirmed that the puppy was very healthy and gave him his vaccine injections, although Mrs Smith did query why such a small dog needed as much vaccine as a large dog.

Three days later the puppy started to have fits and foamed at the mouth. Mrs Smith says he had not shown any signs of this before. About an hour later, the puppy was playing quietly in the garden, seemingly not having suffered from the fit. The next morning, Mrs Smith found the puppy in his basket, almost lifeless. She took him to the vet straight away, who said that it would be in the dog's best interest to have him put to sleep.

Mrs Smith says, "The dog was fully insured, and when I asked the vet for a certificate for the insurers, he stated on the certificate that he was suffering from gastro enteritis which I found very puzzling, because he had shown no symptoms of this illness whatsoever."

Mrs Viv Williams' bulldog pup was vaccinated and, on the way home, started to behave very oddly, jumping around with eyes bulging. She seemed terrified of lights and noise. Upon arriving home, Mrs Williams took the puppy's temperature, which was 'nearly off the thermometer'.

"By this time she was cowering at the back of the settee," says Mrs Williams, "too scared to move. I rang my vet who was puzzled, but he told us to close the curtains and keep her in total darkness and silence, and to take her back if she seemed to get worse." The puppy slowly recovered over the next few days.

"All my vet said was that he had seen this sort of reaction to certain antibiotics, but never with inoculations. Yet in the office there was a warning that vaccination can cause blue eye and fits in Shelties! When I queried this, and told my vet that the puppy had come close to fitting with the vaccine, he seemed to think this was coincidence."

Two years later, Mrs Williams took some puppies for vaccination. Within six hours they became ill with high temperatures, vomiting, and diarrhoea. They were ill for over a week.

"Eventually," says Mrs Williams, "my vet conceded that my dogs may have had adverse reactions to something in the three-in-one vaccine. Since then none of my dogs has been vaccinated. They are just given the jab for leptospirosis. I know of a litter of Pekes who all died within 48 hours of their first inoculation."

Ms R Waters reports that her dog developed fits ten days after his first inoculations at ten weeks of age. After numerous tests, the only one that proved positive was one sent to the Glasgow Veterinary College which showed a `major distemper challenge'. The question was asked whether this was a reaction to the vaccine, or whether the dog had been infected by the distemper virus. Mrs Waters says, "My vet favours the former, as I do, but there is no way of proving that the vaccine caused the fits. We all just have to live with them."

Mrs E Shorrock's Cavalier King Charles Spaniel, known as Marti, was accidentally dropped when he was two months old, two days after his first course of vaccines. All was fine until two years later, when he was given his second annual booster and suffered what appeared to Mrs Shorrock to be a convulsive fit. The next year he was given another booster. Ten days later he suffered a further convulsive fit which appeared longer and seemed more severe.

Mrs Shorrock connected the first fit with the fact that he was a two-year-old dog who had been concussed as a puppy. When he had a second fit, she realised that it was at a similar time of year (August rather than July), and wondered whether the weather could be a factor. It then occurred to her that it was `vaccination time', so she referred to her records. When

Mrs Shorrock mentioned the coincidence to her vet, she was told that any adverse reaction would be immediate, not days later. Mrs Shorrock now worries about having Marti vaccinated again.

Mrs J Silver's Jack Russell had his annual vaccination in March 1994 and was unwell for about a month afterwards. In October 1994, he died aged eight years old. "He had all the symptoms of leptospirosis," says Mrs Silver, "a disease for which he was vaccinated against. My vets were very unhelpful in giving me an explanation as to why my dog died."

Mrs M Broderick says that, in 1989, her Old English Sheepdog contracted parvovirus after his second vaccination. The dog had not been pavement walked, neither had his feet touched the ground in the veterinary surgery.

A few days after his second vaccination, the dog began vomiting. He was given nothing to eat for 24 hours, after which time he tried to eat again, but began to vomit again. Mrs Broderick says, "He just stood in the garden with his head in the rose bushes, not moving. I phoned the vet who said that puppies often get upset tummies as they were always chewing something, and she refused to come out." At 10pm on the Saturday night, Mrs Broderick insisted the vet visit, as the next surgery wasn't until the Monday morning. Mrs Broderick was told to take the puppy to the surgery.

By the next day, the puppy was on a drip, and by Monday Mrs Broderick was told that he had tested positive for parvovirus. Mrs Broderick says, "For five days he was a poorly little dog and, being so young, he wasn't expected to pull through. He was born deaf and brain damaged due to his mother being 10 years old with her first litter. He was one of three of seven puppies to survive, and must have been a born fighter."

Mrs Broderick says that the dog survived the vaccine, and now has the best health of the three. "When I asked the vet how he could have contracted the disease, she said it may have been the batch of vaccine from the supplier, and she would make enquiries. The bill was £200."

When Mrs Broderick asked for an explanation at a later date, the veterinary practice maintained that they had lost the dog's files.

P Garwood's English Bull Terrier, Tess, developed distemper in March 1993, one year after being vaccinated against this disease. She died after more than three weeks' of suffering. Her antibody level was one in eight, when it should have been between one in 500 and one in 1000.

Sam, also an English Bull Terrier who had been inoculated at the same time, showed initial signs of distemper (sticky eyes and nose) but didn't become ill. His blood count was found to be 32.

Mr and Mrs David Beckett's mongrel, Bingo, was born in December 1981. Prior to his visit to the vet's on 21st October 1995, Bingo still had a normal appetite, although he was slowing down with age. The vet looked Bingo over, commenting on his age, the poor state of his teeth, and, at the Becketts' request, investigated a lump on his rump. The vet said that this was only fatty tissue. The vet then administered a vaccine.

Mr Beckett says that Bingo changed almost overnight. The first problem they noticed was that Bingo had difficulty in maintaining balance, especially in his hind legs. Within two weeks he had lost weight, and his back legs appeared stiff at the hip. He had not barked since the injection, and appeared to be unhappy. Mr Beckett, who had seen his father's dog contract distemper, believed that this was what was wrong with Bingo.

The vet, however, rejected the suggestion that it might be a reaction to the vaccine. The vet reminded the Becketts that Bingo was, after all, an old dog - and did they remember the tumour? (previously described as fatty tissue). Bingo was still with the Becketts by February 1996. He maintained a small appetite, but not the strength to sustain a walk of more than a hundred yards.

Ms CA Makins-Barnett acquired a retriever/greyhound cross from the RSPCA who had been vaccinated with no apparent ill effect before Ms Barnett took the dog home. A year later, in 1994, the dog was given his booster which, says Ms Barnett, went badly wrong. "I nearly lost him, and he had daily visits to the vet. After that he gagged at whatever food he was offered, suffered skin disease, diagnosed as eczema, and had three short spells of paralysis in his back legs of a few hours' duration. He also recently suffered cystitis and had to be rushed to the surgery. He is on constant antibiotics, skin tablets, etc."

Ms Makins-Barnett was informed by the vet that the injection was bad, and that several animals had been ill. "The vet told me that they no longer use that brand. When our vet's fees and visits were ongoing I asked if there was any compensation or information they could give me, and they would tell me no more."

Strangely, when Ms Barnett asked why dogs and cats had to have annual injections she was told "it is because they have a number of years' life to our one year"! The dog suffered long-term illness.

Elliot, Mrs Garwood's black and white kitten, was inoculated against leukaemia in the summer of 1992. He died of leukaemia in the spring/summer of 1993.

Mrs Hazel Matthews points out that cats can suffer adverse reactions to vaccines, too. She took her cat for his annual booster for cat flu in the summer of 1995. Two days later he was in the throes of the flu; antibiotics from the vet didn't seem to help. "The poor cat couldn't eat," Mrs Matthews says. "The vet prescribed more tablets but the cat wandered off to die. Needless to say, the vet denied any link between the booster and the cat getting the illness the booster was supposed to prevent. I realised he was probably afraid of being sued, but though I assured him I only wanted to ensure that the manufacturer was aware of the problem so that other cats would not suffer, he dismissed this with the remark that, `I was the only one who had complained'."

On Wednesday, 5th January 1994, Mr and Mrs Collins took their two dogs and three cats for their annual boosters. The cats and two of the dogs were adult, one was a puppy.

By the end of January, the puppy, Rebel, was losing weight at an alarming speed. The vet was consulted, and he took a series of tests and then X-rays, and the couple were advised to feed the puppy white fish, egg and rice. There was no weight gain. By March Rebel was half his normal weight and began to lose energy and alertness.

One Saturday morning, the couple took Rebel back to the vet's, and the duty vet told them that they were waiting for test results to confirm parvovirus. By Monday the puppy was so ill that he was admitted to the veterinary hospital, where he was placed on drips, and swabs were sent off for analysis. Mr and Mrs Collins say that Rebel fought to live during the first week, but by the second he had shown an improvement and was brought home on the Thursday. By Sunday he was refusing food again.

The puppy was immediately taken back to the vet, who gave him a vitamin B injection and explained that this was the puppy's final effort to survive. Later that afternoon, Mr Roberts saw that Rebel was deteriorating, and he sat down with him and cuddled him and talked to him as he slipped into a coma. The vet came out and put the puppy peacefully to sleep.

Two weeks later, one of the vets telephoned to say that the lab had thought Rebel reacted to his annual injection, and asked to test him again. By this time the puppy had been laid to rest, and Mr and Mrs Collins felt the puppy should be allowed to retain his dignity and rest in peace.

Mrs J Gould's dog, Charlie, was vaccinated on the 11th June. Nearly three weeks later he became very weak. For ten days he was treated for kidney disease but it was discovered that this was a misdiagnosis. At this stage, a blood sample was sent to Leeds for analysis. Charlie died on the 17th July before the results were known.

It transpired that immune mediated thrombocytopenia had been triggered by something that Mrs Gould says, "nobody would admit to. I feel that it was vaccine which had made the dog's immune system go out of control and to reject and destroy the blood platelets. His red cells were also malformed and were not being replaced.

"I feel that it was a remote chance of this happening," Mrs Gould says, "but if the vet had been aware that it was possible, treatment could have started earlier. Charlie was in tip-top condition before the vaccination, and much loved."

Mrs V Cavill says, "Six months ago we owned a lovely two year-old Border Collie. We took him to the vet for his booster injection. The vet gave him a very good check over and said he was in perfect condition and very well cared for. He gave the dog the injection, and we walked away feeling very pleased with ourselves to think we were doing everything right in bringing Skip up."

That evening, Skip seemed fine. The next afternoon, however, he was sick. He was sick again in the evening. Mrs Cavill says that his mouth was very pale inside and his "motions were all coming up through his mouth". Mr and Mrs Cavill phoned the vet. It was a Saturday night, and they were told to take the dog to the surgery which was about 11 miles from their home. "By the time we got there he was very thin, as he was losing his body fluids very quickly."

The vet checked Skip and said that he had been poisoned or had picked up something very toxic. However, Mr and Mrs Cavill wonder how this could be, as he hadn't left the garden from the time he had his vaccination to the time he became ill. Skip was left with the vet on a drip and died in the early hours of Sunday morning.

Mr and Mrs Cavill asked for a post mortem. After waiting a week, the vet reported that he could not give a reason for the dog's death, "what with the very hot weather and the rapid deterioration of the dog's body". Mrs Cavill, however, believes that the vaccine killed Skip. He died within 32 hours of the injection.

Mrs Cavill says that they have had five other dogs over the years and none has ever been vaccinated. All lived to between 12 and 16 years of age.

Faith Addis never had any of her dogs vaccinated and, without exception, they all lived long healthy lives, dying of natural causes at ages between 14 and 17 years.

In 1991, Mr and Mrs Addis bought a Bernese Mountain puppy and called her Bess. Bess was bred from unvaccinated parents, one of a litter of eight healthy pups. When Bess was a year old, Faith decided to take her to training classes and, later, on a dogs' activity holiday. None of these places would accept unvaccinated dogs. After giving the matter a great deal of thought, Faith decided that a big robust dog like Bess would be able to throw off the vaccine toxins and so, with some misgivings, she had her vaccinated.

Faith says, "Within days, Bess was suffering from a wheezy chest which the vet diagnosed as flea allergy and treated with cortisone. Shortly after this a small lump appeared on Bess's neck at the site of the vaccination. The vet said this was nothing to worry about."

Faith sought a second opinion and, this time, the diagnosis was cancer. The lump was surgically removed and sent for biopsy, where the cancer was confirmed. The lump grew twice in Bessie's short life. Just before her fourth birthday, Mr and Mrs Addis decided they couldn't put her through any more painful operations and had her put down.

Admitting that there is no firm evidence (except there is!), to connect the vaccine with the destruction of Bessie's immune system, Faith recounted the experience of Bessie's breeder.

"Bessie's breeder is an elderly widow who lives alone," Faith said. "In 1993 she had a bad fall and broke her leg and wrist. She was in hospital for some time so her dogs were put into boarding kennels. Like all kennels, this one had a `vaccinated dogs only' rule, so three hitherto healthy dogs - Bessie's mother, full sister and full brother - were vaccinated. Within a year both bitches were dead, one from liver failure and the other from an internal haemorrhage. The male dog survived."

Faith says, "I feel so angry that the vaccine companies have such a stranglehold on the pet industry. It has been hard for me to tell you about Bess dying so unnecessarily. You can probably imagine the grief and the guilt."

Mrs E Lane apologises for appearing to be bitter, but she says, "I will not give my dogs booster vaccines as they seem to be just as deadly as the serious illness they are supposed to protect the dog from. I have lost two Afghan dogs with the three-in-one booster".

Mrs Julie Caruana took her dog Prince, a cross Weimaraner/Pointer, aged ten, for his booster in July 1995. Later that day he became ill, bowing his head and trying to be sick without success. Mrs Caruana phoned the vet asking whether it could be a reaction to the vaccine, but the vet said no. She was told to take the dog to the surgery immediately. The dog was examined and said to have gastric torsion, and an operation was scheduled. The next morning the surgery phoned to say that Prince had come round after the operation but later died of shock.

Mr David Reekie lost Binks, a hitherto healthy, happy, and active five-year-old tri-colour King Charles Spaniel, in December 1995. The dog received his booster vaccine on the

27th October 1995. This was followed with a gradual loss of appetite and disinterest in exercise. His breathing was laboured, even when at rest.

On the 15th of November, the dog was taken to the veterinary surgery where the vet said that the dog's heart was over-working due to poor circulation. Heart and diuretic tablets were prescribed. The dog occasionally brightened up but continued to refuse food. At this time, Mr and Mrs Reekie were confined to bed with influenza and bronchitis. The dog seemed content to sleep and continued to refuse food. He drank lots of water and there was no sign of weight loss. Because of their illness, Mr and Mrs Reekie asked the vet to visit the dog at their home.

The vet came on the 7th December and gave an injection to reduce the dog's body fluids. He increased the dosage of heart tablets and told the Reekies that even if the dog recovered he would never be an active animal. Mr Reekie says that the dog was most distressed following the injection and seemed unable to control his bodily functions. His breathing became more laboured. There was no food intake whatsoever.

On the 14th of December the dog was taken to the veterinary surgery and a request was made to end his misery. The vet advised that it was too soon to make such a decision. The vet considered that the dog's circulation had improved. Meanwhile, Mr Reekie says that the dog was unable to step to the back door without assistance.

On December 22nd, Binks was taken to the surgery for examination, and later put down. The vet expressed surprise that the end took so long and commented that this proved how bad his circulation had become. The vet was never able to positively diagnose the problem.

Mrs BC Clayton's Cavalier King Charles Spaniel, Celtie, had a booster at Christmas 1993 and was very lethargic for five or six days afterwards. She was boosted again after

Christmas 1994 and, within a week, died in Mrs Clayton's arms of a heart attack. Mrs Clayton says the vet scoffed at the suggestion that the vaccine might be involved.

Mrs MA Read took Sam, a Scottie dog, to the vet for his annual booster Vaccination on Monday, 10th October 1994. On Friday the 15th October, Sam was taken for his regular clipping but, before he could be bathed, Sam collapsed. He was taken straight to the vets. The next day he was taken to the hospital as his condition had deteriorated, and he was kept in all day. Tests were taken to see whether Sam had been poisoned. These proved negative. However, they did show that Sam was suffering from liver and kidney failure.

Mrs Read asked the vet whether the condition could be linked to the vaccine and was told no. Sam was put to sleep on Tuesday, 18th October. Mrs Read says, "It seems strange to me that we had to have Sam put to sleep seven days after he was vaccinated, without showing any indication of being unwell prior to the vaccine."

Mrs P Ariss lost her Westie bitch, a trustworthy companion, in December 1993, and shortly afterwards brought a Westie puppy into her home. This lively puppy had `Westie Disease', a jaw disease treated with steroids. At 15 months, the bitch had her first booster injection and for three days was very quiet and lethargic. On the fourth day, Mr Ariss found the dog dead in the kitchen. A post-mortem revealed a heart attack.

Mrs Ariss is convinced there was a problem with the vaccine but, until she heard that other people had seen similar reactions in their dogs, thought she was probably neurotic. She says that if we were told of the options, we might live better with our consciences.

Jaki McFall bought a beautiful Maltese pup from what she describes as a highly reputable breeder. The puppy had been given a first vaccine at eight weeks old, and was taken to Ms McFall's local vet for a second. The puppy slept through the evening following the second jab, and then appeared to be paralysed, dragging his back end. Taking the puppy, Chico, to the vet the next day, Ms McFall was told that the puppy could have jumped off a chair or twisted his back or spine in some way. The next day the vet rang her to say that he was going to put Chico to sleep as he had a broken back.

"I told him that it was impossible," says Ms McFall. "That puppy was nursed like a baby. I had done everything but wrap him in cotton wool. I quickly drove to the vet and collected Chico, saying that I wanted a second opinion, which I got from a specialist in a nearby town. The specialist told me that the needle may have gone into his neck too deep, or he had had too much of the vaccines. But he didn't want to get involved."

Miss McFall was told to take the puppy home and give him two weeks. Maybe by some miracle he would improve. "I then took him to a third vet who was very gentle and caring," she said. "But Chico got to the stage of severe pain and had difficulty going to the toilet. I prayed he would improve, but agreed that the vet should put him to sleep.

"I'll never forget his little face looking up to me, as I decided I would hold him to the end. I still carry a cutting of his fur in my wallet. It just doesn't seem fair. He only got to live for twelve weeks.

"I am afraid I am very bitter and angry about this. The vet is still sending me the bill, which I refuse to pay. I asked to see the x-ray. It looked to me like the x-ray of a duck, and was completely different to the x-ray taken by the third vet."

KF Warrey's dog lost the use of his legs, seemed to want to go out, and was violently sick on the evening of his booster jab. The same thing happened the following year, but this time it was ten days after the jab.

In October 1995, Mrs S Tilley took her 12-year-old Border Collie cross, Tara, for her annual booster. The vet checked her over and announced that she was very fit and healthy, and then administered the vaccine.

Ten days later, Tara was off colour and shivering uncontrollably. On the Friday, she was taken back to the vet, who diagnosed Kennel Cough and prescribed antibiotics. By Saturday night/Sunday morning, Tara was getting progressively worse, laying motionless on the floor - nothing could be done to attract any attention from her. The Tilleys telephoned the emergency vet who advised giving Tara a Paracetamol. She was violently sick and continued to be for the rest of the day. Tara was then taken to the emergency vet's surgery, where she was given another type of antibiotic.

"During the night," says Mrs Tilley, "we thought we were going to lose her, and we stayed awake with her all night. Her breathing was very laboured and she still continued to be sick, even though she hadn't had anything to drink or eat for more than 48 hours. We took her back to our original vet on the Monday morning, who took her into the hospital for tests and to put her on a drip."

Mr and Mrs Tilley were told that Tara's chances of survival were slim, but then a result from one blood test showed that an enzyme was abnormal and, once this was established, the vet started treating her with antibiotics. Within 48 hours she was able to have the drip removed and managed to keep some water down. On the following Saturday, Tara was well enough to go home and now and, with a regulated diet, she is getting back to her former sprightly self. Mrs Tilley has decided against the booster next year as she feels that the risk of an adverse reaction is greater than the risk of Tara contracting the disease itself.

Ms Mandy Coombes owns an Italian Spinone bitch who suffers from acute pancreatic insufficiency, colitis, and gluten allergy. Ms Coombes says, "our vet and various other individuals suspect that her troubles began when she was given a parvo vaccination at seven weeks by her breeder. We have her conditions mostly under control, but we experienced a flare-up of her pancreatic problems when she received her boosters last autumn. I'm sure this problem needs more investigation."

Mrs D Woodcock's nine-year-old Airedale Terrier bitch was rushed into hospital because she couldn't keep food down. The vet initially suspected a blockage, but after X-rays and a barium test, nothing was found. The problem was eventually diagnosed as gastro-enteritis. The problem occurred 15 days after her vaccination. The dog is now well.

TJ Waring's twelve-week-old Pekingese, Ollie, was given a combined distemper, hepatitis, parvovirus and parainfluenza vaccine. Within two hours he became lethargic, sleeping for extended periods and having little interest in food. The next day he developed diarrhoea which soon became blood streaked. He was taken back to the vet's the next day and the dog was given a Piriton tablet. He rapidly improved within an hour. When asked, the vet said that the condition was unlikely to be a reaction to the vaccine, but the dog may have eaten something. The second part of the vaccine, with the same batch number, was given 14 days later, with no adverse reaction.

Mrs Hylda Reynold's miniature Dachshund Jamie developed colitis shortly after being vaccinated. For three years, Hylda tried to console Jamie and deal with him as he ran around the house screaming in apparent agony. Hylda tells us that her vet and a specialist admitted that Jamie was suffering from a vaccine reaction, but both refused to confirm their comments in writing. After spending some £3,000 with vets and specialists, Hylda eventually resorted to a homoeopath who confirmed that Jamie was suffering from vaccinosis. Although some improvement ensued following homoeopathic treatment, Hylda took the painful decision to put Jamie out of his misery. Hylda was advised by the homoeopath that the powerful steroids used in an attempt to treat Jamie's vaccine damage had compounded the problem. Despite determined attempts to establish a dialogue between the vaccine manufacturer and vets, Hylda feels her attempts were in vain. She is understandably very angry.

Enery, Mrs Lane's first dog, was given his annual booster on the 17th August 1982, the first year in which the vaccine was combined. Enery had a very slow reaction to it, but his coat fell out. Mrs Lane says he had less hair than a Saluki. The vet treated Enery for mange, but Mrs Lane was certain he didn't have mange. All of her dogs shared the same house, and none of the others caught the said mange.

"He had body washes, injections and antibiotics," says Mrs Lane. "We also had some little white pills which gave him a large appetite. We got his coat growing back by February 1983, and the vet thought we had won the battle. We finished the last few white pills and, when they ran out, so did Enery's life. He went into convulsions and died."

Mrs Lane's second dog was called Zippy. He was given his puppy inoculations in May 1983. Because Mrs Lane believed that the combined vaccine had killed Enery, she asked the vet to separate the vaccines. Nevertheless, the vet used the combined vaccine but, says Mrs Lane, the vaccine card now had a warning: `It is not possible to guarantee the response of any individual whether human or animal to a particular vaccine'. Mrs Lane believes that Zippy was lucky because the vet damaged the needle and the vaccine didn't disperse fully into the body. Zippy's skin was, however, very pink around the vaccine site.

At this time, Mr and Mrs Lane were living in the south of England. Zippy's neck, where the vaccine had been administered, developed a lump which wouldn't go away. It got larger and larger, with Mrs Lane describing it as a third ear.

In October 1987, the couple moved to Lincolnshire. In 1989, they discovered a Mr Barker, a vet who treated wild seals. Mrs Lane felt that she trusted him, and took Zippy to see him saying that the vaccine had caused the lump. Mr Barker didn't believe her, but he did say that the lump would have to be removed.

After the operation, Zippy had 28 stitches on the side of his neck, and when Mrs Lane took him back to have the stitches removed, Mr Barker had the results of the biopsy. This concluded that the skin's cells were damaged, and the parvo vaccine was doubling itself every few days. "So that was my proof!" says Mrs Lane.

Zippy fathered nine pups and enjoyed them for two-and-a-half years. "He watched each pup being born," says Mrs Lane, "and for the first three nights stood over the bitch and pups in their whelping box. He had a lovely nature. He died on the 28th April, 1992 aged nine years, three months. Both his lungs collapsed at the same time - twelve hours and it was all over."

Mrs Lane warned the new owners of Zippy's pups not to have them vaccinated. "Of the five that went ahead with the inoculation, four ended up on drips for three days," she says.

Mrs L Eckert and her family have two standard Poodles who enjoy good health. Since the youngest dog has been vaccinated, however, she has been persistently scratching herself and chewing out clumps of fur, as though her skin is very irritated. Mrs Eckert has ruled out the possibility of fleas as her other dog doesn't scratch herself, and both dogs have been sprayed with a flea treatment from the vet. Mrs Eckert says, "We had never noticed any of these symptoms before having her vaccinated, and wondered if there could be a connection."

Nico Venken in Belgium bred a yellow Labrador who was vaccinated with distemper and parvovirus at the age of six weeks, followed by distemper, parvo, hepatitis and leptospirosis vaccines two months later. Two months after the second shot, the dog began to develop skin problems. A blood test was conducted and the owner was told he was allergic. The dog was given an antibiotic lotion.

The next month, with skin problems continuing, the dog's head became swollen. The owners were advised to give him homoeopathic treatment. A urine test confirmed that the dog had an allergic reaction to the vaccination.

Pauline Bishop's American Cocker bitch seemed to be a very healthy and beautifully-coated pup. By the time she was two, the bitch began to pull her coat out across her flanks. No vet was able to give a reason. Eventually, the dog's back legs, chest and stomach were completely bald. The skin turned black and leathery, `like elephant hide' and she was constantly itching. The bitch was taken to five different vets, none of whom were any help. Most thought it was a flea allergy, although they could never find any evidence of fleas.

Mrs Bishop says, "She had steroid injections and creams, and at least eight different shampoos, but the condition got progressively worse. Up to three months ago, she was so disfigured by this complaint that I only exercised her after dark as people used to shy away from her."

The bitch was then taken to three further vets, all of whom suggested she be put down. "She is such a lovely girl and never complains," said Mrs Bishop, "and she's constantly seeking attention. We know the complaint isn't contagious as our other three dogs are all perfectly healthy."

In desperation, Mrs Bishop contacted a homoeopath who did some skin tests and diagnosed vaccinosis. "It seems that the initial puppy vaccines are the ones that have done the damage, aggravated by the annual boosters. She has been given tablets to correct a hormone imbalance caused by the vaccine. She's been on these tablets for three weeks now and has stopped itching, she has hair on her face and chin, her back legs are getting quite fluffy, and her little bottom doesn't look like a baboon's bottom any more."

The American Cocker now has homoeopathic vaccine alternatives.

Moya Panter's Bichon Frise bitch, Katie, was nearly four when the vet diagnosed an impacted gland on the edge of one eyelid. Anti- inflammatory drugs and antibiotic ointment were prescribed, but the eye continued to deteriorate. Katie's temperature was at the high end of normal, and she was given an anti-inflammatory injection. The one lump on her eye became four - two on each eyelid; her eyes were red, inflamed and hot.

Katie was referred to Professor Bedford, an eye specialist, who diagnosed Katie as having a streptococcal infection. Creams, drops and tablets were prescribed. However, the lumps began to bleed and emit pus. An operation was considered, and alternative medication prescribed. By the third month, Professor Bedford said that he felt Katie was having an allergic reaction to `something'.

Distressed by Professor Bedford's prognosis of repeated courses of histamines and steroids, Moya consulted a homoeopath who told her that Katie was suffering from `vaccinosis‘.

Treated by the homoeopath with mineral tablets and homoeopathy, Moya says that Katie began to recover immediately. At the next appointment with Professor Bedford, Katie was given the `all clear'. "He said that her eyes were in excellent condition but he didn't understand why," says Moya. "He told me he thought Katie had a chronic condition and would need life long medication. He put her recovery down to a miracle."

Katie no longer has her annual booster but is given homoeopathic nosodes instead. Moya says, "Katie suffered extreme pain and discomfort for some weeks. To see her suffer caused enormous distress to myself and my family. I never want to see Katie suffer like that again."

Mrs June Goose has bred Skye Terriers for several years with her husband David. She first became suspicious that dogs could have bad reactions to vaccines when Sam - Coruisky Silver Sam - was diagnosed as having hepatitis and jaundice. Sam had been vaccinated before going into kennels whilst June and David went on holiday. June says, "I couldn't believe how he looked when we went to collect him. He'd lost weight, he wouldn't eat, and he was completely yellow."

June took Sam to the vet who, coincidentally, was also the kennel vet. The vet told June that Sam had probably been bitten by a rat. June pointed out that he had been vaccinated and shouldn't react to a rat bite and, anyway, there were no teeth marks. She asked the vet to have Sam's blood tested but the vet refused.

After five weeks of orthodox veterinary treatment, no improvements were noticed - in fact, the two vets involved suggested that Sam should be put to sleep. He weighed 15lbs instead of the normal 30lbs; his coat was falling out, and he had sores all over his back.

June found a practising homoeopath and made an appointment to take Sam along the next day, praying all the while that he would live to keep the appointment. The homoeopathic vet took a blood sample and sent it off for analysis, meanwhile giving June three homoeopathic remedies for Sam. He began to respond immediately and, after five days of treatment, began to eat again.

"When the vet phoned to give me the results of the blood test," says June, "he told me that Sam should, by rights, be dead. In fact, he should have died about two weeks previously. The blood tests confirmed that he had hepatitis and jaundice." Sam had homoeopathic treatment for about a year, and today he is a healthy sixteen year-old dog with a full coat, and he's on no medication at all.

June cannot understand why Sam should have come down with two conditions he was vaccinated against. Further, knowing that hepatitis and jaundice are highly contagious, she can't understand why her other dogs didn't come down with the diseases.

Another of June's dogs, Robbie, developed colitis within a few days of his first annual booster. June says, "He used to pass blood; he used to pass blood clots. It was awful. Despite this, Robbie was a beautiful dog and he did very well in the show ring. Often, when I mentioned to people at the shows that Robbie had colitis, they told me I was a fool for having him vaccinated. One lady actually told me that everyone knows that the parvovirus vaccine is as deadly as the illness itself, and a man called me an idiot for vaccinating my dogs.

"Some years after Robbie developed colitis, my husband came to visit me in hospital where I'd been for a small operation. He told me that Robbie wasn't eating his food. When I got home we took him to the vet who took some blood for analysis. His coat was still lovely, but the weight was dropping off him."

Once home, Robbie was fed with a syringe to get liquid into him, but he was still passing blood. The diarrhoea was black: June panicked and called the vet but Robbie died before the vet arrived. June asked for a post-mortem and the results came back as lymphosarcoma.

But this wasn't the end of June and David's troubles. Having bred a litter from a Skye bitch called Rosie, June decided that, despite her reservations, she was duty bound to vaccinate the puppies. She kept one dog from the litter, Dollar.

One of the puppies, Ben, was sold and the owner rang to say that he'd been taken to the Animal Health Trust with a joint problem, where it had been discovered that he also had a kidney problem. Ben died of renal failure when he was eight months old. Upon hearing of Ben's condition, June rushed

Dollar off to the vet for tests and discovered that he, too, had a kidney problem.

Another puppy, Robbie II, developed severe joint problems to the point where he couldn't walk. He was six months old. The vet advised that he should be put to sleep. Instead, June took him to a homoeopath who told June that Robbie II had vaccinosis. He was treated for vaccinosis and was, June says, cured.

Meanwhile, the late Ben's owners decided to report June to the Kennel Club for breeding Skyes with defective kidneys, and she was also reported to the Skye Terrier Club. At this stage, June was convinced that the vaccines had caused these problems, but she had met a blank wall with the vaccine manufacturer. June says Ben's vet, "laughed in my face when I aired my suspicions and he told me not to phone his surgery again."

June was extremely distressed that Ben's owners had reported her to the Kennel Club, so she wrote to the KC and told them of her suspicions regarding the vaccine. Eventually, one vet offered to take her remaining bitch puppy and her sire and dam to the Royal Veterinary College to have their kidneys checked. All came back clear. June wonders how there can be an hereditary element if they were clear, and the grandfather on the sire's side was then nearly fifteen, and the grandmother on another side was nine.

"I am certain that vaccines caused all these problems," says June, "and nobody will convince me otherwise. I haven't vaccinated any of my dogs since. Quite a few breeders have told me to keep my mouth shut and not say anything, because they think I'll give the breed a bad name. But I'm not ashamed of my breeding. I haven't bred a litter since - because I wouldn't want to vaccinate them."

Mrs J Whiteley wrote:

"I have owned German Shepherds for more than 20 years and, in the last four years I have owned, bred, and been fairly successful with miniature Bull Terriers. My best friend breeds Shih Tzus and Pekingese. We have had several incidents which we believe are vaccine related.

"I have never had any of my dogs boosted, except one GSD bitch, because I've never seen the reasoning behind it. Aside from this bitch, who was boosted at 14 months old, I have never had to take any of my dogs for veterinary treatments apart from the routine puppy inoculations, a caesarean section, one castration, and a course of antibiotics once or twice. My friend has a similar record.

"My GSD bitch, now four, was the only bitch in a litter of three. She was a completely healthy puppy in every way until she was inoculated, after which she developed ear infections and a very sparse and itchy coat, and skin requiring constant veterinary treatment. She seemed to grow out of it when she was approximately a year old. Her brother, who belongs to a friend, developed identical symptoms but, if anything, they were worse.

"My friend, unknown to me, booked my bitch, along with her litter brother, at her vets to have their boosters at 14 months old. Unwilling to upset her, I took my bitch. She was, as I have already said, the first of my dogs to have a booster.

"Within a month, both my bitch and my friend's dog went down with the same itchy hypersensitive skin and ear infections. We also had a job to keep weight on both of them, even though their appetites were good and their stools perfectly normal. It goes without saying that she never had another booster!

"By the time she was three, she hadn't had an ear infection for 18 months and her coat was beautiful, and she was at last well covered. But despite pleading with my friend not to have her dog boosted annually, she always did up until this year. Her veterinary bills have been horrendous.

"All symptoms occurred at their worst within four weeks of his annual booster. This year, in desperation, she stopped the booster and looked into homoeopathic treatment because, unless he had an annual booster, the insurance company will not cover her dog. At the time of writing her dog has never looked so well: fat, shiny and no skin irritation. Coincidence - I think not!

"My bitch was mated at three years of age, healthy, fit and well. She whelped and reared 12 puppies. I kept one of the puppies and he had his routine puppy inoculations at eight and 12 weeks, and he's never had a day's ill health. However, the last puppy to be sold was inoculated at 12 weeks. Two days after he was found in the new owner's kitchen, practically comatose. He was on a drip for two days then seemed to make a remarkable recovery.

"His new owners took him on holiday with them and he received his second inoculation at a different vets where they were on holiday. Again, within two days he was comatose: hospitalisation, around the clock treatment, and then his kidneys, liver and heart and lungs packed up. He died the next day. His owners, I, and a lot more very experienced dog people, believe it was an adverse reaction to the vaccine. The vets at both the practices of course never really could pinpoint the exact cause of death.

"My friend with the Pekes and Shih Tzus has had a Pekingese puppy, again sold to new owners, at death's door after its inoculation. He began fitting within days. He was referred to a large veterinary hospital for intensive tests, and thankfully he recovered and hasn't fitted since. No conclusive evidence of any medical condition was found. The lady who bred my friend's original Pekes told her that she doesn't vaccinate her pups until they are at least 14 to 16 weeks old.

She says she had many adverse reactions when the puppies were vaccinated at a younger age.

"As I write, she has a Shih Tzu puppy who was inoculated last week. She was a picture of health until four days ago when, within the course of an afternoon, her eyes clouded over and became a milky blue. She is now on a course of steroid eye drops.

"I could go on and on, each time I hear of yet another illness, sickness, or death after inoculations. It just makes me more determined to do things my way. I do believe puppies need protection and will continue with their first jabs, but nothing will convince my friend or I that a cocktail of drugs yearly does a dog anything but harm. I believe I know the outcome of your survey but will the veterinary profession listen? I doubt it."

Your notes.

Chapter Ten

The Alternative to Vaccination

Had I known what I now know about vaccines, I would never have vaccinated Oliver, Prudence, or Samson - or, indeed, any of my other dogs. I would have had a choice. As a caring, responsible, dog owner I would have been able to make an informed decision, as we all morally have a right to do.

Given that contagious diseases do exist, and do affect our dogs, and given also that vaccinations against these diseases present their own risks, where does this leave those of us who want to do the best for our dogs? Are we left with an all or nothing situation? Too scared to vaccinate, but scared also that the dog will contract leptospirosis, or parvo, or distemper, or rabies?

In common with a vast number of conventional vets, Steve Dean dismisses the only alternative open to us. He wrote in Dog World (UK):

"My reader rightly states that distemper is now rare, as is hepatitis, and they are so because of the tremendous success of the vaccines. In fact parvovirus is also dwindling for similar reasons. It is against this background of low incidence that other schemes such as homoeopathic nosodes flourish, for if there is no infection then even water will work!

"I know some of you are persuaded to rely on alternative medicine in place of vaccines and I admit that I am sceptical of the success you can expect, but I do think homoeopaths are occasionally wrong and in trusting nosodes as substitutes for proven vaccines I think homoeopaths are being foolhardy.

"I do occasionally poke fun at homoeopathy only because it seems to be based on amazing trust and faith rather than proven scientific fact.

"There is one over-riding thought persuading me I am right to be sceptical - homoeopathy is an art steeped in history. In historical terms, homoeopathy was there well before the advent of modern medicines, anatomy and physiology. It must seem strange to a homoeopath that we can cure more diseases today than 100 years ago. If homoeopathy is such a great substitute, how come so many people and animals died of so much disease when it was all that was available?"

Answer: hygiene, diet . . . and the fact that 'conventional' medicine was there long before homoeopathy. Also conventional medicine of the day was just as blinkered against homoeopathy then as it is now - they wouldn't use it. It is also questionable that we do cure more diseases than we used to do; we seem, rather, to have swapped one set of diseases for others. In the words of the author Arabella Melville, "people are not living longer - they are just taking longer to die." Further, many of the diseases were waning before the drug that was claimed to cure them ever came on the market, and this is due to hygiene, and diet, and other such factors.

In fact, it was reported during January 1997, that a UK government social trends survey has concluded that whilst people are living longer, our healthy lifespan has shortened. To put it another way, we have replaced deadly diseases with long-term chronic diseases. I think you have read enough now to refrain from throwing out the idea that vaccines might be involved in this trend.

One trial was quoted in Hansard, concerning the cholera outbreak in London in the 19th Century where the Royal London Homoeopathic Hospital scored so much better than any other attempts, but the result wasn't published. Hahnemann was curing typhus, losing two out of 180 patients in Leipzig in 1813, while other medical practitioners were losing 70% of their patients. After Hahnemann published his method for curing cholera, a gentleman in Hungary took up his writings and only lost between 16 and 20% of patients, as opposed to the usual 50-60%.

So let's examine the homoeopathic alternative, and make up our own minds about the options.

The principle of homoeopathy

The word homoeopathy comes from two Greek words: Homois, which means like or similar, and Pathos, which means feeling, passion, or suffering.

Homoeopathy is a science which treats a disease using remedies chosen because they have produced in healthy volunteer people under test - when given in large or poisonous quantities - symptoms that are similar to that disease.

In Latin, this rule is expressed by the term Similia Similibus curentur - let like be treated by likes. The objective is to stimulate the body to respond to the homoeopathic `energy', and re-balance itself. The second cornerstone of homoeopathy is that 'less is more'. So, giving a simple example, someone who has ulcers in the mouth might be given the homoeopathic remedy Merc. Sol. which, if taken in large quantities, would actually cause mouth ulcers - but in the minute homoeopathic dilution it will have the opposite effect. The greater dilutions in homoeopathy increase in curative power.

In fact, vaccination is to homoeopathy what marching boots are to ballet shoes. The two may seem to follow the same course to the uninformed, but there are significant differences between the two.

With vaccination, we inject a (hopefully) attenuated virus into an organism in the belief that the organism will mount a response and develop antibodies against the virus. In homoeopathy, we take the virus and dilute it until it cannot even be measured by scientific instruments, and give it orally in tablet form. The homoeopathic 'nosode' (vaccine alternative), if given under skilled veterinary advice, is known to protect from disease and to be without side-effect. I say 'known to be', although homoeopathy does not accept conventional scientific methods of 'proof', and conventional science does not accept homoeopathic methods of proof. More of this later.

Conventional scientists suggest that if the virus contained in the homoeopathic nosode can't even be measured by scientific instrument, then it can't be there. My answer is that they haven't developed sensitive-enough instruments - instruments that measure the energy field rather than the mechanical body. (Dr Viera Scheibner contends that her Cotwatch system does measure the effect of homoeopathic remedies.)

Homoeopathy - an energy medicine

This energy is called 'vital force' in homoeopathy, and 'Chi' in Chinese medicine; in Indian Ayurvedic medicine it is called 'prana'. Einstein's quantum physics and Benveniste's work put this energy in a modern scientific light.

The basic premise is that each person (and dog, and flower, and stone) vibrates at cellular level at a certain dynamic frequency. When a person's dynamic frequency is off balance, then cellular imbalances occur, and this gives rise to physical and/or mental illness. The correct homoeopathic remedy gives a gentle jump start to the subtle energy, allowing the body to resonate at its proper rate and allowing the immune system to function properly.

As an aside, a growing number of people are finding themselves hyper-sensitive to modern electromagnetic radiation - emitted by electrical appliances, for example. Diana Crumpler is one such person; not long after the local authorities sprayed DDT and herbicides directly into her water supply, Diana became hypersensitive to light, electricity and chemicals. Since then, she has been trapped in a specially-built allergy-free home. Tiny amounts can cause blackouts, headaches, muscle spasms, partial paralysis, double vision and memory loss. Not surprisingly, Diana has a great deal of time in which to investigate her illness. She writes:

"Medicine, as much as physics, needs to accept that energy and matter are one, that bio-electricity is as much the basis of life as is bio-chemistry, and that man is an electrical entity interacting with all other energy sources - as Eastern medicine and philosophy have long recognised."

Einstein had no problem with this viewpoint - he placed energy and mass in the same equation: as something approaches the velocity of light it becomes infinitely small and infinitely heavy. If travelling at the speed of light it would disappear and weigh an infinite amount.

In her book, 'The Pleidian Agenda', Barbara Hand Clow says that we all have 'miasms' in our bodies that we must release. She writes: "These are etheric masses that hold memory of genetic or past-life disease patterns; memory of present-life diseases that were not cleared due to vaccinations, which prevent you from manifesting the disease memory and erasing it; or memory of disease that you drive deep into your bodies by taking antibiotics, chemicals or radiation when your body actually wants to heal by means of its own immune system or by letting go into total healing by dying."

Marilyn Terry, a dog owner, expresses it thus: "Modern medicine works like a formula. A certain disease has a certain cure, using suppressive drugs to suppress the symptoms, which only serves to drive the real disease inward, to emerge in a deeper, more serious disease some time later."

A basic distinction between conventional and homoeopathic medicines is the belief in homoeopathy that symptoms are an indication of a disease pattern, but not the disease itself. Homoeopaths see symptoms - such as diarrhoea, skin rashes, and fever - as products of an expression of the patient's fight against disease: it is adapting to an underlying problem. Homoeopaths believe that the body can cope - adapt to - most chronic and acute illnesses. Remedies are given to assist the body in its own healing process. As Chris Day explained in a previous chapter, the body tries to maintain a state of equilibrium: balance . . . electrical or energetic balance (she said putting words in his mouth).

Conversely, conventional medicine tends to see the symptom as the problem in itself. Conventional doctors and vets therefore try to make the symptoms go away. They will, for example, prescribe an aspirin to cure a headache, but rarely the agent or imbalance that caused the headache in the first place. This, to homoeopaths, is a short-term solution. They believe that if you simply suppress the disease manifestation, the disease itself will go on to wreak havoc elsewhere at a deeper level.

Homoeopaths, however, rarely claim to have all the answers. They willingly work side by side with the orthodox medical and veterinary establishment to effect a cure and/or alleviate suffering.

Samuel Hahnemann

Samuel Hahnemann, the founder of homoeopathy, was born in Germany in 1755 and qualified as a physician by the age of 24. Becoming disenchanted with the medical practices of the time - bloodletting, purgation, and suppression of symptoms - Hahnemann gave up his work as a doctor and turned to translating medical texts. Whilst working on *Cullen's Materia Medica,* he read a reference to quinine which stated that quinine cured malaria due to its bitter and astringent qualities. Having suffered from the disease himself, Hahnemann began experimenting.

No. He did not put a rat in a cage and give it quinine. Instead, Hahnemann took half an ounce of the bark (quinine is made from the cinchona bark) twice a day for several days. He came down with malaria's intermittent fever like symptoms - cold extremities, drowsiness, flushed cheeks, and thirst - but without the shivering fever itself. When he stopped taking the bark, the attacks ceased. He repeated the exercise, achieving the same results.

Hahnemann felt he had discovered `the law of similars' which, he recognised, Hippocrates had originally referred to in his 4th century BC writings. Yet another important figure, the Swiss physician, philosopher, and alchemist Paracelsus (1493-1541), had also emphasised the use of `similars' - substances that make one ill but can also cure in small enough doses. Paracelsus is reputed to have successfully treated victims of the 1534 plague with pills made from bread and minute pinhead-sized amounts of the patients' excreta.

So Hahnemann continued to experiment with a long list of substances, and recorded the effects. He discovered that some of the tinctures seemed too strong, causing toxic effects in a few patients and, later, that dilution and succussion (shaking and banging down heavily to release the energy of a substance) not only eliminated toxic effects, they also increased the remedy's power, scope and depth of action. Interestingly, homoeopathic remedies rely upon nature: they are the essences of naturally occurring substances derived from plants, animal materials, and natural chemicals.

The homoeopathic response to vaccine damage

The homoeopathic doctor, Dr James Compton Burnett, was perhaps the first person to recognise that vaccines can cause serious side effects. Although believing at the time that vaccination does protect against smallpox, he wished to show that a) a diseased state is engendered by the vaccinial (smallpox) virus, which he called vaccinosis, and b) that homoeopathic remedies, in particular Thuja, are able to counteract vaccinosis.

Burnett wrote that an acute reaction to vaccination, the febrile state, was not the only effect of vaccinosis. *"One suffering from vaccinosis may not be ill in the ordinary sense. But he must be in a subdued morbid state"*.

Having spoken with people who no longer vaccinate their dogs - that is, the puppies are never vaccinated but treated homoeopathically from day one - it seems that non-vaccinated dogs support Burnett's premise. Their owners report that they are generally healthier than vaccinated dogs, and their temperaments are usually brighter. Anecdotal evidence, but interesting at that.

Burnett noted that a few people dated their ill-health from a so-called unsuccessful vaccination . . . paresis, neuralgia, cephalgia, pimples, acne, etc., he felt could stem from vaccination. He gave many examples where Thuja had cured illnesses which he believed had been brought about by vaccines.

Many people were successfully treated for vaccinosis by Dr Burnett. Countless homoeopaths - and their patients - have since witnessed similar successful outcomes, which are, it seems, invariably dismissed by the mainstream medical profession.

Please note, however, that homoeopathy has over three thousand remedies at its disposal, and the successful treatment of a disease relies upon an accurate diagnosis. I would therefore recommend anyone interested in pursuing the homoeopathic route to consult a trained homoeopath. Many who have tried their own DIY jobs fail, and consequently believe that homoeopathy itself has failed. Thuja, for example, is not to be used for all cases of vaccinosis. The person's own constitutional type indicates the remedy to be used.

It must also be noted that remedies can create powerful reactions. This is known by homoeopaths as `an aggravation'. The reaction often indicates that it is the right remedy - and it is here that the skill of the homoeopath comes to play. S/he will know the correct dose and timing - and when to stop treatment.

Where animals are concerned, the law of the land stipulates that only a vet can offer treatment.

Homoeopathy is not necessarily a quick fix therapeutic alternative. The remedies work gently over time, giving the homoeopath time to observe and respond appropriately. Vaccines, on the other hand, are administered by injection straight into the body, and serious irreversible damage can be caused. The damage is compounded by the fact that few vets are aware of the possible dangers of vaccines. If they don't connect the vaccine with, say, epilepsy, or allergies, or colitis, they cannot get to the root and cure it. Furthermore, vets only have two main remedies at their disposal: antibiotics and steroids. When these fail, there is little else for them to resort to. (Yes, I know, a little bias creeping in, here!)

A good homoeopathic vet will only prescribe homoeopathic nosodes - the alternative to vaccines - after they have explained to the animal's guardian how the nosodes work and are to be administered. They should also give a full breakdown of evidence concerning efficacy so that the guardian is able to make a decision. S/he will also want to keep in contact with the patient to ensure that the patient remains in good health. Some homoeopathic vets will, however, vaccinate because it is financially difficult for them to stay in business by offering nosodes instead, and some are worried by the legal situation regarding nosodes (see `the Question & Answer section' towards the end of this book).

Scientific 'experiments' that proved homoeopathy works

There are, indeed, tests which prove homoeopathy is effective. The difference is that they are not always conducted in laboratory experiments where animals are given a disease so that the scientists can watch what happens.

Christopher Day MA, Vet.M.B., M.R.C.V.S., Vet.F.F. Hom. says: "I will not submit animals to laboratory testing, nor will I willfully create disease in animals in order to test efficacy, so there is a problem in providing accepted 'scientific' proof of efficacy. However, I have known many unvaccinated, homoeopathically-protected dogs survive known contact with the major viruses without taking on the disease. I have never known of a breakdown, except in the case of one young Golden Retriever who suffered only transitory mild vomiting and diarrhoea after exposure to and contracting (proven by laboratory tests) parvovirus. This experience will presumably have strengthened his immune system enormously."

However, Mr Day was able to test, in a controlled manner, the efficacy of the kennel cough nosode. It wasn't necessary for Mr Day to inflict a canine disease on any dog - but merely to seek to cure that disease in a controlled way once it had occurred naturally.

A local kennel came down with kennel cough. Mr Day was invited in.

There were 40 dogs in the kennel; eighteen had been vaccinated against kennel cough, 22 had not. Of the vaccinated dogs, all 40 had developed a cough, whereas only 19 of the 22 unvaccinated dogs had developed a cough.

A homoeopathic nosode was given to all the dogs who entered the infected boarding premises subsequently: one dose on entry, and twice daily for three days. There were 214 dogs entering the kennel during the rest of the summer, all of whom received the nosodes - 64 had been conventionally vaccinated, and 150 had not prior to entry into the kennel.

Of the 214 dogs, three of the 64 vaccinated dogs contracted kennel cough; one of the 150 non-vaccinated dogs contracted kennel cough. Apparently, the homoeopathic nosodes had halted the outbreak in its tracks.

As a further exercise, any dogs showing just one very transient sign of kennel cough were recorded. This showed that 51 of the 64 vaccinated dogs showed evidence of slight symptoms, whereas only 40 of the 150 dogs who were not vaccinated showed any symptoms. Chris Day felt that this actually showed that vaccines were harmful in this situation!

Mr Day, a gentleman not given to black and white statements, says:

"What *appears* to emerge from this study is:

> a) Nosodes can very effectively stop, in its tracks, an outbreak of a highly transmissible disease (viz kennel cough)
> b) That it does so, in this case, more effectively than the presently available vaccines
> c) That vaccination impairs the ability of the animal to respond to the nosode."

John Saxton MRCVS VetMFHom, in IJVH Volume 5, No 1, 1991, presented a paper describing the use of the canine distemper nosode in disease control. Although not presented as a clinical trial, it was presented as a report upon a clinical problem which was significantly relieved by the use of nosodes.

This involved a boarding kennels dealing solely with stray dogs under contract to the local police authority. As such, vaccination status was unknown. All animals not claimed or rehomed were destroyed on the 8th day after arrival.

When the dogs arrived at the kennels, they were screened by experienced lay staff and those with no obvious signs of disease or injury were admitted directly into the main kennels. All others were placed in an isolation block for examination by the veterinary staff.

It became clear that there was an unacceptably high incidence of clinical distemper associated with the kennels, despite all possible screening and management procedures. It was therefore decided to use the canine distemper nosode as a control measure in addition to the general management measures. The homoeopathic nosode was prepared from a local clinical case, using nasal and ocular discharge, plus a swab from the tonsils. Prepared as a liquid, the nosode was administered via the dogs' drinking water.

The results showed that, of dogs kept in the kennels for eight days, 11.67% showed clinical signs of distemper on the 5th day prior to the introduction of nosodes, dropping to 4.36% after the nosodes were introduced. Where the entire kennel population was taken into account (including those dogs who left prior to the eighth day), the incidence of distemper dropped from 8.05% to 2.81% after the introduction of nosodes.

Interestingly, the incidence of distemper rose markedly in the 8th and 11th months of the trial. Upon investigation, it was realised that one of the kennel staff had left the homoeopathic supply in direct sunlight for several hours prior to administration. When this storage practice was remedied, incidences of distemper dropped once again - indicating that the homoeopathic remedies were, indeed, having a positive effect.

The principle of homoeopathy was proven in the human field in a significant breakthrough which took place in 1986, when it was shown, in controlled trials, that homoeopathy was helpful in preventing hay fever. Also, in 1995, a team from Glasgow University succeeded in proving, in controlled trials, that 30c (homoeopathic) potencies of pollen and house dust mite were more effective than placebos in treating hay fever and asthma respectively. You see, the work does exist but it is dismissed through a protective mythology built around orthodox medicine.

Finally, I am including one clinical trial - not because I want to, on ethical grounds, but because we can't allow the allopathic veterinary fraternity to get away with the statement that homoeopathic nosodes are unproven.

The trial was conducted by W Jonas, A Fortier, D Heckendorn and C Macy during 1991, and a paper was presented at the 5th LIBI meeting in Paris. The paper was entitled `Prophylaxis of Tularaemia Infection in Mice Using Agitated Ultra High Dilutions of Tularaemia Infected Tissues'.

Homoeopathic dilutions from reticulo-endothelial tissues of mice infected with Tularaemia were administered orally to a group of mice; a control group was treated with dilutions of ethanol. An LD of F tularensis was then administered and survival time and mortality were evaluated. After 15 experiments, the very high homoeopathic dilutions produced a significant increase in survival time and a significant reduction in total mortality compared to non controls. (Homoeopathy - a frontier in medical science, published by North Atlantic Books.)

Something has been causing me a great deal of frustration since the publication of the first edition of this book. I had been aware of clinical trials conducted by Ronald Schultz and Susan Wynne which looked into, supposedly, the effectiveness of nosodes against canine parvovirus. Because the paper had not been published, I honoured a request by Jean Dodds, a close friend of Ronald Schultz, to refrain from including details of that trial here.

But because so very many conventional vets have seized upon this unpublished trial as proof positive that nosodes don't work, I am forced to reveal the reality of this trial. It is wrong for so-called scientists to be blind to examples of efficacy and seize upon unpublished information to support their bias.

Basically, puppies were given a strange regime of various potencies of nosodes and then injected with live parvovirus, and they died. This is taken as proof that nosodes don't work. But puppies don't contract parvovirus by injection in normal circumstances. The trial proves only that nosode-protected pups don't survive when injected with live parvovirus.

Dr Dodds tells me that Drs Schultz and Wynne were well aware that the trial was only a paranteral challenge. "This was only a preliminary study and was specifically designed to determine whether or not dogs prepared by nosode protocol could withstand the same paranteral challenge that vaccinated dogs undergo."

As much as I respect Dr Schultz, and I do, I have to say that I find these clinical trials rather difficult to cope with. So much relies upon the methodology employed. Further, it would have been much better if someone could leak the unpublished results of a trial involving naturally challenged puppies. Trouble with this, though, is that the conventional scientific community wouldn't be rubbing it's hands in glee at the results.

Homoeopathically protected dogs - case studies

Christopher Day states: "While the motivation for vaccination is quite clear and irreproachable, it is sad to me that there appears to be neither an open-mindedness about the possibility of serious side effects of the process, nor an openness about information which could lead to an objective reappraisal of the system. I have become so convinced that vaccination can represent a risk greater than that posed by the target disease that I will never have further vaccination myself, nor will I use or sell vaccinations for my own animals or for animals brought to me.

"That is not to say that I advocate no protection. We use the homoeopathic nosodes as a preventative regime for all the major dog diseases, and although we only have anecdotal evidence of efficacy in the cases of distemper, hepatitis and parvovirus, the kennel cough trial we performed was very convincing."

Marlene Jordan has kept dogs for many years. She currently breeds German Shepherd Dogs and Shar-Peis, and has been directly or indirectly responsible for the Crufts Shar-Pei best of breed for the last four years. She currently shares her home with eighteen dogs.

Marlene's dogs are regularly exposed to the risk of viral disease. They are, for example, prominent members of the show ring, mixing with hundreds of other dogs at each show. Some five years ago, Marlene took a Shar-Pei puppy called Sumo for his vaccine jab. Within 30 hours his body `blew up'. *"His entire body was swelling,"* Marlene says. *"He was shivering, and he had a temperature of 107F. He was literally dying: he was staring death in the face. His skin began to split. There was a split on his forehead; his side split, and all the skin round his hocks split and fell down.*

"You have never seen anything like it in your life. There was a foul green smelly gunk pouring out of him from everywhere, including his eyes. Part of his face fell off. I swear the exorcist was at work."

Marlene took Sumo straight to the vet, stating that the vaccine had caused the condition. The vet told her she had no right to say so. "I asked him what else could have caused it?" says Marlene. "Sumo's face literally fell off - right under his nose on one side of his face. It was swinging, hanging on by a quarter of an inch of skin. The vet said he had never seen anything like it. I told him that he'd vaccinated his last. I've had it before where the dogs have been shivering and dribbling, and the vet always said it wasn't the vaccine. I told the vet it was the vaccine - what else could it possibly be?"

Marlene took the dog straight to Chris Day, and Sumo underwent treatment to save his life. Extensive skin grafts were involved.

As a result of this experience, Marlene refuses to sell a puppy unless the owner undertakes not to vaccinate the dog, but to protect homoeopathically. "If the purchasers refuse, then I tell them I'm sorry, but they must go somewhere else."

In the last five years, Marlene's homoeopathically protected dogs have been taken to many high risk areas and have not contracted any of the viruses they are protected against. Marlene also believes that the homoeopathically protected dogs are healthier than those who have been vaccinated. "They have excellent coats, they don't have off days, they're just exceedingly healthy," she says. "Their health shows in their eyes. I firmly believe that vaccines do not help a dog's general well-being."

Incidentally, a report appeared in one of the British tabloids of a young child whose mother twice refused to subject the child to the measles jab due to a family history of asthma. But when Amy Gregory's mum mentioned this to the doctor giving the jab to children at Amy's school, the doctor said not to make Amy look a fool in front of her friends. Within 45 minutes of the injection, Amy's skin started to peel off from her head to her toes - just like Sumo. Amy was later diagnosed with an inflammatory form of arthritis called zero negative spondyloarthropathy, and she also suffers from Crohn's disease. Amy's mother says that doctors had previously warned her not to have Amy vaccinated as she had breathing difficulties as a baby and her step-brother had fits.

"Amy's life has changed dramatically and no-one will admit responsibility," she said.

Angela Price breeds Rough Collies. On 11th October 1995, Angela consulted James L Newns BVetMed, AMFHom, MRCVS, as there was a parvovirus outbreak in the area, and Angela had unwittingly brought a six-month-old rescue bitch with the virus into the kennel. All of Angela's dogs, however, are routinely given the homoeopathic 'combination canine' nosodes for distemper, hepatitis, leptospirosis, parvovirus and parainfluenza, and had been nosode-protected for the past three years.

The depressed 'import' was allowed free contact with six of Angela's dogs, three of whom were the rescue dog's six-month-old siblings, and three of whom were pups aged three months. Within a week the rescue bitch started to vomit and produce dysenteric stools, and was by now extremely depressed.

Angela took the rescue bitch and one of the three-month old pups to the vet. Despite being nosode protected, the pup was beginning to show signs of the illness displayed by the rescue bitch although, at this point, Angela had no idea that it was the parvovirus. The puppy was left at the vet's on a drip, and was dead within 24 hours.

The remaining two three-month-old puppies also began to show symptoms of parvovirus, and Angela decided to treat them at home homoeopathically, reasoning that the veterinary treatment had hardly been a success. As with the first puppy, the two home-based puppies had been dehydrating with haematemesis and dysentery. "I couldn't believe how quickly the homoeopathic remedies worked," Angela exclaims. "Ipecac tincture stopped the haemorrhaging within two hours. Nobody could have been more surprised than I was - having already lost one puppy, I must admit I thought we were fighting a losing battle." Both puppies survived the virus and are now alive and well.

Five nosode-protected adults were totally unaffected by the virus. These dogs had never been conventionally vaccinated. The three six-month-old dogs who, once again, were protected only homoeopathically, exhibited a slight depression and a temperature, but none came down with the virus. "These dogs had been playing with the rescue," says Angela, "they were all running on the same ground with her."

Meanwhile, a litter of seven-week-old puppies had been isolated and put on the homoeopathic 'combination' course. Three were sent to new homes and are alive today, two were retained by Angela. "The vet insisted that the two puppies I kept should be inoculated," says Angela. "I was told they would die if I didn't vaccinate them." Within 24 hours of the jab, both puppies were dead.

"My sister helped me through all of this," Angela adds. "and then her three dogs contracted parvo. She took the first dog, a Labrador, to the vet and he died. I urged her to use homoeopathy on the two remaining dogs, and both have survived the virus.

"Afterwards, my vet told me I was foolish to place my trust in homoeopathy. It seemed an outrageous statement in view of the fact that the only dogs who survived had been treated homoeopathically."

It is interesting to note that most vaccine manufacturers admit that their vaccines may be ineffective until a puppy is 12 weeks old (three months) due to maternal antibody. Taking a reasoned view, it seems clear that neither vaccines nor nosodes can guarantee to protect very young puppies, although homoeopathic treatment did, in this case, prove more successful than conventional veterinary treatment, and the nosodes did appear to protect the older puppies and dogs.

It could also be argued that the puppies were successfully fighting the viral challenge with the help of nosodes, until the vet insisted upon injecting the live vaccine into them, at which point the total challenge became too severe. This, of course, would support Chris Days theory that vaccines impair an animal's ability to respond to the nosodes.

Angela's sister's dogs had been given the homoeopathic nosodes in the past, but she had allowed the course to drop off. This seems to indicate that dogs are protected when nosode protection is continued (as Angela's protected dogs escaped the disease).

Sue Lambelle breeds and shows Cavalier Spaniels. Three years ago, Sue took a litter of puppies for their first course of vaccines. Within 24 hours, one of the puppies - Holly - had her first fit. "She was the largest puppy of the litter; one of the best I've ever bred," says Sue. "She had fits roughly every eight days. The vet said that there was no connection with the vaccine, and the reaction was never reported."

Holly continued to have severe fits. "She would be unconscious for an hour and then come round and scream," says Sue. "At nine months old we decided to have her put down. I took her to the vet and she wouldn't keep still, and I just couldn't do it. I took her home, thinking that the next time she was unconscious I'd take her back to the vet. From that point on she started to pick up. The vet had put her on phenobarbitone, which did keep the fits under control, and Valium for when she was having several fits in a row."

About six months later, Sue decided to breed a litter of puppies and was worried that they might be at risk if Holly wasn't revaccinated. "Looking back, I realise I was stupid," she admits. "It started the fits off again."

After a long time on phenobarbitone, Holly became zombie-like. Sue realised that at a year old, her life expectancy wouldn't be long on these tablets, so she started to wean her off very gradually. "Then I heard about Chris Day and got a referral to go and see him," she says.

Chris Day treated Holly with a number of different remedies. Sue says she was like a different dog, so very much better. Sue was told about the homoeopathic nosodes, and decided to stop vaccinating her dogs, but to use the nosodes instead. Sue's adult dogs and puppies are now protected homoeopathically.

One-year-old Annie, and seven-month-old Crystal and Duncan have never been vaccinated. Sue, too, notices a difference between these Cavaliers and Cavaliers who have been vaccinated. "For a start, they never go to the vet, apart from routine heart and eye checks," she says. "They don't get diarrhoea which, looking back, often happened between the first and second set of vaccines with other puppies. They used to pass blood in their faeces. The other difference is temperament. They're much calmer."

Sue and her husband dedicate a lot of their time to running the local ringcraft society. Sue is secretary, and her husband is the chairman. "The subject of vaccination came up at the last AGM," says Sue. "Normally, 'responsible' people involved with dogs in groups would insist upon vaccine certificates. However, it was soon discovered that the society would lose its secretary, chairman, and three of its committee members if they continued to insist upon vaccination for members. We organised a talk by a homoeopathic vet, and now we compromise. We have a poster saying that dogs and puppies must have some form of protection against distemper, lepto, parvo and hepatitis, with a note saying that dogs who have been in contact with an infectious disease within the last three weeks shouldn't come to class."

Sue doesn't insist that new puppy owners protect their dogs with nosodes, but she does take care to tell them Holly's story. Meanwhile, her own dogs are not subjected to the vaccine risk. The nosodes have continued to protect them in their hectic, far-travelling, lives.

Mrs Hilary Jupp uses nosodes rather than vaccines for her dogs, as well as for her sheep. Mrs Jupp says: "Ours were the only sheep on the show circuit one year which did not contract Orf and we have had no further problems with coccidiosis or toxoplasmosis since we started using the relevant nosodes, which is more than we could say while using the conventional treatment, which had very little effect. We even keep worming to a minimum with a worm nosode, and have to worm our lambs only about three times a year despite having no clean ground for grazing."

Jean Kenny has been protecting her dogs with homoeopathic nosodes for fourteen years. Caring for a maximum of five dogs at any one time, Jean has three dogs at time of writing. In fourteen years, none of Jean's dogs has contracted any of the canine diseases which others vaccinate against.

"My dogs are walked in areas which are frequented by over a hundred dogs," Jean says. "It's been known to have distemper and parvo in the area, also kennel cough which I also use the nosodes for. If there's a problem of, say, kennel cough in the area, I just re-dose the dogs and walk straight in. My show dogs are taken all over the country and, again, if I know there's a problem of distemper, then I simply give them the nosodes before we go."

Jean says: "I don't believe we should be pumping dogs full of man-made chemicals and viruses just for the fun of it. There's a real danger that they'll go into toxic overload and their bodies will simply say enough is enough. I know someone who lost an entire litter by giving a vaccine and worming tablets at the same time - I always tell people not to worm their puppies for at least a week after the vaccine. I know it's only my theory, but I really do think we have to be careful about putting too much into a body at once."

So why does the medical/veterinary profession generally dismiss homoeopathy?

I think an accurate history lesson will be of use, here. Let's take a trip around the globe.

History

Hahnemann published his findings in 1810, and a keen following soon ensued. The first homoeopaths emigrated from Germany to America in the 1820s, and their medical practice spread quickly throughout the 1830s and 1840s.

'Allopathic' (what we know as conventional) medicine, had been following a different course. Largely rooted in the Industrial Revolution, allopathic medicine tends to believe that the body is a machine. For the first time in the history of healing, medical practitioners divided the body into its smallest functioning parts. Surgery was based upon the premise that if it didn't work, cut it out. Medicine was based upon the premise that if a disease entity attacks an organism, one should attack/remove the disease entity or symptom.

Ready for the mass markets of the post-industrial world, scientists began to look for treatments which could be produced en-masse by machines. Doctors were counselled to treat the body as a distinctly separate entity to the person who lived in the body, and almost as though they were treating the body as if each of its components function independently.

Homoeopaths, on the other hand, insisted they could treat the whole person: a different remedy might be prescribed for the same condition, depending upon the `constitution' or natural tendencies - physical, mental and spiritual - of the patient. This led the allopathic fraternity to accuse the homoeopaths of mysticism and quackery: `scientists' saw the world, and the people in it, as machines with moving parts, and not as spiritual beings. They were proud of their intellectual astuteness, methods of observation, organised testing, and `rigour'. So there was a division.

As is usually the case, the division bell sounded to the peel of cash registers. The American Medical Association (AMA) was founded in 1847 to protect the professional and monetary status of allopathic doctors (illustrating the parallel development of the two disciplines). Homoeopaths were not welcomed.

The first code of practice laid down by the AMA stated that the patient's view was not to be entertained: "The obedience of a patient to the prescriptions of his doctor should be prompt and implicit." Another rule in the code of ethics warned that patients should not permit their 'own crude opinions' to influence attention to treatments given them by doctors. (Martin Walker, *Dirty Medicine,* Slingshot Publications)

Behind this, of course, was a belief in the absolute correctness of 'science' which had now been hired by commerce. Ordinary people simply didn't have the intelligence to understand. This, of course, is not too different to the way many vets treat their clients in the twentieth century. We are not supposed to participate in the treatment of our animals; we are not supposed to ask why a certain drug is administered, or what the side effects might be. We are supposed to believe vets when they say vaccines are perfectly safe, and to continue to believe them when the results of vaccination stare us in the face.

Anyone visiting a good homoeopathic vet, on the other hand, will soon realise that the owner's observations are vitally important in the diagnosis. A homoeopathic vet will listen to you - and must do so to be successful. Everyone who loves and respects their dog (to respect is to heed, to pay attention to), knows when their dog is unwell. We know that when our dog starts lagging behind on walks or starts sitting in places he never used to sit, or suddenly refused to come with us in the car, that something is wrong.

We recently took Sammie to a conventional vet because we felt there was something happening in his stomach. The vet refused to take an x-ray. We found another vet and asked again for Sammie to have an x-ray. Once again, they dismissed our request and instead wanted to give him a blood test. We kicked up a fuss, Sam got his x-ray, and he underwent emergency surgery the following morning, when a tumour was removed from his spleen which, together, weighed 5lb. I have heard so many similar stories, where vets dismissed animal guardians, and the guardians were right. Of course, sometimes we are wrong - but we live with our dogs and often have inside knowledge to impart.

So back to the history lesson. As is usually the case, the opposing sides back in the 1800s - allopathic/conventional medicine and homoeopathy - opposed one-another, books were written, `anti' societies were formed, and something simply had to happen to break the deadlock.

Enter John D Rockefeller.

As the AMA moved into the twentieth century, it sought and secured the backing of major industrial foundations which saw profit for themselves in the rapidly developing field of medical science. With Rockefeller money behind it, money that came originally from oil, the conventional medical profession developed a new model. A model which leant heavily towards industry and biological research, whilst using copious quantities of synthetic pharmaceuticals - synthetic pharmaceuticals made (you've guessed it), mostly from oil.

In classic marketing terms, it seems that John D Rockefeller had a product and was looking for a market. He found it in the pharmaceutical/ petrochemical industry. And if you think that this is too cynical a view, please note that John D Rockefeller had a lifelong belief in homoeopathy. His own family did not, at that time at least, take the drugs his petrochemicals produced.

So, by 1909, the AMA had begun to rationalise medical education. Cutting a long story short, the medical schools which supported the industrial/medical model were allowed to teach medicine; these schools were also allowed to award meaningful professional qualifications. Within a decade the AMA had achieved total control over the administration of medical education, and had also found the necessary financial and political support for the scientific development of allopathic/conventional medicine.

Eustace Mullins wrote in, Murder by injection, the story of the medical conspiracy against America (Staunton, VA: *National Council for Medical Research*):

"Rockefeller (junior) and Carnegie began immediately to shower hundreds of millions of dollars on those better medical schools that were vulnerable to control. Those that did not conform were denied the funds and the prestige that came with those funds, and were forced out of business."

For over half a century the Rockefeller Foundation determined the direction and the content of medical research, without competition. Other organisations later joined in. The Ford Foundation (motor cars), the Kellogg Foundation (cereals), the Commonwealth Fund (created by Edward Harkness of Standard Oil), the Sloan Foundation (General Motors) . . . these gigantic organisations were sharing their wealth, but sharing it in a tunnel.

Billions of dollars were spent in helping scientists to travel and hold conferences, buy equipment and laboratories, and generally ensure that the industrial/medical scientific model would win. More money was put into seeing off the opposition. 'Quack busting' organisations were founded and funded. Even the American Food and Drug Administration (FDA) was enrolled in the fight. Ostensibly established to protect the American public against false medical and health claims and harmful products, the FDA has tended to defend the interests of the large American food producing corporations, the pharmaceutical industry, and medical orthodoxy. (Morton Mintz. *By prescription only*. Beacon Press, 1967)

More recently, in 1994, the alarm bells sounded for the ancient practice of herbalism. Despite the fact that herbs have been used successfully for centuries, Britain was being pressurised by the European Union to ban herbs unless they went through extensive - and expensive - laboratory testing. Anyone with any sense will realise that you can't patent a naturally growing herb - so who is going to put up the money to conduct these tests?

Those of us who used herbs, for ourselves and our animals, were desperately asked to contact our MPs, MEPs and the press, to block the effective ban. So strong must the response have been, that the British government decided to hold off their decision for a few years. The axe still hangs over the herbal head.

At time of writing, the UK's Veterinary Medicines Directorate has issued consultation papers to groups and individuals expressing an interest in veterinary use of homoeopathic remedies. This consultation paper follows a EU Directive, and the fear is that new homoeopathic remedies may be on the way to being denied to our pets. One thing in particular worries me about the proposals: it is being suggested that remedies in use before 31 March 1997 can continue to be used, but remedies after that date must be licensed. But what happens if a new disease, like Aids, emerges? Are they suggesting that only big business, with the necessary funding, can search for a cure? And how unbiased will this consultative process be, and will our government support freedom of choice?

Biassed representation?

Looking at the UK government's Register of Members' Interests (1997), we find that quite a few of our elected representatives are associated with the pharmaceutical and oil industries.

Spencer Batiste, MP for Elmet, consults on health issues for Magellan Medical Communications, whose clients include Schering Health Care, The Parkinsons Disease Society, Knoll Ltd, and the National Osteoporosis Society. He is also a director and company secretary for Sheffield Analytical Services Ltd and subsidiaries, involved in laboratory analysis and sales.

The Rt. Hon. Alan Beith, MP for Berwick-upon-Tweed, is also a consultant to Magellan Medical Communications.

Stuart Bell, MP for Middlesborough, had his expenses for a Franco-British Colloque paid for by British Petroleum.

Henry Bellingham, MP for North West Norfolk, has a directorship with Lothian Plc, a chemical manufacturer, and has shareholdings with Lothian Plc and Knightsbridge Medical Services.

Abbott Laboratories Limited gave the Rt. Hon. Betty Boothroyd MP two tickets for Wimbledon in 1995. Dr Michael Clark MP had his rail fare to France paid for by Shell. James Couchman MP is a paid adviser to Pfizer Ltd, a pharmaceutical manufacturer. Alan Duncan MP is an owner of Harcourt Consultants, trading as oil broker and adviser on energy matters.

Harold Elletson MP is a paid director of Harold Elletson Ltd, a management consultancy acting for BP Exploration and Omega Oil and Gas, amongst others. Roger Evans MP received a donation to the Monmouth Conservative Association through sponsoring a lunch in the House of Commons for Surgicraft Limited.

Roger Gale MP receives payment from the pharmaceutical companies Rhone Poulenc and Organon UK Ltd, and receives a contribution towards the running of his parliamentary office from Magellan Medical Communications. The Rt. Hon Tristan Garel-Jones is a paid consultant to BP Exploration.

Dr Charles Goodson-Wickes MP is a consultant to UPjohn Ltd, pharmaceutical company; Forum Holdings Ltd, chemicals and food products; and Chelgate Ltd, a public affairs company. Mrs Teresa Gorman MP is an unpaid director of a family business that makes scientific teaching aids.

John Greenway MP is a paid Parliamentary Adviser to General Healthcare Ltd. Sir Michael Grylls MP has paid directorships from four industrial companies, and is a paid trustee of Sanofi Winthrop Ltd, a pharmaceutical company. Sir John Hannam MP is a paid Parliamentary Adviser for the Royal Pharmaceutical Society of Great Britain. Sir Alan Haselhurst MP consults for Albright and Wilson Ltd, chemical manufacturers. Jerry Hayes MP is a public affairs consultant to Ivax Corporation, a pharmaceutical company.

The Rt. Hon. Sir Peter Hordern MP is a paid director of Fina PLC, the UK subsidiary of an international oil company. Andrew Hunter MP is a paid consultant to Lilly Industries, a pharmaceutical conglomerate. Robert Jackson MP was a paid consultant to Wessex Pharmaceutical Group in connection with a project on NHS reform. And we've only got to the `Js' - not even half way through the alphabet!

Toby Jessel MP, declared in the Register that he had played the piano at two concerts sponsored by South Eastern Electricity and BT. He very honestly remarked: "In both concerts I performed unpaid, but the sponsorship has affected my attitude to the sponsors."

UK readers will be interested to hear that Members of the House of Lords, who are not elected, are frequently retained by commercial concerns but there are no laws to prevent this, nor to force them to declare their interests.

How can our elected and non-elected representatives possibly believe that they are able to represent the interests of their constituents, and the interests of big businesses who are giving them money? I am sure that all of the above-mentioned MPs are men and women of the highest integrity and honour. But what do they do when, say, one of their constituents comes to them claiming that a drug manufactured by a company of which the MP is a director, appears to have damaged their immune system?

But, according to Edwina Curry MP, in an interview given for Channel 4's Dispatches programme, in connection with the `cash for questions' scandal, it's not what we see in the Register of Interests that should worry us, it's what we are not shown.

It is quite probable that MPs with vested interests will do the right thing. The problem is, as citizens in a society that is supposed to be a democracy, how do we know?

How do we know that the veterinary and medical establishments of education are similarly unaffected by the wishes and desires of their sponsors?

And will anyone forgive me for asking why these big businesses should want to give gifts and favours to our democratically elected representatives? Are we to believe they are doing it out of the goodness of their corporate hearts?

Today, it is still the practice of 'big business' to donate funds to academic, medical, and veterinary establishments. To receive these funds, the fear is that these establishments must be vulnerable - or amenable - to control.

This means that, should a veterinary or medical establishment wish to research the effectiveness of homoeopathy, someone somewhere might threaten to withdraw their big bucks. If a veterinary establishment wishes to independently test the inherent value of processed pet food, someone somewhere might take their bursary or grant or free hospital food away if the findings are not to their liking. And, as happened to me, if a veterinary college wishes to hold a seminar to raise funds for research, and if that seminar includes speakers who talk about vaccine damage, or processed pet food, the big businesses who are giving critical money to the college can, and do, threaten to withdraw that critical money if the seminar goes ahead.

In fact, one pet food company has tried to stop me speaking at more than one seminar, and a vaccine manufacturer has also tried to stop me being heard. In both cases, money was the lever. I have to say that it demands some courage to stand against wealthy multi-national businesses. But, in my experience, life only becomes worth living when you find a cause you are willing to die for, and somebody somewhere has to stand up and face the dragon. Animals and children have no voices - who else do they have if not us?

Sadly, money pays for the silence of a good many people. If, for example, a research fellow or PhD chappie is impressed by the merits of homoeopathy or natural food for pets, or anything that doesn't support the interests of the college's sponsors; and if that open minded individual publicly expresses the view that the college should look into the subject, the poor chap could well be put in a back room somewhere, have his funding withdrawn, and get told to keep his mouth shut. I have personally seen it happen.

There are vets who genuinely believe that vaccines are beneficial. There are vets who know that they are harmful but keep their mouths shut. One vet wrote to me saying: "I suspect the profession will ignore your survey results, as they deliberately ignore anything remotely threatening to financial interests." There are vets who choose to further their career in the commercial arena and put their families and personal interests before their conscience. Just like any kind of human being, from any walk of life.

And on, and on, all down the line. In my experience, and I've asked a lot of vets, if homoeopathy is mentioned at all in medical and veterinary colleges, the purpose is to deride it. Doctors and vets are, I postulate, brainwashed by the system. Similarly, if the colleges wish to teach doctors and vets about, say, vaccines, they draw upon the knowledge, and often the teaching skills, of vaccine company employees. Ditto for animal nutrition, where the pet food manufacturers are wheeled in as visiting experts.

If the Veterinary Medicines Directorate, or the Ministry of Agriculture, Fisheries and Food (and equivalent 'protective' bodies outside the UK) wish to establish expert panels or committees to look into a specific subject, they draw their members from the commercial arena - the so-called experts who have been employed by big businesses because they are supposedly the best in the field. But if the best in the field also includes an open-minded affiliation with healing treatments which do not involve big business interests, I suspect that they do not get employed by the big companies, and they do not get invited to sit on government committees or panels.

In fact, the British Ministry of Agriculture grants product licenses on the recommendation of the Veterinary Medicines Directorate. In turn, the VMD relies upon expert scientific advice from the Veterinary Products Committee (VPC). According to Dr Goran Jamal, speaking in the BBC 2 Programme, 'Disasters', broadcast on 30th January 1997, concerning organophosphate poisoning, "The VPC depends on data provided solely by the manufacturer of the product. There is no independent work, independent of the manufacturers."

Steve Dean, who has made his views on vaccines perfectly clear, who is known to be positively biassed in favour of vaccines and whose background includes being an employee of a pharmaceutical company, announced during 1996 that he is to be employed by the Veterinary Medicines Directorate to record adverse drug reactions. The Veterinary Medicines Directorate is, interestingly, funded by big business. (ie. those organisations it is intended to control - source: VMD's own brochure!) We have already heard from scientists within these pages who admit that much of the information about vaccine reactions is held by vaccine companies, and is considered proprietary information.

Meanwhile, the alternative practitioners, starved of funds, rely instead upon generating enough income from their practice work, and at the same time finding enough time and funds to conduct their own research and spread their own message.

In the UK today, it is illegal for anyone who is not a vet to heal an animal. They could have a doctorate in homoeopathy; they could be curing hundreds of dogs or cats or horses a year; but if the Royal College of Veterinary Surgeons wishes to do so, it can put the healer out of business and be supported by the law in doing so.

However, the people who obtain orthodox qualifications and then go on to acquire homoeopathic qualifications are the people who, generally speaking, become disillusioned with the allopathic model and have the courage, the funding, and the time, to stand against their more orthodox peers.

I must add here, before quoting any homoeopathic or conventional vets, that the above information was written by me, and not by any of the people I am now bringing into the debate.

Richard Allport B.Vet.Med., Vet.M.F. Hom., M.A.P.M.C., M.R.C.V.S is a homoeopathic vet. A gentler, more affable, more reasonable and open-minded man does not exist. But Richard moved away from conventional veterinary medicine because he simply didn't find it working. He began to look at the alternatives, obtained official qualifications in the alternatives, and in 1995 he had stopped treating animals with pharmaceuticals altogether. By 1996, he had opened a natural medicine veterinary centre using natural therapies only.

"No conventional drugs cross our threshold," he says. "We have a healer, an animal masseur, a behaviour counsellor, an osteopath, and an aromatherapist, plus counselling and therapy for pet owners."

Of vaccines, Richard says, "Whilst conventional vaccines may give protection for dogs and cats, there are obvious dangers associated with them. Conventional vets might say that homoeopathic nosodes don't work - although I trust them enough to protect my own dog using nosodes - but it is a known fact that you can't guarantee vaccines, either. In the final analysis, vets should provide their clients with the necessary information so that they can make their own informed decisions. I don't believe in imposing one's will on other people."

Homoeopaths do not experiment on laboratory animals

There is one so-called 'downside' to homoeopathy - a downside that enables the scientists to dismiss it but, to me, represents its greatest strength. Homoeopathic remedies are not routinely tested on animals in laboratory experiments. No true homoeopath has ever broken this ethical code, and we should all pray that they never do. Instead, following in the footsteps of Dr Samuel Hahnemann, homoeopathic remedies are tested on the physician and not the patient. They are used on animals to cure disease, but not to inflict disease.

This, in itself, strikes me as a very good reason for favouring homoeopathy rather than conventional medicine: you, your loved-ones, and your beloved pets can be protected without having inflicted suffering on others. As Dr Chopra has pointed out, we know more about death than we do about life: the first thing that is killed in the laboratory is the delicate web of intelligence that binds the body together.

Christopher Day, who is the Honorary Secretary of the British Association for Homoeopathic Veterinary Surgeons says, "I will not be involved at all in laboratory animal experimentation and I believe I still hold enough influence to ensure that homoeopathic vets don't do it. While I'm in charge it is not going to happen."

Could you imagine the manufacturers of the parvovirus vaccine injecting it into themselves just to make sure the vaccine is benign? The typical scientist will respond by telling me not to be so stupid: "Humans don't get parvovirus," they will say in an indignant and irritated tone.

"But rabbits and mice and rats and dogs don't get . . . smallpox, or measles, or . . ." I will answer. "But you tell us that if you test drugs for humans on animals, we will be safe."

In fact, the supporting structure for animal experimentation soon crumbles when you look at the facts. What happens to an animal in a laboratory bears little resemblance to what might happen to a human in the real world - because humans and animals are biologically different to one-another. Even individual humans are different to one-another, which is why some humans cannot tolerate pollen while others can, and some humans cannot tolerate gluten and others can.

The vivisector Dr HF Kraybill, states: "Response data from one laboratory sometimes cannot be duplicated elsewhere because of a different strain of the same species, variance in environmental conditions such as type and composition of diet, biorefractories (contaminants) in the water, pollutants in the air, animal care and/or husbandry, and others. The question then arises: Which experimental findings and which reports are authentic and recognised as a basis for an informed decision?" (Dr HF Kraybill. "From Mice to Men")

A study of the scientific use of laboratory experiments reveals that a substance producing a reaction on a rat or mouse or monkey or dog cannot be expected to produce the same reaction on a human, nor indeed any other species. Laboratory experiments are there for another reason, which I shall put to you in a little while.

A friend commented that some people are unable to see how wrong experiments of this type are: some simply do not have the consciousness to understand. But look at the dog sitting beside you now and ask yourself whether you would allow him or her to test the efficacy of vaccines for the entire dog population. And then consider that the tests themselves are often designed to prove a commercial point rather than establish the truth.

A Course in Miracles states that laws are devised to protect the system in which the lawmaker believes.

The fact that the law supports the restrictive practices of the veterinary establishment made absolute sense to me when I realised that almost all of industry is dependent upon animal experimentation. If big businesses test their poisons on animals, then when the humans get ill, they can hold up their hands and say: "but we did all the tests".

Of course: it is necessary to ensure that vets are 'educated' to believe that animal experimentation is necessary. Whilst those of us who have looked into the facts behind the scenes understand that animal experimentation is nothing more than a marketing ploy, the rest of us believe our wife/father/brother/child will die unless we inflict pain on animals.

We received a remarkable e-mail from a research scientist at one of the world's largest chemical companies. He said: "It's true. Most research is conducted to prove a commercial point - not to discover the scientific truth."

And yet, at a recent seminar, a pro-vaccinating 'scientist' stood up and told the assembled audience that the safety of British veterinary medicines and vaccines was superior to American safety standards, because we have rigorous testing and the Yellow Form scheme (which fails abysmally). The same man proudly told us all that British veterinary medicines are rarely, if ever, withdrawn: the safety standards are so high. Yet a misalliance injection for bitches comes with the warning that one in a hundred bitches injected with the substance will die of bone marrow failure. Perhaps the standards aren't high enough - if they were, this particular drug might be illegal. And carbaryl, a flea control product, is still for sale for use on dogs and cats whereas it's been withdrawn for human use due to its risky cancer-producing properties.

In fact, apart from testing products intended for humans on species that are distinctly different to humans, the research findings are themselves routinely ignored. Apartame serves as an illustrative example, taken from an abundantly overflowing box of reasons to be worried, in this case from the UK magazine '*What Doctors Don't Tell You*':

Apartame is an artificial sweetener, sold under the brand names NutraSweet, Hermesetas Gold Choice and Canderel; it is found in some 9000 foods in America and in hundreds of products in Britain: diet soda, fruit drinks, lollies, chewing gum, cocoa, and more.

Dr Erik Millstone of the Science Policy Research Unit at Sussex University maintains that aspartame was accepted in the UK on the basis of animal tests which weren't properly conducted. According to his evidence, the 15 pivotal studies leading to aspartame approval both in the US and UK had serious flaws or demonstrated risks.

In one of those studies, seven monkeys received varying dosages of aspartame in powdered milk formula. According to the study, all the monkeys exhibited grand mal seizures after 218 days, and one monkey in the high dose group died, although the cause of death wasn't determined.

Once the aspartame was withdrawn, the monkeys were kept under observation for three months on unsweetened powdered milk formula. No further convulsions were detected. Despite being `safe', aspartame accounts for more than 75 per cent of the adverse reactions to food reported to the FDA. Some of these reactions are very serious, including death (Department of Health and Human Services, "Report on All Adverse Reactions in the Adverse Reaction Monitoring System", 25-28 February 1994).

Apart from ignoring the results, the results are sometimes fraudulent. A Sunday Times article described the fate of a group of scientists who exposed a colleague's 'fudging' of results. The Sunday Times reported: "Meanwhile, the scientists who first suspected Evans feel that they are the victims. Many of them have since left the department for jobs abroad and are unwilling to talk publicly about the case for fear of jeopardising their careers still further. 'The whistle blowers are always, without doubt, the ones who get hurt', one of the scientists said."

The Sunday Times quoted a small-scale survey of 80 scientists carried in the British Medical Journal in 1988. More than half of the scientists knew of some instances of misconduct and in more than half of these cases fabricated or dubious results had been published in the scientific literature, and hence taken as fact by other scientists. Only six retractions had subsequently appeared and all were apparently too vague to indicate what had gone on. None of the guilty scientists was formally disciplined, and only one was dismissed.

But despite the fact that scientific fraud is widespread, scientists are still taught to discard homoeopathy on the basis that it isn't subjected to 'rigorous scientific analysis'. Maybe we should thank the Lord that it isn't - we have to rely, instead, upon the empirical evidence of those of us who have seen homoeopathy alleviate suffering.

A debate about homoeopathy took place on BBC 2's Newsnight on January 22nd, 1997. The anti-homoeopathy representative stated that homoeopathy only appears to work because the people who take the remedies believe they will: the placebo effect. Yet those of us who have treated our dogs homoeopathically know that this can't be true. We also know, now, from the research detailed in this book, that homoeopathy has been proven as a principle.

If ordinary people - people who care for their dogs and cats, for example - use homoeopathic remedies and witness their dogs and cats responding, we can legitimately overrule the scientific viewpoint. When Chappie ruptured his cruciate ligaments we asked our (conventional) vet to refer us to a homoeopath. He quite literally went ape, phoning us and sending us letters to tell us that homoeopathy was religious mumbo jumbo, and we might as well take Chappie on a visit to Lourdes for all the good it would do.

We were somewhat surprised by the force of our vet's reaction, but we felt that Chappie deserved any chance of recovery we could find for him. The conventional vet had nothing but painkillers that didn't kill the pain to offer. So off we went to the homoeopathic vet, and Chappie showed instant signs of improvement. At that moment I stopped trusting scientific judgement implicitly, my brain came out of my back pocket.

Allow a vet to become a homoeopath, however, a science which tangibly demonstrates that all living organisms have bodies, minds and spirits, then the vet would soon be unable to stomach vivisection. We who love our animal brothers and sisters must hope that the current anti-vivisection stance of the British Association for Homoeopathic Veterinary Surgeons continues. We need to be strong, and protect the innocent.

The fallibility of vivisection is, of course, regularly demonstrated when new drugs are released onto the market, cause human beings serious harm, and then have to be withdrawn.

The success of modern science

Steve Dean told Dog World (UK) readers in one of his articles that modern `science' has stretched itself to the limits to do so very much good to the planet. Rather a risky statement at the time, as hundreds of thousands of cattle were then being slaughtered in Britain, thanks to 'science'-induced BSE. So how successful has modern science been? And how much credence should we give to the `scientists' who tell ordinary people - like you and me - that we know nothing and should listen to them?

In May 1995, Canine Health Concern issued a press release warning dog and cat owners of the dangers of many chemical-based flea treatments. No-one published it. Between December 1996 and January 1997, the manufacturer of Droplix, an organophosphate flea killer, admitted that its product had killed several dogs and cats - demonstrating clearly that if you play with fire, you are bound to get burnt sooner or later. `Science', however, maintains that these chemicals are safe.

In 1950 the British National Health Service cost £300 million; the cost for 1995 was projected to be over £35 billion - an increase of 116 times the original (over 10% compound annual growth for every person in the U.K.), whilst the population had increased by around 15 per cent of the 1950's figure. Now, around two out of five people have, or will develop, cancer; 20 million people suffer some form of arthritis; 800 people die daily from circulatory disease; 30,000 new cases of diabetes are diagnosed each year; and there are 30,000 new cases of epilepsy - 10,000 of which are children. Combined with ME, multiple sclerosis, asthma, autism, bowel disease, and over 20,000 other maladies, the spectacle of an economic-disease gridlock seems inevitable. The British National Health Service is slowly being wound down by the current government to reflect this, and we're being encouraged to write off our National Insurance payments and opt for private insurance.

Doctors are now shelling out some 460 million prescriptions annually. Up to 98 per cent of children in some areas are being vaccinated with a cross section of animal-derived viruses and proteins, mucus, urine, faeces, blood, aluminium, mercury, and formaldehyde. Cancer-inducing X-rays are used like sunshine; fluoride waste is dumped into our drinking water. The food, air and environment is saturated with a lethal concoction of synthetic chemicals, and the prospects for the future include cross-species transplantation and the genetic engineering of God-given foods.

Is the world mad?

"Far from making a useful contribution to health care, the medical industry is making huge numbers of people ill," says Dr Vernon Coleman " . . . as many as one sixth of patients in European hospitals are there only because they have been made ill by doctors. In Britain more than a million people a year are admitted to hospitals because of medical errors, incompetence, or the side-effects of drugs. Doctors rate alongside cancer and heart disease as a major cause of serious illness and death."

The hundreds of thousands of petrochemical synthetics - pesticides, herbicides, solvents, tars, dyes, detergents, paints, and cosmetics - which are polluting the air, water and land; and killing people and animals, birds, fish, trees, lakes, rivers and seas - have all been passed as safe following tests on animals. Animal experimentation - a deceitful web of intrigue and agony - is literally costing us the earth.

Every thinking person can see the 'benefits' of 'science'. Without the skill of a good veterinary surgeon and antibiotics, Samson would never have survived the cancer in his spleen. My father would never have survived several heart attacks. But Samson was also offered antibiotics several years ago to deal with a hot spot: I said no thank you and took him home and treated him homoeopathically. And what caused his cancer in the first place, and why is heart disease so prevalent in the modern world? Chemicals, drugs, inappropriate food, vaccines . . . Brought to us by the wonders of `science' which is, in effect, no more than the lackey of commerce.

Dr Albert Schatz, who discovered the antibiotic Streptomycin, wrote in the forward to a wonderful book (MAP, The Co-Creative White Brotherhood Medical Assistance Program, Perelandra Ltd, USA):

"Man's localised destruction of nature has been responsible for the extinction of many animal species. Now our global assault on nature threatens our survival. We have chosen a collision course with the Four Horsemen of the Apocalypse. We are running out of natural resources, out of natural environment, out of space, and out of time. In our suicidal assault on nature, we are approaching the point of no return. "We obviously will not be saved by our anthropocentric science, which has given us chemical dumps, deadly radioactive waste that we do not know how to dispose of, air and water pollution, carcinogenic pesticides and food additives, ineffective and harmful synthetic drugs, nerve gas, nuclear weapons, biological warfare, the profligate waste of natural resources, the global devastation of nature, and much more. This is what science means to many people.

"We obviously will not be saved by academic scientists whose research is supported by grants from and, in turn, supports the pharmaceutical, agricultural, and chemical industries - and the military. Indeed, the military-industrial complex that Eisenhower warned us about has metastasised into a military-industrial-educational complex."

What I, and countless individuals, are saying is that science is literally killing us. It started out with good intentions, but it has been hijacked by commercial greed. The academics and scientists who do not recognised this have simply been brainwashed to ignore what is now striking us firmly between the eyes.

You, a thinking person, can do something about this. You can stop buying the lie. Investigate the homoeopathic and natural alternatives. Satisfy yourselves that you are happy with a different course. Save the planet by taking one small step for yourself, your dogs, and the whole of Creation.

Strong words, perhaps? So start paying attention to the scientific items on the news. I don't think we have time to wait for the scientists to wise up and put life before a living. We must all be part of the solution - or we are, by default, part of the problem. It has taken me all this time to realise the significance of Pontius Pilate in Christ's death. Wash your hands at the peril of the world.

Who killed the darling Buds of May? I did, you did, we did. Every time we can't be bothered and we go for the easy option without knowing why or what we are doing; every time we abdicate responsibility and place all of the decisions in the hands of the experts, we negate life and our purpose for being here.

A last word about vets

Some readers might imagine that I don't like vets. I wouldn't want you to think this, because nothing could be further from the truth. Vets are just as much victims of the system as we all are. They have a very tough job on their hands, a job that is very stressful. I honestly don't believe, as some people do, that all vets vaccinate dogs annually because it's a money-spinner, knowing that the vaccines create disease and an ever-increasing supply of sick dogs to make more money from.

Most vets genuinely believe that vaccines protect against viral disease, and that the benefits far outweigh the risks. They real problem is that they are not taught the truth about vaccines - and for some strange reason they don't go searching for the truth. Actually, tell a lie: some vets <u>do</u> go searching for the truth and, to this end, we have reason to be extremely grateful to vets like Chris Day, Jean Dodds, Peter Gregory, John Saxton, James Newns, and others. In fact, without these people, I would have been unable to share my life with another dog. After losing Oliver, Prudence and Samson, any other dog would represent a tragic death waiting to happen. With vets such as these, I have hope - hope that, with good food and no vaccine risk, there is every reason to believe that my dogs, your dogs, can live long, happy and healthy lives.

In the original edition of this book, I wrote that I hope that this book will at least cause vets to be aware of the possibility that vaccines can create the reactions we have described. But I have to be patient. Really, I wanted vets to pay immediate attention to the vaccine tragedy, but my book was met with considerable resistance. I guess you have to expect that - the world has been brainwashed into believing that vaccines are the medical miracle of the twentieth century.

We rob vets of their humanity if we imagine that they put money above the lives of their patients. Call me naive if you like, but I simply do not believe that there are many people who are that short sighted. The issue is much more complex than that, and most of us are deliberately blinded by 'science'. In The Republic, Plato put forward the view that sin is merely ignorance: if we knew the results of our sin, then we wouldn't do it. And if we dog owners hand all the decisions over to the experts, then aren't we just as culpable?

Gibran wrote, in the Prophet, that the victim is never innocent of the crime. Many years ago, when I first read it, I didn't understand that. But by abdicating responsibility and letting 'the experts' decide whether we should inject our dogs, cats or horses every year with something we know nothing about, aren't we being rather careless with the lives of the animals who trust us?

Mystics say that we live in a world of delusion - which means that all of us are capable of adamantly believing in something that is totally unreal. For all I know, these vets might be right and the anti-vaccinators might be wrong. Each individual must listen to all of the views, and take responsibility for their own decisions. We must stop giving our power away.

But even then, I still struggle to not be angry with vets, especially when they put their heads in the sand and refuse to look at the evidence.

My Dad always used to say: "He who is mad and knows he is mad is not mad, but he who is mad and knows not that he is mad is mad." It's quite scary to realise that experts and views and 'facts' are fallible and capable of being erroneous. But it's also very exciting, and the knowledge of this opens the door to freedom.

You know, many humans claim that they are superior to animals - but animals never sell their friends out. Vets, and all of us whose lives are blessed by the animals, must remember this fact.

I asked Richard Allport why vets have such a high suicide rate. He told me that, "vets are not taught communication skills at college. They are taught to diagnose illness and treat animals, and I think it is sometimes very stressful when dealing with the public. Also, we always think we're going to get used to watching our patients die. This is not the case. We never get used to it. We find it even harder when we have to kill an animal. We give it different names, like euthanasia or put down, but the fact is, it's killing, and we don't like doing it."

I also had an interesting conversation with a chiropractor recently. She was telling me about a patient who complained that she went to the doctor with back pain, and was disgusted when he only gave her pills. "but that's what doctors do," she said. "You go to a doctor for pills, and a chiropractor to have your back fixed."

Specialisation: vets are good when surgery is required or violent drugs are needed to combat violent ailments; homoeopaths are good where a gentler course is more appropriate; faith healers have been seen to produce excellent results; herbs and nutritional therapies work wonders . . . no human being has all the answers to everything, and you don't have to stick with one model. You can make choices, the best choices in the circumstance.

Few conventionally trained vets know very much about homoeopathy or herbs, or any other alternative forms of medicine. As such, they only have opinion and a specialised education, which you should bear in mind when they seek to offer advice on these subjects.

One last word for dog owners

Thank you for reading this book. It means that you care so much about your friends, that you are willing to wade through quite a lot of technical information so that you are better informed.

Thank you, also, to every dog lover who has taken part in the Canine Health Concern vaccine survey. I believe that dog owners have a vital and valuable contribution to make. A contribution that can not only help our dogs, but also the spirit of life on this planet. Around the world, countless children and animals have been killed or seriously damaged by vaccines. By giving your attention now, you have done something very positive to prevent unnecessary risk, and to nurture creation.

For evil to thrive, all that is required is that good men and women do nothing. You cannot be sold duff products if you refuse to buy them.

And, finally, I would like to share another sentiment my father - Fred Mullin - taught me as a child: "You are superior to no-one, and inferior to no-one." You don't need letters after your name to know the truth and speak the truth. Just keep questioning, keep your mind open and become, as Christ told us, like little children. Being smart isn't about what you know; it's about what you ask.

Now it's your choice. Read, learn, ask questions - and make your own mind up. No-one, no matter how qualified, has the moral right to compel you to do anything that you don't understand, or don't agree with. Your dogs look at YOU with love and trust in their eyes - not at some stranger in a white coat. God has given you a brain. Importantly, He gave you free will.

The planet is in serious trouble. This is what Oliver, Prudence and Samson, and your own dear animal friends, came to tell us. Perhaps, when you think of the planet, it seems too large and remote a problem, and there's nothing you personally can do about it. But you can start from where you are: move the mountain a stone at a time. By making conscious decisions about your life and the lives of those in your care; about the type of products you choose to buy; even about using less detergents, or slightly less shampoo; by consciously choosing products that haven't been tested on animals, and pulling the weeds out instead of treating them with chemicals, we can make the world a better place.

All I know is that I, personally, used to have my dogs vaccinated annually like a 'good responsible' dog owner should. The vaccines didn't stop Samson, Pru and Ollie dying, they hastened their deaths. Chappie, Sophie and Gwinnie have lived their lives under the cloud of chronic disease. Had our own personal nightmare been due to a naturally occurring disease, I wouldn't have needed to wail why out to the heavens, to be met by a stern dark silence on the part of the established veterinary community.

Thankfully, I have met vets along the way whose candles are still burning brightly. Together, the cats and the dogs and the cattle and the sheep, and even the humans, can spread light where there is darkness.

All life is precious: think for yourself

We are in the vet's, and the vet is coming at Prudence with a needle. And she looks at it, and her eyes roll in their sockets, and she starts to climb onto my back. I say: "It's all right Prudence, it's good for you." And I hold her so the vet can give Prudence her annual vaccine. I don't listen to Prudence.

Later, we go for a walk. Prudence is ahead with John. She's on the lead because there are cars about and we want to protect her. But she stops, and she looks at me, and I smile at her and say, "Come on then darling," and she sparkles and effervesces like a bottle of lemonade with the lid coming off. And she walks with her mummy, and her eyes are looking at me with such love, such trust. She's looking at me. She isn't looking at any man in a white coat. She trusts me.

Chief Seathl's testament, given when the white man was virtually exterminating native American Indians, applies just as powerfully today as it did in the 19th Century. The following words speak to all of us - the animal guardians, those who seek to heal the animals, those who legislate, and those whose livelihoods depend upon the multi-billion pet industry.

How can you buy or sell the sky,
the warmth of the land?
The idea is strange to us.
If we do not own
the freshness of the air
and the sparkle of the water,
how can you buy them?
Every part of this earth is sacred to my people.
Every shining pine needle, every sandy shore, every mist
in the dark woods, every clearing and humming insect is
holy in the memory and experience of my people.
The sap which courses through the trees
carries the memories of the red man.
We are part of the earth and it is part of us.
The perfumed flowers are our sisters; the deer,
the horse, the great eagle, these are our brothers.
So we will consider your offer to buy our land.
If we decide to accept, I will make one condition;
the white man must treat the beasts of this land as
his brothers.
What is man without the beasts? If all the beasts were gone,
men would die from a great loneliness of spirit.
For whatever happens to the beasts, soon happens to man.
All things are connected.

Vaccination - the issues

Questions and Answers

Q: I would like to explore the possibility of protecting my dogs against viral disease, and leptospirosis, homoeopathically. How do I go about doing this?

A: The first course would be to ask your conventional vet whether he or she offers this option. If not, you can ask your vet to refer you to a homoeopathically qualified vet. If for some reason your vet cannot or will not refer you, you can contact the homoeopathic veterinary association in your country. If you are in the UK, or you are unable to locate the relevant association overseas, you can write to The British Association for Homoeopathic Veterinary Surgeons, Chinham House, Stanford-in-the-Vale, Farringdon, Oxon SN7 8NQ, England. Please enclose stamps or money to pay for return postage.

Q: Is there anything to stop a conventional vet from offering the homoeopathic alternative?

A: No. It would not take much for a conventional vet to receive training in how to administer the nosode vaccine alternative, although it may be that your conventional vet is unwilling to offer them. This is his or her right, but it is also your right, as your dog's guardian, to choose whichever course of treatment is best and legally available. You are, for example, entitled to select another vet.

Q: My homoeopathic vet has never mentioned the nosode alternative to vaccination. Why?

A: Although most homoeopathic vets protect their own animals homoeopathically, not all are sure of their legal position when it comes to offering advice to clients in this respect, and some may lack experience.

For example, the Royal College in the UK has introduced the Cascade System under the Veterinary Surgeons Act. Some homoeopathic vets mistakenly believe that they are, under the System, legally obliged to prescribe first a licensed drug. If no suitable licensed drug exists, they believe that they must then use an unlicensed drug which has a recognised use in that area. Only when the first two options have been explored and discounted, are they able to recommend 'alternatives'.

This belief is, however, incorrect. Having sought clarification from Dr JM Rutter, head of the Veterinary Medicines Directorate, we are advised that:

"Firstly, decisions on the appropriate treatment in any particular case remain matters for the professional judgement of the veterinary surgeon who has care of the animal or animals in question. The veterinarian should consider whether a suitable authorised product is available, in accordance with the cascade. If the veterinarian concludes that a homoeopathic treatment is required then there is nothing in the regulations to prevent use of such treatment.

"There is no requirement for an allopathic (modern chemical-based) treatment to be prescribed where professional judgement indicates that a non-allopathic treatment is more suitable."

Some homoeopathic vets believe that homoeopathic nosodes are unproven scientifically, even though they trust them to protect their own animals. You must also be aware that some homoeopathic vets, just like conventional vets, are very reliant upon the income generated by vaccines.

I hope that you will be able to enlighten your vet with the studies contained in this book, and that you will ask your homoeopathic vet to explain about the nosodes if he or she fails to do so. Ultimately, you must make the choice for yourself and your animals.

Q: Why are homoeopathic remedies not licensed?

A: There are two basic reasons. The first is that homoeopaths have historically resisted animal experimentation, which is an inherent part of the licensing procedure.

Secondly, it would be difficult to patent homoeopathic remedies. Anyone can make them if they know how, as they are made from naturally occurring substances. Further, you can't patent anything which is already in the public domain. These facts combine to make it financially unviable for homoeopathic remedies to go through the licensing procedure. Each 'product' costs many thousands of pounds to license and, as the drug companies are unlikely to see a return on any investment in homoeopathic remedies, they are unlikely to invest.

However, a recent consultation document issued by the VMD under EU guidance suggests that homoeopathic remedies not in use before 31 March 1997 must be licensed. The implication of this is that if, say, a new disease like Aids emerges, then individual homoeopaths will be legally prevented from producing a homoeopathic remedy, whereas wealthy drug companies will be able to.

Q: Do conventional vets recognise that vaccines create side-effects?

A: I don't know. Some vets I speak with tell me that they do; others tell me that they don't. It will probably take some time before they reach a unified decision, and this depends very much upon the profession's ability to view the facts objectively. I have been less than impressed by the 'professions' unwillingness to consider the information contained within this book, or the vaccine survey findings.

Q: I believe my dog was killed or damaged by a vaccine, but no-one will listen to me. I feel so alone. What can I do?

A: Contact Canine Health Concern. We will at least listen, and we may be able to help with impartial advice.

Q: I have been told that vets would go out of business if they didn't make money out of annual vaccinations. Is this true?

A: It is true to say that between 18% and 40% of a vet's turnover is directly vaccine related, and that many vets are reliant upon vaccination to be profitable. Vets also rely upon the ability to negotiate discounts with drug companies, so there is some pressure upon them not to speak out if they witness the adverse effects of vaccines.

Christopher Day comments: "I have suffered, and continue to suffer, serious economic disadvantage from not using vaccines in practice, but I feel quite unable to do so until such time as the issues can be resolved in vaccine's favour by proper and extensive study of all the circumstantial evidence."

Even now, some homoeopathic vets will vaccinate dogs if their owners ask them to. One vet told me that he felt as though he was committing a crime every time he vaccinated a dog, but he felt trapped by the system. Rather than view this as an 'us and them' situation, wouldn't it be better if we supported our vets as they struggle with ethical decisions of this sort?

For example, I would ask all dog owners to support their vets financially if they can afford to do so by taking their dogs for annual checkups. This will help soften the blow for vets in practice, and it will also help them to examine the vaccine issue with a degree of fear removed from their examination.

Q: But won't people start suing vets and vaccine manufacturers in the light of the evidence?

A: Possibly, although I have to say that I hope animal guardians will take steps to become informed about what is done to their dogs - before it ever gets to law.

Whilst some vets believe that the vaccine manufacturer will be sued, rather than themselves, it is quite possible that the vet may be joined as a party in any legal battle. Indeed, under the UK's Trade Descriptions Act and Sale of Goods Act, the primary responsibility rests with the person who supplied the service or sold the product, i.e., the vet. The vet, in order to protect his interests, may choose to join the vaccine manufacturer as a third party.

However, if, for example, a dog is being given steroids and is vaccinated, and dies, the vaccine company will most likely defend its interests by claiming that the vet's inappropriate administration killed the dog. (If it admits the vaccine's involvement in the first place.) Similarly, if a vet fails to ask questions about the dog's diet or genetic or stress status, then there is a case to suggest that he or she was negligent. Also, if pet owners are not warned of the possible adverse reactions, it could be argued that the vet failed in his duty as a fee-earning consultant.

It could go further. If a vet vaccinates a dog who he knows has previously suffered adverse reactions to a vaccine, without warning the owner of possible side effects, he or she may well risk criminal prosecution as it could be argued that his actions were designed to obtain a pecuniary advantage by deception, contrary to S16 of the Theft Act 1968. (Source: p 312 et seq, Criminal Law, Card, Cross & Jones, ISBN 0 406 03255 6), or worse contrary to S15, Theft Act 1968.

The same case could be argued against vets who vaccinate sick dogs, dogs on immune-suppressant drugs, and so on.

Q: What about the rabies vaccine? Some of us are obliged by law to vaccinate our animals against rabies.

A: Firstly, vaccines are licensed for use in healthy animals. It may be possible to build a case against mandatory vaccination if your animal is unwell. Use of the homoeopathic alternative may make your case stronger. If anyone out there wants to test this one through the courts, I'd be pleased to hear from you. In fact, you have my promise that if rabies vaccination is made mandatory in the UK, I shall be taking it as far as I can through legal channels.

Q: I want to put my dog in kennels, but they always insist upon vaccination certificates.

A: More and more kennel owners are willing to accept homoeopathically protected dogs. Kennel owners in this position are invited to write to Canine Health Concern so that we can circulate your details to members. Another alternative is to find a friend who is a dog lover and doggie sit for each other, or use a dog sitting service. The same is also true of dog clubs - many are beginning to accept homoeopathically protected puppies and adult dogs.

Q: Well, I'm now convinced that I'll never vaccinate my dog again. But aren't you concerned that the drug companies will retaliate?

A: This is inevitable. No-one's going to say goodbye to a multi-million dollar industry without a fight, and it is natural that they should seek to respond. You can expect to see the drug companies taking more advertising space in dog-related magazines, and you can also expect to see an increase in articles supporting vaccination. Please keep an open mind when you read these articles, and ensure that you are satisfied by the scientific arguments. You should ask yourself what motivates the writer.

For example, when I replied to Steve Dean's letter in Dog World, he replied with sarcasm and ridicule. He also 'corrected' statements I had never made, presumably with the intention of discrediting the central message. I have been able to answer these tactics now, but I may not have the opportunity to do so in the future - which means you must be vigilant when weighing up the interests of your dogs against the interests of big business and strongly held views.

All writers take on karmic responsibility for their work, and I have thought long and hard, and prayed, that the outcome of this work will be positive - if not for me, then for the animals. We must all of us examine our consciences and our talents, and do our bit now.

If you are convinced by the arguments put forward in this book, please encourage as many people as possible to read it. We cannot force anyone to agree with us, but everyone who needs to decide whether they should vaccinate their animal or not has a right to at least see the evidence. We did not know, when this book was first published, whether the dog magazines would air the views and scientific evidence expressed in this book, nor did we know whether the bookshops would stock it. I am particularly concerned that the pet owners - who do not go to shows or have the opportunity to speak to more learned dog owners - are allowed to study the facts. So please help if you can by spreading the word. You never know, together we may be able to breathe new life into the ailing pet population. Incidentally, many people have told me that they have lent this book to dozens of friends. This is great, because the word is being spread - but please bear in mind that the work of Canine Health Concern can only continue if we have funds.

So if you can afford to buy a copy or make a donation, that would be much appreciated.

Summary:

Top experts tell us that:
* Vaccines come with proven risks.
* Vaccines can cause the disease they are designed to prevent.
* Vaccines can lead to hypersensitivity, encephalitis, autoimmune disease and death.
* Annual vaccination is not necessary - once is said to be enough for viral disease; the leptospirosis vaccine, for bacterial disease, is not yet effective and presents significant risks.
* Indeed, there is growing catalogue of evidence to support the view that vaccines cause more problems than they alleviate. Animals can be shown to develop natural immunity, so long as they are not overcrowded, stressed and/or malnourished.
* Vaccines keep disease in the eco system.
* There are, arguably, safer alternatives to vaccination.
* You have the right to choose.

Chapter Eleven

Canine Health Census Vaccine Survey

Interim Results

February 1997 and August 1998

As a result of the debate between Steve Dean and myself and others in *Dog World*, John and I decided to put the argument to proper scientific test. I had been researching and writing this book for some two years at this stage, and felt sure that we could unearth some significant information by implementing a vaccine-specific survey.

We knew for a fact that adverse reactions were possible from vaccination - even the vaccine manufacturers admit this. But what we didn't know was how common these side effects might be. We had many testimonies from owners whose dogs had become ill or died immediately after vaccination, but few of these reactions had been reported to the Veterinary Medicines Directorate. Further, as our case stories have shown, vets will rarely acknowledge that an illness occurring within a few hours or days after vaccination is vaccine-related, so there was little hope that they might acknowledge a vaccine reaction several weeks or months after the jab.

The homoeopathic vet Christopher Day on the other hand, told us that he suspected that around 80% of the diseases he treats in his surgery are vaccine related, and occur within three months of vaccination where the start date of the illness is known. Chris is a referral vet, which means that he tends to see mostly the cases where every other avenue has been tried and failed, so the 80% figure was, by his own admission, likely to be exaggerated.

It was, then, with only very slight unease that I agreed to my husband John's suggestion that we put Christopher Day's hypothesis to scientific test. If we were wrong, not only would two years' work go down the tubes (my book), but I would also receive a blow to my belief system. That said, it was important that the findings be truthful and accurate because our aim all along has been to save unnecessary suffering and death. In this respect, our results have always been open to independent audit, but - so far - no-one has taken us up on this offer. Instead, some vaccine manufacturers and vets have chosen to denigrate the work but without taking the trouble to ask for clarification on any issues; and none of them have even seen the data.

The CHC vaccine survey was first launched during October 1996. A questionnaire was devised with the help of Christopher Day, Jean Dodds DVM, and Dr Viera Scheibner. Some 30,000 readers of *Dog World* magazine were invited to participate: we paid an advertising rate to have the questionnaire printed within the publication. In addition, all members of the Canine Health Concern were mailed with a questionnaire, and some members of CHC (very kindly) circulated the questionnaire to friends and neighbours. The first edition of this book carried our first interim findings. This edition adds over a thousand dogs to the picture. If we had more, we could achieve a lot more, for example, we could be more specific about individual breeds - so please contact us for a questionnaire.

At time of publication of the second edition of this book, 770 detailed questionnaires have been received. These cover 523 dog owners and a total of approximately 3,800 dogs. Based on this data, our second set of provisional results do add emphasis to the alarm raised in the first analysis and confirm many of the fears previously outlined in this book. The second set of analysis, updated for this edition, gives no cause to doubt the principles outlined previously.

Indeed, we have been able to show a definite statistical correlation between a vaccinate event and the onset of a number of specific illnesses. The graph on the next page shows how the profiles of the two batches of source data compare. Mathematically these are identical confirming that the initial analysis was fundamentally sound.

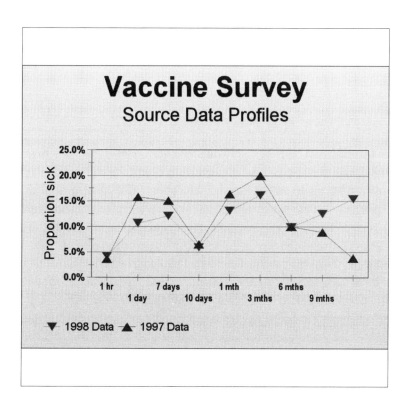

First Interim results

The following published provisional conclusions have all satisfied mathematical or inferential statistical tests at a level of confidence of 99% or better. That is, we have rejected, unless otherwise stated, any result with a z alpha of less than 2.56. In mathematical terms, an alpha score of 4 would mean that the chance of a false conclusion is less than one in about 33,000. In many cases, the data we have is greatly in excess of 4, making the following conclusions a certainty for all practical purposes.

The second analyses initially used the Chi square test. This test was used to compare the expected number of illnesses over the twelve months following vaccination against the actual results. We have rejected any illness with a Chi test statistic of less than twelve. That is to say, any Chi test statistic higher than twelve gives a 95%

confidence about the conclusions. A Chi test result of 13 or greater gives a 99% confidence, and a Chi test of 17 gives 99.5% confidence. Only one test, heart conditions, was accepted at the 95% level as being vaccine-induced. Arthritis and pancreas problems are, at a 99% level of statistical certainty, vaccine-induced. Hepatitis is 99.5% certain to be vaccine-induced.

Meningitis, CDRM, asthma, leukaemia and thyroid problems did not pass the statistical test, although the term 'meningitis' is often the name given to encephalitis. However, the numbers of dogs in the survey with such ailments were extremely small and as leukaemia is a form of cancer, if cancer and leukaemia are combined, then one can conclude that leukaemia, like other cancers is vaccine related. Strong research does exist in the human field to link these illnesses with vaccination. To clarify this position, we need more dogs to study. We also know that thyroid disease is very commonly undetected in the dog and therefore undiagnosed, and diseases like leukaemia may have varying incubation periods depending upon the inherent health of the dog. In Pru's case, I had been saying to John that she seemed to be lacking in energy for some three months before we took her to the vet; John couldn't see any difference in her. The owner's observation and the vet's diagnosis will therefore distort observed start date records where underlying disease is concerned. Meningitis may escape diagnosis.

For the purposes of this survey, we asked all participants to list their dogs' illnesses, and tell us how soon they started after the date of vaccination. Our aim was to test whether there was a time frame bias between vaccination and the start of illness. This in itself would enable us to see whether illnesses which developed within three months after vaccination might be vaccine-linked.

The hypothesis is that, if vaccination has no adverse effect or even bearing on subsequent illness, then illnesses will occur in equal numbers at any time during the twelve months after vaccination. In fact, the results so far gathered show a distinct skewness or bias towards illness occurring within the first three months after vaccination.

No data was recorded in respect of lupus, lyme disease or rabies in the first analysis, but one dog with lupus was incorporated into the second analysis. Obviously, no statistical conclusions can be drawn on such a sample size. Some diseases showed a distinct bias towards occurring at nine months or more after vaccination had taken place. These are arthritis and heart conditions. We do, though, ask why these illnesses should all be clustered together at around the nine month period? It may, in fact, suggest that it takes longer for these illnesses to manifest overt symptoms, and consequently for diagnosis to take place. If vaccination had no bearing, then there should by rights be an even spread of occurrence throughout the twelve month period.

In a paper published in the *Journal of Veterinary Internal Medicine*, Vol 10, No 5, September/October 1966, entitled *'Vaccine-Associated Immune-mediated Haemolytic Anaemia in the Dog'*, the authors state: "Because vaccine components can remain in the body for extended periods of time, chemical reactions caused by these vaccine components may continue to occur later than with other drugs that are excreted or metabolized more quickly." This statement in its own right would appear to support the belief that vaccines can cause reactions some time after the jab.

Although samples are small in terms of the number of dogs in each breed, it is clear that some breeds have a distinct propensity to heart conditions and additional data would permit us to assess whether or not such heart conditions were affected by vaccination. These breeds are Beagles, Bernese Mountain Dogs, Cavalier King Charles Spaniels, Irish Wolfhounds, and Miniature Poodles.

The first, astounding, finding of our initial survey results showed that, overall, 55% of all illnesses reported by participants occurred within the first three months of vaccination. This has risen to 66% in the second analysis. **If the vaccine had no bearing on the illness, you would expect to see no more than 25% occurring within that three month time frame.** The graph on the next page clearly shows the high incidence of illness in the three months following vaccination.

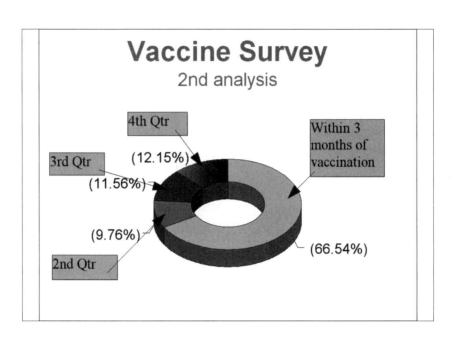

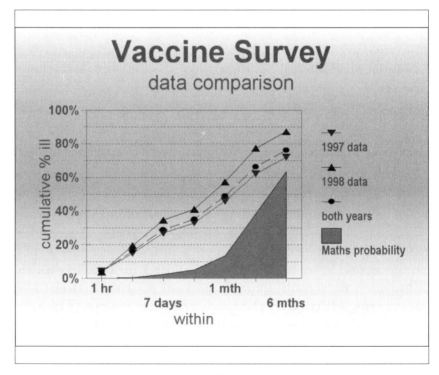

The graph on the previous page demonstrates how data from both batches of survey data significantly exceed the mathematical expectations if vaccines were innocent. Note how, during the first two quarters, the actual survey results are so different to the mathematically expected levels.

This demonstrates that a significant percentage of canine diseases arise in the first quarter following vaccination. Further analysis of the data shows that 41.75% of all illnesses start within 30 days after vaccination; this figure rose to 49% with extra data. This is over five times the expected percentage (if vaccination had no bearing on subsequent illness, you would expect only 8.22% of the dogs to become ill during the 30 days after vaccination.)

The original observation was tested using a standard t-Test which resulted in a t value of 5.39 with alpha at 0.001%. This means that a statistician would be 99.999% confident that vaccines are related to the subsequent illnesses.

In respect of the illnesses occurring seven days after vaccination, the case against vaccination is even more dramatic. The first interim survey results showed that 24.56% of illness occurred within seven days, when statistically it should only be 1.92%. This rose to 29% when more dogs were added to the survey. *That is to say, the risk of illness is 12.8 (now 13%) times greater than would be expected if vaccines had nothing to do with the illness. This t-Test gave a t value of 4.69, with alpha at 1%. For the non-statistician, this means that the vaccine/illness connection can be expressed with 99% confidence.*

The pie chart on the previous page shows how significant illness is during the first three months following vaccination. 66% of illness occurring during this period compared with a mathematical expectation of 25%: almost three times the number of illnesses you would expect if vaccines had no bearing on the outcome.

Specific diseases highlighted by the first interim survey now follows. Significant new information arising from the second interim analysis is listed at the end of this chapter.

2.7% of all dogs surveyed had arthritis. Of these, 71.8% were diagnosed nine months plus after vaccination. Arthritis in humans has been positively linked to vaccines. The fact that the onset of arthritis clusters at the nine month period indicates that vaccine-induced arthritis has a longer incubation period, or takes longer for overt physical symptoms to manifest. At a 95% confidence interval, we believe that arthritis is caused by vaccination.

The New England Journal of Medicine (vol. 313 no 18, 1985), carried a research report entitled 'Persistent rubella virus infection associated with chronic arthritis in children'. The report confirms that infection or immunisation with rubella virus has been recognised in producing an acute synovitis (inflammation of the joint) . . . which has been reported to recur in certain persons for months or years after the acute stage'. It is also reported that it is often possible to isolate the virus from affected joints in children, vaccinated against rubella, many months after the vaccination.

Arthritis can be either inflammatory or noninflammatory. Stratton *Vaccines:* 97 carries case reports linking tetanus and diphtheria vaccines with arthritis and skin eruptions. The US National Academy of Sciences IOM report concluded that the measles vaccine can cause death from measles-vaccine-strain infection, thrombocytopenia, fatal shock and arthritis. Measles and distemper are, as you know, virtually the same virus. Transient arthritis follows rubella vaccination (Am J Child Dis, 1969), and pain in wrists, hands and knees (JAMA, 1970). One study reported that as many as 26% of children receiving rubella vaccination develop arthritis (Science, 1977). A study by the Institutes of Medicine in America concluded that there was evidence of a causal relationship between the rubella vaccine and acute arthritis in 13-15% of adult women.

As arthritis has been clearly linked to a number of different vaccines, it would be blinkered to discount the possibility that canine vaccines can also cause arthritis in the light of these survey findings.

Indeed, a paper appearing in the British Veterinary Journal during May 1995, by Bell, Carter, May and Bennett, tells us that dogs with rheumatoid arthritis showed higher anti-heat shock proteins (HSP) antibodylevels in both their sera and synovial fluids, compared to control dogs. The paper states that there was a significant correlation between anti-HSP65 and antibodies to the canine distemper virus, and discussed the relevance of the presence of canine distemper virus within the joint. As humans are known to develop vaccine-induced arthritis, then it is perfectly obvious that the distemper vaccine could also cause this condition.

Diarrhoea

Where dogs had diarrhoea, 68% of cases occurred within the first three months after vaccination. 4.9% of dogs surveyed had diarrhoea at some stage. This could be a mild anaphylactic reaction. Anaphylactic reactions can be an indication that encephalitis might follow. You will already have seen how encephalitis (inflammation of the brain) has been shown to follow vaccination, even where no overt reaction has occurred. Incidentally, anaphylaxis and anaphylactic shock are not the same thing. Anaphylaxis is a Type 1 hypersensitivity reaction which involves the release of histamine. Anaphylactic shock is an extreme allergic reaction that could result in death. At 99% confidence interval, diarrhoea is highly likely to be vaccine related. The data satisfies the one-tail test but not the two-tail test, so more data (more completed survey questionnaires) will help.

Allergies

Where dogs had allergies, 55.6% occurred within the first three months after vaccination. 3.8% of dogs surveyed had allergies. This indicates that vaccines do, indeed, 'sensitise' an organism. At 99% confidence, we are certain that allergies are triggered by vaccines.

Of course, Merck has already told us that patients suffering from B and T cell immunodeficiencies should not receive live virus vaccines. Deficiency symptoms include atopic (inherited) diseases such as allergies. Dr Robert Gouch of Baylor University, Houston, Texas reported to the US Public Health Committee in 1982 that a worsening of allergic symptoms occurred in six out of seven people immunised against flu. It wouldn't take too great a leap of imagination to understand that other vaccines can provoke hypersensitivity reactions and could quite easily invoke or worsen allergic conditions. Frick and Brooks, in 1983, demonstrated that vaccines can trigger atopic dermatitis. As over half the dogs in the CHC survey first became allergic within three months of vaccination, we strongly suggest that further research be conducted to establish the relationship between vaccines and allergic conditions. **This research, rather than being based upon experiment, could be simply accomplished if vets or the Veterinary Medicines Directorate took a serious look at patient records.**

Ataxia

At 95% confidence, it is very probable that ataxia (muscle incoordination caused by lesions throughout the nervous system) is caused by vaccines, with a high percentage starting within three months of vaccination.

Merck has already told us that encephalitis can extend to the central nervous system, and encephalitis can result in lesions.

Autoimmune disease

54.8% of dogs in the survey had this condition within the first three months after vaccination. However, there were abnormally low incidences occurring at the six month and nine month intervals, which may be explained by delays in diagnosis. We can now say that AI related diseases, at a 95% confidence interval, are vaccine-related.

Merck acknowledges that autoimmune disease can follow rabies vaccination in which, 'cross-reaction probably is initiated by animal brain tissue in the vaccine'. As dogs in the UK are not yet subjected to the rabies vaccine, we must either assume (upon the evidence that nearly half of dogs in the survey with autoimmune disease developed it within three months of vaccination) that either other canine vaccines are developed on brain tissue, or that vaccines not cultured on brain tissue can also initiate autoimmune diseases. Merck tells us that details of the autoimmune response are incompletely understood. We do, though, know from other research that autoimmune haemolytic anaemia, Hashimotos thyroiditis, cancer, leukaemia, atopic dermatitis, and other autoimmune diseases are positively associated with vaccination.

Colitis

Where dogs had colitis, 56.9% occurred within the first three months after vaccination. 2.7% of dogs surveyed had colitis. This finding may help current research seeking to establish the vaccine/colitis/irritable bowel link in humans. At 95% confidence, the survey indicates strongly that colitis is a sequel to vaccination. As colitis and diarrhoea overlap, the case could be considered to be even stronger.

The Concise Oxford Veterinary Dictionary defines colitis as inflammation of the colon and says it is also associated with concurrent enteritis, which it defines as an acute or chronic inflammation of the mucosa of any part of the intestines. Crohn's disease, an inflammatory bowel disease which can affect any part of the digestive tract in humans, has been associated with vaccination by Dr Andrew Wakefield of the Royal Free Hospital in London (*The Lancet Vol 345*, 1995).

Dry eye/conjunctivitis

Where dogs had dry eye or conjunctivitis, 56.9% occurred within the first three months after vaccination. 2.5% of dogs surveyed had this complaint. According to the homoeopathic vet Richard Pitcairn, the vaccine has induced chronic (long lasting) conjunctivitis, rather than distemper-induced conjunctivitis. At 99% confidence, we are certain that dry eye and conjunctivitis can be caused by vaccines. Frick and Brooks' research highlighting the incidence of atopic dermatitis following vaccination showed that conjunctivitis could also be involved. Conjunctivitis is described as a Type 1 hypersensitivity reaction in the *Concise Oxford Veterinary Dictionary*.

Epilepsy

Where dogs had epilepsy, 65.5% occurred within the first three months after vaccination. 2.1% of the dogs surveyed had epilepsy. Epilepsy is essentially a neurological condition; scientific evidence has already been given to explain that vaccines can cause brain palsy and lesions, leading to epilepsy (this is tied in with encephalitis, admitted by vaccine manufacturers to be a possible effect of vaccination). The surveys allows a 99% certainty that epilepsy can be caused by vaccines, and that the most common cause of epilepsy in dogs is vaccines.

Loss of appetite

Where owners reported a loss of appetite in their dogs, 79.8% were within 3 months after vaccination. 3.4% of dogs surveyed suffered a loss of appetite at some stage. Loss of appetite is vaccine related at 95% confidence.

Nasal discharges

Where dogs showed nasal discharges, 84.1% occurred within 3 months of vaccination. 1.7% of dogs surveyed had nasal discharges. At 99% confidence interval, it is a certainty that nasal discharges are vaccine related. Indeed, as Dr Richard Pitcairn has stated, "a dog with distemper would have watery discharge of eyes and nose; a dog with chronic vaccine-induced distemper would have a tendency for watery fluid to drip from the nose".

Nervous/worrying disposition

Where dogs exhibited a nervous or worrying disposition, 54.8% began to do so within three months after vaccination. 2.8% of dogs surveyed suffered from this complaint. **This is THE certainty of** the survey! It has the highest t-score of any group, i.e., 19.9. Combined with another category - behavioural problems - we can say without a shadow of a doubt that vaccines cause total personality changes in dogs. Of course, we know that encephalitis can be caused by vaccines. This fact is irrefutable.

Skin problems

Where dogs had skin problems, 46.2% started within three months after vaccination. 5.4% of dogs surveyed had skin problems. This, again, supports the contention that vaccines sensitise an organism. Again, with a 99% confidence, we can be certain that vaccines cause skin problems. Research conducted by Frick and Brooks in 1983 illustrates graphically that skin problems can be induced by vaccines.

Vomiting

Where owners reported vomiting in their dogs, 72.5% occurred within 3 months of vaccination. 3% of dogs surveyed were reported to have vomited. This, of course, can be described as an anaphylactic reaction which can develop into encephalitis. Dr JA Morris, a leading US infectious disease expert declared: "We only hear about the encephalitis and the deaths, but there is an entire spectrum between fever and death, and it's all those things in between that never get reported". Vomiting after vaccination can be expressed as a vaccine reaction, as a certainty at the 95% confidence interval.

Weight loss

Where owners reported weight loss in their dogs, 63.1% were within three months after vaccination. 2.5% of dogs in the survey had lost weight. At 99% confidence, weight loss is directly connected to vaccination.

The legal firm Dawbarns has been acting on behalf of parents whose children were vaccine damaged. Their fact sheet describes vaccine-induced Crohn's disease which, it says, 'can also be accompanied by joint pains and swelling, and conjunctivitis of the eyes. It can take many years to develop, but with children the first symptom is often malabsorption and failure to thrive'.

Behavioural problems

Where owners reported behavioural problems, 55.4% occurred within three months after vaccination. 2.5% of all dogs surveyed had behavioural problems. This, then, supports Dr Harris L Coulter's hypothesis that much human violence, sociopathy and criminality is vaccine linked, and has its basis in brain damage caused by vaccines. At a 99% confidence interval, we are now certain that behavioural problems are largely vaccine related.

The law firm Dawbarns says of autistic children (autism is thought to be a range symptoms including brain damage): "Before they were vaccinated they (according to their parents) were developing perfectly normally, passing all milestones and showing none of the classical signs of autism. After being vaccinated they regressed (sometimes only within a few days), losing metal, physical and social skills." Dawbarns adds, "*If a teenager takes Ecstasy and becomes ill or dies, it is IMMEDIATELY concluded that the illness or death was caused by the drug. But if a child becomes ill or dies after vaccination, it is dismissed as mere coincidence.*"

Tumour or growth at vaccination site

Where dogs had tumours or growths at vaccination site, 67.9% occurred within three months of vaccination. 1.1% of all dogs surveyed suffered from this occurrence. It is well recorded in the medical/veterinary literature that cancer/tumours can (and do) grow at vaccine sites. With 95% confidence, we are certain that tumours or growths at vaccination sites are caused by the vaccination process itself.

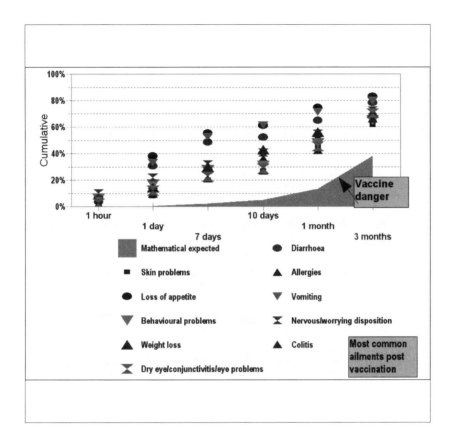

All of the above figures had z alpha scores of greater than 5, and showed a distinct tendency to occur during the first three months after vaccination. This means that there is a link between vaccines and the above illnesses which, in turn, means that the vaccine/illness link is a certainty.

The graph above, based on consolidated survey data, shows how so many illnesses occur during the first three months post vaccination and how many types of illness cluster so closely together. Such clusters indicate that vaccine induced diseases are not a matter of fluke situations.

To increase statistical confidence, we need more completed questionnaires to study the patterns of each of the following diseases, although the interim figures do give rise for concern:

Cancer - 31% within 3 months

Chorea - 63.2% within 3 months (note: although we would like more data, the data that we do have indicates at a 99% confidence interval that this disease is vaccine-related. Chorea is, in fact, involuntary jerking of the muscles due to degenerative lesions of nerve cells. It is common in dogs with distemper when the fever has subsided; residual brain damage is revealed as chorea. This, once again, supports Harris L Coulter's proposition that vaccines can cause brain damage.)

Encephalitis - 75% within 3 months (note: at 95% confidence, it is highly probable that vaccination caused the encephalitis.)

Heart conditions - 26.8% within 3 months (note: even though only 26.8% occurred within the first three months after vaccination, we can say that, from the statistical evidence, it is very likely that heart conditions can be caused by vaccination. More data would help us resolve this.)

Kidney damage - 40.5% within three months (note: we are only 90% confident that it is probable that kidney damage follows vaccination.)

Lameness - 52% within three months (note: statistically, it is a 99% certainty that lameness can be caused by vaccination.)

Liver damage - 47% within three months (note: we are 90% certain that, statistically, liver damage can follow vaccination)

Paralysis of rear end - 64.7% within three months (it is very likely - at 95% confidence interval - that this condition is caused by vaccines)

Pancreas problems - 31.6% within three months (note: these are likely to be related to vaccines at a 90% confidence interval)

Short attention span - 68.4% within three months (note: we would like more data concerning dogs with this problem, although we can say that, even with the limited data, we are 99% confident that this is vaccine related)

Dogs contracting the diseases they were vaccinated against:

Hepatitis - 63.6% occurred within three months of vaccination

Parainfluenza - 50% occurred within three months of vaccination (note: it is highly probable that parainfluenza can be caused by vaccines, at 95% confidence interval)

Parvovirus - 68.2% occurred within three months of vaccination (note: at 95% confidence, this satisfies the one-tail test but not the two-tail. More data would allow us to prove whether vaccines cause the disease they are designed to prevent, in this case parvovirus)

Distemper - 55.6% occurred within three months of vaccination

Leptospirosis - 100% of dogs contracted leptospirosis within three months of vaccination (note: according to the data we have, leptospirosis is related to vaccination at a 90% confidence interval.)

With the exception of distemper and leptospirosis, where not enough dogs with the disease were recorded, all of the above satisfy a z alpha score of more than three. This means that we are 99.53% certain that there is a strong causal link between vaccination and the onset of the diseases.

In all cases, at least half of the dogs with each of the viral diseases contracted them within three months of vaccination. This supports the view that vaccines either don't protect, or can cause the disease itself.

A paper published in Vet Microbiology during October 1993, by Blixenkrone-Moller, et al, showed that in a distemper outbreak during 1991, severe clinical cases were diagnosed in both vaccinated and unvaccinated individuals.

Probability of vaccine reaction

Although we need more dog owners to participate in the survey, we are able to make tentative prognoses regarding the likelihood of a vaccine reaction in an individual dog.

Critics might say that the survey attracted dog owners whose dogs appeared to have experienced a reaction, thereby creating a bias in the survey. This is answered by the fact that a good number of people with perfectly healthy dogs participated; many participants were approached at random (by knocking on doors); and many participants had several dogs, only some of whom, and in some cases none, were said to be ill.

We know that the initial analysis showed that 55% of illnesses occurred within the first three months after vaccination. We have compared this data with the total number of dogs (2,628) in the survey.

One veterinary vaccine manufacturer claimed that 15 adverse reactions occurred in three million administered doses (.000005 probability). If this is realistic, then our personal experience of having six dogs (100%) experience a vaccine reaction is mathematically impossible. Mathematically it only requires a cluster of seven adverse reaction reports coming in during a narrow time frame for the claimed probability of 0.000005 to be rejected. **Resulting from the combined data we can now estimate that the likelihood of a reaction to vaccination in a dog is at least 3%. This is about 30,000 times more risky than that accepted for human vaccines.**

According to the Pet Food Manufacturers Association, the UK dog population is approximately 7 million, a figure that we believe from other data to be on the high side, but which we will use for the purposes of the argument.

We also extrapolated that the maximum number of dogs whose owners were aware of the survey was about 270,000. Assuming that out of this population, only 607 dogs had any illnesses and the healthy dogs' owners therefore decided not to participate (an extremely unrealistic hypothesis), then the probability of a vaccine related illness or reaction drops to .0077778. Even at this highly unlikely level, this means that the risk of adverse reaction to vaccination is at least 1,556 times greater than admitted by one manufacturer.

In reality, we can be reasonably sure that the probability of a vaccine related illness is vastly under reported/admitted by manufacturers and authorities such as the Veterinary Medicines Directorate. It demonstrates clearly the need for a proper system of verification and compliance regarding the use of vaccines and other manufactured medicines.

Looking at the reactions/illnesses reported after vaccination in the survey, we have a probability of .7990868. In view of some of the above statistics, it is not unreasonable to conclude that the probability of a vaccine-related disease occurring is in the order of 1% (i.e., one in a hundred).

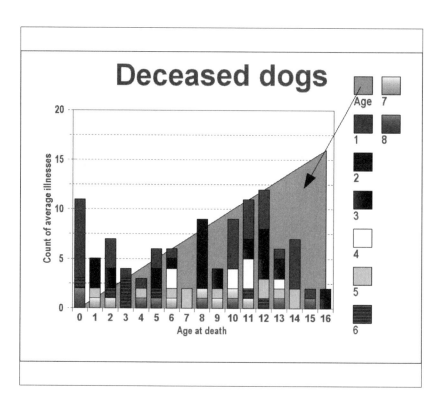

Age and illness

It is commonly believed that, as a dog gets older, the incidence of illness will increase. This has not been our personal experience, and the vaccine survey does not support this view, either. Pictorially shown in the graph above.

The data we have relates to dogs ranging from a few weeks old to over 19 years of age. The conclusion from this survey is that a dog can become ill at any age - there was no statistical bias between the incidence of illness and the ages of the dogs covered in the survey.

Neither was there a correlation between the number of illnesses per dog and their respective ages. This suggests that vaccine reactions may not simply be a hereditary/genetic problem, as is often suggested by vaccine manufacturers, but more related to environmental factors. It might also support the statement by Dr Ronald D Schultz, that these reactions are a result of "the accumulation of many antigens over many years. I believe that adverse effects are increasing because we are putting more and more components into these animals."

Environment

The majority of respondents were UK residents (England, Scotland and Wales). The remaining respondents were from the USA, Canada, New Zealand and the Channel Islands. After analysing the two batches of combined data we can rule out environmental factors having any relevance to illnesses in dogs.

Dogs who were never vaccinated

Only a small number of dogs in the survey had never been vaccinated. We need more data about unvaccinated dogs, including dogs protected exclusively with homoeopathic nosodes, before conclusions can be drawn. So if you have an unvaccinated dog, please contact us for a questionnaire. It will take you only ten minutes to complete.

Dog ownership

A person who has kept dogs for many years is just as likely to experience illness in their dogs as a person who has had a dog for a short time, indicating that experienced husbandry has little bearing on the rate of illness.

Type of vaccine used

Based on combined survey data, we checked to see if it might be better to give annual boosters, or to give a puppy its initial course of vaccines and none thereafter. The risk of vaccine reaction appears to be the same irrespective of regime - initial only or annual vaccination. Nor are killed vaccines any safer than modified live vaccines.

Additional Analysis

Based on the data gained after publication of the first edition of this book, we compared the profile of the second batch of data with the first. The objective was to ascertain whether or not we had received any different data that would invalidate previous conclusions. The second batch of data was a very close match to the first batch and statistically it can be concluded that the first and second batches of data are identical as to content. Consolidating the two batches of data together allowed some more detailed levels of investigation. Significantly, the rankings of different diseases and ailments following vaccination did not change materially compared with the previous analysis.

In order of most significance, the following diseases occurred within three months of vaccination. Where we have large Chi scores, this tends to reflect that the disease was reported in large numbers of dogs in the survey, highlighting the fact that more dogs to study = more valid conclusions:

> **Ataxia** - 91% occurred within three months of vaccination. This can be caused by lesions throughout the central nervous system (Concise Oxford Veterinary Dictionary). The previous analysis showed that, with a 95% confidence, Ataxia was caused by vaccines. Additional data allows us to attribute a Chi score of 29 and, as stated previously, a Chi score of 13 gives a 99% confidence. On which basis, without any

hesitation whatsoever, we say that the most common cause of Ataxia is vaccination.

Nasal discharges - 87% occurred within three months of vaccination. Previous analysis was 84%. The Chi score is now 125.

Loss of appetite - 83% occurred within three months of vaccination. Previous analysis was 79.8%. The Chi score is now 213.

Tumour or growth at vaccine site - this has climbed from 67.9% to 81.1%. There is a Chi score of 62.

Chorea - this has climbed from 63.2% and is now 81%. Chi score is 36.

Vomiting - climbed from 72.5% and is now 79.7% with a Chi score of 190.

Encephalitis occurring within three months of vaccination has risen from 75% to 78.6%. The Chi score for this is 22. It's interesting that this is a known and acknowledged vaccine reaction, and our survey shows well above a 99% certainty that it's vaccine related - but some other diseases which are not acknowledge as vaccine reactions show even higher Chi scores.

Diarrhoea - first interim results showed that 68% of the dogs in the survey with diarrhoea developed it within three months of vaccination. This has now risen to 78.4%. The Chi score is 290. Thus it is absolutely certain (not surprisingly) that vaccines can induce diarrhoea. Not too much of a problem if underlying encephalitis isn't involved.

Hepatitis - initially 63.6% and now risen to 75%. Chi score is 17, i.e., 99.5% confidence that hepatitis was caused by vaccines in the dogs in our survey.

Short attention span - was 68.4% and now risen to 73.1%. The Chi score is 34. Again, this offers extremely strong proof (99.9% certainty) that dogs with short attention spans are vaccine damaged.

Epilepsy/fits/convulsions - 65.5% of dogs in the first interim analysis developed epilepsy within three months of vaccination. This has now risen to 73.1%, with a Chi score of 96. We would say that the majority of dogs in our survey with epilepsy are vaccine damaged.

Nervous, worrying disposition - this was the certainty in the previous survey, with 54.8% developing the condition within three months of vaccination, bringing a t score of 19.9. The percentage has now risen to 72.5% and a Chi score of 112. Yet another cast iron example of vaccine-induced brain damage.

Weight loss - was 63.1% and has grown to 70.3% developing within three months of vaccination; with a Chi score of 101.

Dry eye/conjunctivitis - was 56.9%, now risen to 70.2% with a Chi score of 95. Again, this is a vaccine-induced condition.

Paralysis of rear end - was 64.7%, now risen to 69.2% with Chi score of 28.

Allergies - was 55.6%, and has now risen to 69.2% with a Chi score of 136. Allergies are caused or worsened by vaccines with a certainty above 99.9%

Parvovirus - in the previous analysis 68.2% of dogs with this disease developed it within three months of vaccination. This has now risen to 69%, giving a Chi score of 33. We were only able to say with a 95% confidence in the first analysis that parvovirus can be vaccine-induced. We are now able to say with a 99.9% certainty that it can (was).

Lameness - was 52%, now 66.7% with a Chi score 66. A vet was reported in the UK media during 1998, saying that we shouldn't allow our dogs upstairs as this is the cause of lameness!

Distemper - was 55.6%, now risen to 66.7%, with a Chi score of 12. Despite scientific research which shows that distemper can be vaccine induced, we can only give you a 95% confidence level of this fact.

Colitis - was 54.8%, now 65.9% with a Chi score of 79. Obviously, colitis can be vaccine induced. Vets: please check your practice records.

Behavioural problems - 55.4% of dogs in the first analysis developed behavioural problems within three months of vaccination. This has risen to 64.9% with a Chi score of 80. This gives a 99.9% certainty that the dogs with behavioural problems in our survey were brain damaged by vaccines.

Liver damage/failure - the number of dogs in the survey with liver damage/failure within three months of vaccination rose from 47% to 61.5%, with a Chi score of 29. Previously, we were only able to offer a 90% confidence that liver damage and/or failure was vaccine-induced. It is now 99.9% certain that liver damage/failure is a vaccine-induced condition.

Skin problems - 46.2% of dogs in the first analysis developed skin problems within three months of vaccination. This has risen to 61.2% of dogs, with a Chi of 130. A certainty at 99.99%.

Autoimmune disease - was 54.8%, now risen to 55.8% with a Chi of 26. As it is acknowledged by Merck that vaccines can initiate autoimmune disease, all we can do is confirm the experts' opinion.

Parainfluenza - 50% of dogs with parainfluenza within the first analysis had been vaccinated against it within three months of getting it. This has now risen to 55.7% with a Chi score of 39. In the previous analysis we could only offer a 95% confidence that the parainfluenza vaccine could cause the disease. Now we are 99.9% certain.

Pancreas problems - was 31.6% and is now 54.2%, with a Chi score of 13, i.e., a 99% confidence that vaccines can induce pancreas problems.

Kidney damage - was 40.5% and has risen to 53.7%, with a Chi score of 20. Again, if you don't want your dog to develop kidney damage, steer clear of vaccines.

There were only small numbers of dogs with leukaemia, asthma and meningitis in the survey and although around 50% of the dogs with these diseases contracted them within three months of a vaccine event, because of the small numbers involved, we can only give low Chi scores. Dog owners - please contact us for a questionnaire.

Heart condition - 26.8% of dogs with a heart condition first developed the condition within three months of vaccination. This has risen to 39.2% with a Chi score of 12, offering a 95% certainty that vaccines can induce this condition.

Arthritis - the original analysis revealed that 71.8% of dogs with arthritis developed it within the third quarter after vaccination. Further data reveals that 37.8% got it within the first three months after vaccination, and only 21% in the third quarter. Our Chi score is still 13, giving a 99% confidence that arthritis in dogs in our survey is vaccine induced. It is interesting to note that the New England Journal of Medicine (vol 313, 1985), reported that it is often possible to isolate the rubella virus from affected joints in children vaccinated against rubella, many months after vaccination. The report tells of isolation of viruses from the peripheral blood of women with prolonged arthritis which followed vaccination. As, statistically, our survey indicates a strong vaccine-arthritis association, we feel that further research should be carried out. It could be that many viruses can stimulate arthritis and, particularly, the immune mechanisms following vaccination with a live virus vaccine.

Cancer - 31% of dogs in the first analysis with cancer developed it within three months of vaccination. This has risen to 35.1%, with a Chi score of 15. This raises serious alarm. Indeed, we urge that those with the ability should look seriously at the vaccine link in relation to cancer. More research - looking at the onset of disease in relation to a vaccine event - could benefit animals and man.

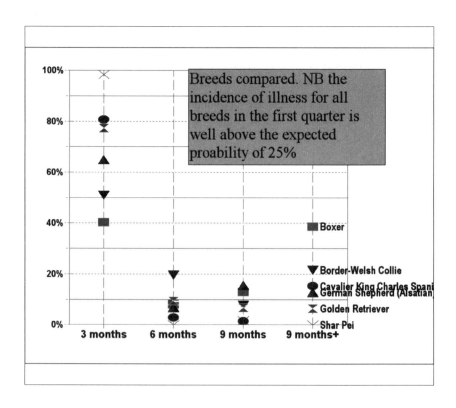

Breeds compared. NB the incidence of illness for all breeds in the first quarter is well above the expected proability of 25%

Genetic Pre-Disposition, or Vaccine Damage?

Although John and I have never bred a dog, we have always intuitively doubted the assertion that most illnesses in dogs can be attributed to irresponsible or faulty breeding practices. We have sufficient data from a number of breeds to say that the genetic issue is a red herring without justification. We had sufficient data to look specifically at a number of breeds, and found that Golden Retrievers, German Shepherds, Shar-Peis, Border Collies, Boxers, and Cavalier King Charles Spaniels all showed a high incidence of illness in the first three months following vaccination. Mathematically speaking, the propensity to illness within these breeds is the same. The myth has told us that Border Collies, bred predominantly as workers, were hardier than other breeds, and that Shar-Peis hadn't been westernised for long enough to suffer from irresponsible breeding. German Shepherds and Goldens, on the other hand, are said to be genetically compromised as they are so popular and therefore bred like rabbits. Or maybe, on the other hand, all these breeds are genetically defective . . . . in which case, maybe all dogs are genetically defective and vaccination should not - as indicated by Merck - take place.

As can be seen in the graph on the previous page, these breeds all showed a marked propensity to illness in the first three months following vaccination and the clusters for the other quarters were very tight.

Dr Dodds has questioned why it is that big dogs and small dogs should have the same amount of vaccine. We have therefore checked to see whether illnesses are more common in small dogs than large dogs, or vice versa. **We have found that size makes no difference, nor does it matter whether or not the vaccine used was killed, live, or a mix.**

Similarly, a puppy is just as prone to a vaccine reaction as an adult. Although illnesses can appear to clear up and then get worse upon re-vaccination, any vaccine, at any time, at any age, can invoke disease. And reactions can happen at any time of year. This raises a question about the quality of the vaccines used, and suggests variability in manufacture. **It also highlights the false assumption that a puppy shot plus a booster is safe. It is not. Each time you vaccinate, you are relying upon luck.**

Each class was subdivided into type of vaccine - killed, live or mixed with a fourth column where dog owners were unsure as to type. Statistically there is no difference in the results of any of the data at 99% confidence. The hashed bars show the incidence of illness for dogs which only received an inital vaccintion on the graph below.

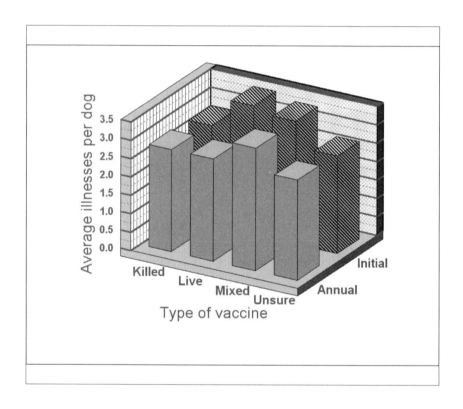

Geography?

We can also now rule out geographical environment as having any bearing on the likelihood of vaccine reaction. Comparing data from England, Scotland, Wales and North America, a dog is just as likely to have a vaccine reaction irrespective of the country involved.

Epilogue

Much has happened in the first year of this book's existence. Jo Knowsley of *The Sunday Telegraph* (a quality UK national newspaper) featured our survey findings, and this caused quite a stir with the media. I was invited to talk on several radio programmes, and also on TV. But each time the researchers spoke to vaccine companies or the veterinary establishment, the programme seemed to change dramatically and I was frequently dis-invited. One journalist who works in the national press told me that if she mentioned my name in a column, she had angry letters and phone calls from vets who felt that the views expressed in this book shouldn't be given space.

The veterinary establishment came out against the vaccine survey before it was even published. That is, they made statements to the media that the research was wrong and vaccines were incredibly safe before they even got to see what they were commenting on. One local radio programme gave me about two minutes to explain the contents of this book before cutting me off and allowing a media vet to rant and rave about the wonders of vaccines. Very frustrating. The next time I went on the radio with a vet, I had the station fax me a confirmation that I wouldn't be cut off - but the vet simply shouted over me, drowning me out. I'm learning as I go along!

The survey findings went to Dr JM Rutter, head of the Veterinary Medicine's Directorate, before the book was published. Dr Rutter offered no adverse comments about the research. Although he didn't seek to take matters further, he did define an adverse reaction for us:

> *"A serious adverse reaction is defined as one which is fatal, life threatening, lesion producing, disabling, incapacitating, or which results in permanent or prolonged symptoms in the animal treated."*

. . . which sort of covers every animal in this book.

A few weeks after publication of this book, and five days after Samson's death, The National Office of Animal Health (a trade association representing drug and vaccine manufacturers) held a press conference to launch a briefing document for worried pet owners. *'The Veterinary Record'* reported, "Aimed at the pet owner, the document is intended to help veterinary surgeons in practice give clear information to clients on the safety and importance of vaccinating pet animals."

A veterinary spokesman at the press conference spoke of the dreadful diseases we vaccinate against, and how important it was to continue vaccinating. "Veterinary surgeons needed to convince their clients that vaccines were safe, effective and necessary," the report stated, without which, "killer diseases could be very difficult and expensive to treat."

Peter Bowen, a retired vet, urged veterinary surgeons to make clear to their clients how much cost and suffering would be involved should their pet contract one of these diseases. "If a dog gets a disease like distemper," he said, "apart from the distress caused, and assuming it survives, the cost will be much, much higher than that of giving an original vaccination."

After I had spoken at one seminar, a vet came up to me to say that distemper and parvo are very, very rare these days. At another seminar, John Saxton, a homoeopathic vet, pointed out that the diseases induced by vaccines can be just as cruel as the diseases we're vaccinating against. In fact, vaccine-induced disease can be every bit as costly and expensive as the diseases NOAH wants us to vaccinate against.

Personally, while I'm not rich, I would say that cost doesn't come into it. We want our dogs, cats, horses, rabbits, ferrets and children to be safe. And we don't want to be frightened into doing something to our animals by people who stand to benefit financially from our decision. True, vets and vaccine manufacturers might genuinely believe that vaccines are necessary and safe - but they should start trying to convince us on the science, not the psychology of fear.

Meanwhile, dog owners in America had compared notes and felt that over a hundred of their puppies had died as a result of one batch of one brand of vaccine - from a manufacturer supplying worldwide. So the owners contacted the vaccine manufacturer, who said: "Not our problem, pal."

In America, you can buy vaccines yourself and inject them yourself, and consequently one of the owners had quite a few of the vaccines left. She tried to have it tested but could find no-one who was both willing and able. So we contacted Professor Richard Lacey, an eminent microbiologist and man of integrity, and asked him if he would test it. He agreed.

The trouble was that, in order to test the viral component of a vaccine, you need a license. And guess who has the licences? The vaccine manufacturers. So Professor Lacey was only able to test for bacterial contamination. As it happens, they were bacterially sound which, according to Professor Lacey, was bad news. If the vaccine did kill all those puppies, and if there's no bacterial contamination, then it's a process problem - i.e., an ongoing problem.

Professor Lacey worked with us to prepare a press release which went out to the dog papers in the UK. It read:

> *"Professor Richard Lacey, one of the UK's most eminent scientists and the man who exposed the BSE problem to the world, has lent his weight to Canine Health Concern's campaign which seeks to protect dogs from unnecessary and harmful vaccine practices.*

> *"Professor Lacey, who served on the Ministry of Agriculture Veterinary Products Committee (VPC) between 1984 and 1989, told CHC that veterinary vaccine manufacturers are totally without proper control. 'The Veterinary Medicines Directorate and the VPC are reliant upon data supplied by the manufacturers themselves, but no one makes them supply that information. It is my belief that serious side-effects are far greater than the number reported. There is no proper*

*monitoring system, no independent check, and there
should be.'*

*"Professor Lacey has confirmed to CHC that only
vaccine manufacturers are able to test vaccines, which
means that if there are any problems, no one except the
vaccine manufacturers need know about them. Professor
Lacey further confirmed that bovine products are used in
vaccine manufacture which, he believes, could certainly
pose a risk of cross-species spongiform encephalopathy
(BSE).*

*"Professor Lacey echoes statements from top US
veterinary immunologists that once immunity to a virus
exists, it generally exists for the lifetime of an animal.
'Vets and kennels are demanding that pets be vaccinated
unnecessarily,' he says, 'and owners are being fleeced.
The veterinary profession and the vaccine manufacturers
should be subject to adequate external monitoring.'"*

Richard Lacey subsequently received a phone call from David
Sutton of Intervet, who told him that he represented NOAH.
Richard called me, feeling that maybe we might face legal action as
a result of the press release. Because David Sutton had placed so
much emphasis on the need to vaccinate against leptospirosis
annually, Professor Lacey decided to do a literature search on the
disease. He discovered that there are around 150 strains of the
virus, and you can't get all 150 in the vaccine. He concluded that
the vaccine is all but useless and should be withdrawn from the
market, especially in view of Australian research that poses serious
questions about side-effects (and remember, the vaccine lasts for
only between three and nine months).

The magazine, *'Mad About Dogs'* printed the story, as did *'Dog
World'*. I didn't see any other reports in the half-dozen or so dog
publications in the UK. *'Mad About Dogs'* has since been put down.
A report in *'Media Gazette'* attributed this to the fact that two major
pet food manufacturers, which accounted for between 35 and 40

per cent of advertising revenue, had decided to focus their advertising budget for the next two years on TV.

Meanwhile, before publication of the book, we offered our survey findings as an exclusive to 'Dog World'. The editor declined to accept the findings on the basis that they should be published in a scientific journal. Half page advertisements from Intervet, a vaccine manufacturer, did appear, though. We obtained back issues of the publication and conducted a media analysis - Intervet's advertisements for SA37, a food supplement, had not appeared in 'Dog World' for several months before my article about vaccine reactions appeared, but did shortly afterwards. Not that I'm suggesting for one minute that dog-related publications would allow advertising revenue to affect editorial content. 'Dog World' is one of the few papers that has given space to both sides of the argument.

We offered free copies of the first edition of this book to all the UK's dog publications, as well as veterinary publications. Only the now defunct 'Mad About Dogs' requested a copy. I would have thought that they would at least want to see what all the fuss was about. Surely, as publications for dog lovers and those concerned with animal health, you might expect them to want to be aware of the issues. It was largely left to the non-dog-related media to help raise the concerns. More recently, 'Dog Training Weekly' has taken up the cause, although this publication doesn't rely too heavily on advertising revenue. 'Sporting Dog also carried one of my articles, chiefly because the editor suspected a reaction in one of his dogs.

Canine Health Concern (CHC) also campaigns for healthy diets for dogs. In June of 1998, the Pet Food Manufacturers Association held an external affairs committee meeting with CHC on the agenda. The minutes read that Grayling (a large London PR firm) had been instructed to counteract 'inaccurate information' coming from CHC and that, to this end, a list of friendly journalists was being compiled, as well as a list of friendly processed petfood favouring vets. If you have the budget, it seems you have a greater chance of having your views represented in themedia.

Vets have now had over a year to take note of the evidence contained within the first edition of this book - and not only of the evidence presented within these pages. In September '97, a vaccination symposium was held in America, organised and attended by the world's top vets and immunologists. Unofficial recommendations from this symposium (The First International Veterinary Vaccines and Diagnostics Conference) say that boosters should be given every three years unless required more often by law, but not if the animal has a history of adverse vaccine reaction, immune-mediated disease, or some other immune dysfunction. Geriatric animals do not need booster vaccinations. And animals should only be vaccinated if there is a current risk of disease in the locality. The advice to vets and pet owners was that immunity to viruses following vaccination lasts at least three years and probably more than five years.

In Sweden, Dr Dodds informed me, 83% of dogs vaccinated more than four years previously still had adequate vaccine titers against distemper (Olson, et al, *J Vet Int Med* 11:148,1997, abstr). However, the experts suggested that antibody titers be measured annually between boosters.

Meanwhile, vets continue to vaccinate sick dogs. I know this because a considerable number of their owners have phoned us in tears.

I was invited to sign first edition copies of this book at a bookstand at Crufts, and found myself talking to a vet. He told me that there is no evidence that vaccines are harmful, so I spent some time trying to convince him otherwise. At the end of the conversation he repeated his 'vaccines are harmless' assertion, and then he left the stand without the book - no doubt so that he could continue in his ignorance and retain his fee income levels. Or maybe professionals have trouble listening to dog owners.

Another girl was looking at the book on the stand, so one of the girls went to her and asked if she'd like to speak with the author. "Certainly not!", she said. "I am a veterinary nurse!" And then she stomped off.

Another vet phoned from overseas, having read the book. "I have to tell you that I have experienced equally horrific cases of vaccine damage in my practice," he said. "In fact, some more horrific than are illustrated in your book." He continued: "When I left veterinary college in the '70s no-one considered annual vaccination necessary. But in the '80s we were approached by vaccine manufacturers who told us that annual boosters would increase practice income, and allow us to do an annual checkup. We knew it was fraud at the time, but we all went along with it. Now, boosters just seem to have been accepted into the mythology." This particular vet is still giving boosters.

Another vet came to visit from overseas. She told me that she was aware of the issues long before my book was published. However, as she is a locum, she has to do as she's told and vaccinate. She said she tries not to think about it when she does it. I could understand this, but afterwards I thought that if she had vaccinated Oliver, Prudence or Samson knowing the risks and without telling me, I might be less understanding.

Not that I judge anyone. We all do the best we can with the knowledge and the resources available to us at the time. But it kind of illustrates how we must become our own experts, and not rely upon the political, economical, and scientific status of the advice-giver.

But I have some good news for you. The phone rang one day while Sammie was struggling to survive. It was Sue Hawkins, a breeder of Golden Retrievers who hasn't vaccinated for many, many years. I don't know why she phoned, but she did. Sue told me that she had a litter of puppies due in the next few weeks, and she was planning to give them homoeopathic nosodes rather than vaccines. I mentioned that I'd never seen a puppy being born, and Sue invited me to come along and attend. She phoned me one night, but I wasn't able to make it there as I had planned to take Samson to see a healer the next day.

In the meantime, Sammie died. Sue phoned and suggested I come and see the pups, it would cheer me up. So John and I went along to cheer ourselves up, but not to buy. Decoy was there - he was a two-year-old Golden who looked so like Sammie, and he grabbed our arms in his mouth just like Sammie used to do. We wanted to steal him. Unfortunately, Sue wouldn't let us - but fortunately, she did allow us to have two pups. We couldn't resist it. We're real suckers.

Edward and Daniel came to live with us around two months after Sammie went home. I don't know, but I have a feeling Samson went looking for them for us. (Didn't you know that dogs can astral travel?)

So Edward and Daniel have never been vaccinated; they have received the homoeopathic nosodes. Both are unlike any Golden Retriever puppy I have ever known. They are much calmer, for a start - and neither has suffered more than a day's illness in the 18 months of their lives. Quite a novel experience for a reformed Golden Retriever puppy owner who once thought vaccines were necessary. So calm have Edward and Dannie been that I seriously question whether everyone - animal or human - is brain damaged to some extent by vaccines.

We also had our own controlled, albeit unplanned, trial. Believing that geriatric animals would be immune to viruses (if Sophie had reached the age of 14 and Chappie 15 without dying of distemper or parvo, I figured they must surely have developed immunity), so I didn't bother with nosodes for my older dogs. But I forgot about kennel cough, which mutates. Sophie came down with it first, then Chappie, then Gwinnie. It was the middle of winter, snow was thick on the ground outside, all the windows and doors were closed shut . . . but my homoeopathically protected pups *did not contract kennel cough.*

We have since had full blood work done on Edward. He has antibody titers to distemper and parvo - which means that he has come across the diseases or shed vaccine whilst out on walks, but he has not contracted the diseases.

326

So I have to conclude that the nosodes have protected Edward and Daniel against kennel cough, parvo and distemper. Still not a day's illness from either of them. This gives me hope that our hearts will not be broken again - either by vaccine-induced illness, or by the diseases we vaccinate against.

Other good news. The first edition of this book became a word-of-mouth best-seller, and the second edition has a distributor, which means it will make it into the shops and will be more easily available to animal lovers (providing the shops order it). This means that there are thousands of people out there who now have a choice. Many of them, who now realise why their dogs died unnecessarily, have already organised seminars for me to speak at, or volunteered to help in some other way to spread the message.

I've even been invited to speak to about a hundred vets down in the South of England. This hasn't taken place yet, and I can tell you I'm both nervous and grateful that they, finally, are beginning to listen.

I wrote the previous paragraph while feeling particularly optimistic. Since then, Intervet has offered to sponsor the seminar. I had a phone call to tell me that I would receive a fee, and my expenses would be paid. Sounds good - but is it? First a big business offers to sponsor a seminar. Then they offer to sponsor a bursary at your college. Then they pay for a few research projects, and then a new library wing, and pretty soon you're frightened to upset them lest they take their money away. So Canine Health Concern offered to pay the room hire charge and buy dinner for the vets. It's good, anyway, that a group representing vets' clients should host this breakthrough dialogue.

The seminar takes place the day after a television documentary - World in Action - is due to air. Readers of The Celestine Prophesy will understand what I mean when a say that a coincidence led me to meet the producer (on a Reiki course, of all places). Having introduced the production team to every 'expert' on the subject I know, and also pointed towards the key people 'on the other side', I have no idea how the programme will turn out. But you have to walk through the door when the Great Mystery opens it for you.

Many continue to say that I (and others) are talking rubbish, but I think this is because they have turned their backs on the words we have so painstakingly set out for them. Vaccine-associated ostrich disease. But have patience. For there is hope. Ordinary people, from around the world, are making change happen. Our animals are not voiceless - for they have us to defend them. Eventually, the 'experts' will hear us. For I know one thing: annual vaccination is going through the last painful spasms of death. Soon it will be gone for good. RIP.

I wish you long life, joy and an abiding sense of wonder and gratitude. For this is a beautiful world, made more beautiful by the dogs, cats, horses and children we share our lives with. I am so thankful, despite the pain of loss, to have been blessed by the presence of Oliver, Prudence and Samson - for if they have died in order that others can live, I know they would be so pleased with you who have listened.

Thank you for giving their lives meaning.

Conclusions

There is a building catalogue of evidence to suggest that vaccines, whether by specific batch or by brand, are a cause of significant ill health and death in the canine species. It is clear that the current methods of compliance are inadequate, and will always be in doubt whilst there is a lack of common mathematical standards and an absence of objective, open-minded regulation.

We believe that the first and second interim reports demonstrate the significant value of dog owners comparing their experiences, and hope that it prompts other dog owners to participate. Participation in the CHC vaccine survey is free and should take only a little of your time. Importantly, no animals were used in laboratories to arrive at these results.

Additional analysis needs to be performed, as we require considerably more completed questionnaires if mathematically valid conclusions are to be made across the board. A great deal more analysis could be done - and a great deal more could be discovered - if we had more completed questionnaires to add to the database. Dog lovers are therefore invited to take advantage of this opportunity to gain valuable insight for the benefit of dogs and dog owners. Vaccine questionnaires are available from the CHC at the address below - please enclose a large (12" x 9") stamped, self-addressed envelope.

Veterinary surgeons interested in this work are also invited to participate and are urged to study their own patient records to see whether a similar pattern can be established.

Canine Health Concern,

PO Box 1, Longnor,

Derbyshire SK17 0JD

Selected References/Bibliography - and suggested further reading.

To locate a qualified homoeopathic vet, ask your local vet to refer you.

To investigate whether your dog might have thyroid disease, you can either ask your local vet to conduct a blood test, or you can send a blood sample to Dr Jean Dodds (you need to ensure that it arrives the next day). Dr Dodds' address is: Hemopet, 938 Stanford Street, Santa Monica, California 90403, USA. Hemopet tests beyond the normal T4 analysis to detect underlying thyroid disease.

To participate in the Canine Health Census, please send a large self-addressed envelope (stamped in the UK, but with an international reply paid postal coupon if outside the UK), to The Canine Health Census, PO Box 1, Longnor, Derbyshire SK17 OJD, England.

In addition to looking at the vaccine question, we are also studying the effects of other genetic and environmental factors.

Contact addresses

for further information on vaccines, animal issues, and environmental issues
- Association of Parents of Vaccine Damaged Children 2 Church Street Shipston on Stour Warwickshire CV36 4AP UK
- BAVA (British Anti Vivisection Association) PO Box 82 Kingswood Bristol BS15 1YF England
- Campaign to Ban Genetically Engineered Food Natural Law Party Mentmore Buckinghamshire LU7 OQH UK The International Vaccine Newsletter Louise Maguire Foundation Krekenstraat 4 B-3600 Genk Belgium
- Green Line newsletter PO Box 5 Lostwithiel Cornwall PL22 OYT UK
- JABS 1 Gawsworth Road Golborne Nr Warrington Cheshire WA3 3RF UK

- PeTA (People for the Ethical Treatment of Animals) PO Box 3169 London NW1 2JF UK
- Plan 2000 234 Summergangs Road Hull HU8 8LL UK
- The Fellowship of Life 43 Braichmelyn Bethesda Bangor Gwynedd North Wales LL57 3RD
- The Informed Parent 19 Woodlands Road Harrow Middlesex HA1 2RT UK
- The Truth Campaign PO Box 70 North Shields NE29 OYP
- Vaccination Information PO Box 3 Hull HU1 1AA UK

Overseas:

Austria

- Schutzverband fur Impfgeschadigte Herztstrasse 23 4020 Linz

Australia:

- Australian Council for Immunisation Information Inc POB 177 Artarmon NSW 2064
- Immunisation Investigation Group POB 900 Katoomba NSW 2780
- Vaccination Awareness and Information Service POB 9086 Manly West QLD 4179
- Vaccination Awareness Network NWS POB 177 Bangalow NSW 2479

Belgium:

- The International Vaccine Newsletter Louise Maguire Foundation Krekenstraat 4 B-3600 Genk Belgium
- Zelfhulpgroep Vaccinatieziekten vzw Edelweisstraat 45 3530 Houthalen-Oost

Canada:

- Vaccination Risk Information & Alternatives Resource Group 49, Benlamond Ave #1 Toronto Ontario M4E 1Y8
- Vaccines & Alternatives 485 Montford Dr Dollard-des Orneaux Quebec H9G 1M7

France:

- Association Liberte Information Sante 19 rue de l'argentiere 63200 Riom

Germany:

- Schutzverband fur Impfgeschadigte e.V. Postfach 1160 57271 Hilchenback

Israel:

- Brain Damaged Children Rehabilitation Association POB 484 Kefar Saba 44 104

Italy:

- Coordinamento del Movimento Italiano per la Liberta di Vaccinazione Via Milano 65 25126 Brescia

Netherlands:

- Nederlandse Vereniging Krities Prikken Leuterhoek-weg 25 6171 RW Stei

New Zealand:

- Immunisation Awareness Society Inc POB 56 048 Dominion Road Auckland
- Vaccination Information Network POB 149 Kaeo Northland

Switzerland:

- Arbeitsgruppe fur differenzierte MMR Impfungen Postfach, CH-3000 Bern 9

USA:

- National Vaccine Information Center/Dissatisfied Parents Together 512 W Maple Ave Suite 206 Vienna VA 22180

Internet

World Wide Web

Http://members.aol.com/abywood/www/index.htm

Note this site contains many articles written by the author and other research material.

Email

abywood@aol.com

CODriscll@aol.com

What Can Canine Health Concern Do For You?

Canine Health Concern is an international group of dog lovers, ethical vets, and animal healthcare professionals who recognise that dogs these days are generally in a very poor state of health. A high proportion of dogs - nearly half of all dogs over the age of ten, and a quarter below that age - die of cancer. Other killer diseases like leukaemia and autoimmune haemolytic anaemia are also rising in number.

In addition, our dogs seem to suffer from an incredible array of chronic illnesses. Arthritis, epilepsy, digestive disorders, skin problems, allergies, behavioural problems, encephalitis, and a whole host of conditions connected with the immune system, seem normal rather than exceptional. If you visit the vet so often that he thinks you fancy him, then maybe Canine Health Concern can help you! Because the fact is, your dog doesn't need to be so ill.

Back in 1994, when CHC was first formed, we set out to prevent our beloved friends from suffering and dying years before their time. We asked why our dogs were so ill, with the aim of developing a preventative healthcare regime. Today, thousands of dogs around the world are enjoying a new lease of life, thanks to information that CHC has unearthed and shared. And it's all so incredibly simple.

The fact is, good health is a natural state. If your dog is ill, then most, if not all, of the following factors will be involved:

❖ The basic constitution - the genetics - of your dog may be at fault. It is known that certain breeds have very specific genetic weaknesses. Bearing in mind that all of us are genetic weaklings in one way or another (some human families, for example, are prone to allergies, others are prone to cancer, others to heart disease, and so on), a lot can be done to help overcome these weaknesses, and even ensure that they don't express themselves in the first place.

✓ Diet - this is one of the few factors you, as a loving dog owner, have any control over. Hippocrates, the father of modern medicine, understood the importance of diet. He advised physicians to attend to their patients' diets before anything else. In 1995, the American Surgeon General announced that over 70% of human illness is diet related.

❖ It is a sad fact that most commercially available pet foods are nothing more than garbage - quite literally, the rejects from the human food chain and other sources. In addition, they contain many suspect chemicals that are implicated in, or proven to cause, degenerative disease. The solution is therefore very simple: stop feeding a sickly dog processed garbage, and a health transformation (providing it hasn't gone too far) is more than likely.

And we have proof! Members who put their dogs on a CHC- recommended natural diet attested to an 85% drop in veterinary visits, and their vet bills fell significantly, too. Even better, many CHC members now have their puppies on a natural diet from the day they arrive home. Apart from enjoying remarkable health, many members tell us that the naturally reared dogs are winning at the shows, too!

Annual vaccination, combined with poor diet, is largely responsible for the appalling state of our dogs' health. We have all heard of human children who have been damaged by vaccines - but we are told to vaccinate our dogs every year, substantially increasing the risk! Why? The answer to this question is also simple. When annual vaccination was first introduced, nobody realised it could be so harmful. It represented a good way for vets to give patients an annual check-up, and it also boosted their practice income significantly.

According to Robert Kirk, writing in Kirk's Current Veterinary Therapy XI, a textbook used in all American veterinary schools, there is no immunologic reason that would make annual vaccinations necessary. He tells us that it is a practice that lacks scientific validity or verification. Immunity to viruses persists for years or for the life of the dog, and revaccinating does not add to that immunity.

Vaccine manufacturers are defending annual boosters by saying that the leptospirosis vaccine, which is a bacterin rather than a virus, needs boosting annually. But please be aware that there are around 150 strains of the bacterin, and the chance of the strain in the needle matching the strain in the field is remote. Further, this vaccine generally protects for only between three and six months - leaving your dog potentially unprotected for nine months each year.

Sadly, we have to say - up front - that if a vet tells you that your dog must have a complete booster every year, then the vet is either ignorant of the true facts, or thinking of his profits rather than your dog's health. We are sorry to make such a shocking statement, but your dog does not deserve to suffer vaccine damage.

Today, in America, veterinary colleges are announcing that they no longer advocate annual vaccination. The veterinary establishment in the UK, and other countries, will have to follow or risk professional disgrace. Vaccines are known, scientifically, to be a cause of cancer, autoimmune haemolytic anaemia, leukaemia, epilepsy, skin disease, behavioural problems, allergies, and a whole lot more. **Fact!**

Canine Health Concern invites you to study the true facts, and makes information available - through newsletters, books, audio tapes and videos - so that you can make an informed choice about your dog's preventative healthcare regime. Many top vets and immunologists have stated - on the record - that the benefits of many vaccines are outweighed by the risks.

There is also a growing number of dog lovers who use the homoeopathic alternative to vaccines. Canine Health Concern invites you to examine the evidence regarding the safety and efficacy of the homoeopathic nosode so that, once again, you may make an informed choice on behalf of your canine friends.

Veterinary medication is used, once your dog is ill, to correct the results of poor genetics, poor diet, and over-vaccination. However, sometimes the medication itself has the potential to kill your dog faster than the illness it's treating. Steroids and antibiotics fall into this category - the two most commonly used pharmaceuticals in the veterinary repertory.

But there are so many safer ways to help your dog to overcome non-life-threatening illnesses. Dietary supplements (and good fresh foods), herbs, homoeopathy, Reiki, acupuncture, chiropractics - these and other gentle therapies are available through fully qualified holistic vets, and many CHC members can attest to the fact that they work. CHC does all it can to help you to find appropriately qualified, holistic, open-minded veterinary care for your dogs. Self help is also a key factor in our work - we encourage dog owners to study the alternatives. This has the potential not only to transform your dog's life, but also your own.

Chemicals

in the environment, and chemicals sold for use on your dog, have the potential to kill your friend. During 1997, for example, an organophosphate flea control product had to be withdrawn from the market after it did just that. Canine Health Concern warned of the dangers of these products back in 1995, fearing that many further deaths could arise from use of these products (for example, your dog develops cancer six months after you use a flea control product . . . but who is to say whether the flea control product did or didn't cause the cancer, despite the fact that they've been shown to cause cancer in laboratory animals?), so we look for ways of ridding dogs of fleas without ridding them of their lives at the same time. Once again, the answer is very simple. A good natural diet, together with vitamin and mineral supplements, usually solves the flea problem for good. And if that fails, we can point you towards a few essential oils or herbs that should do the trick.

The bottom line is this: you and your dog are customers of a multi-billion pound international pet products industry that exists, first and foremost, for financial profit. With gigantic advertising and sponsorship budgets, and the money to give to veterinary colleges and research establishments in return for their allegiance, the likelihood of the real truth getting through to you - you who love and care for your dogs - is remote.

Consequently, Canine Health Concern grew from need: a real need for independent research, free of commercial bias. The group's role has now expanded to include education for pet owners; and a consumer protection group.

Please understand that Canine Health Concern does not go out of its way to attack the veterinary profession, or any other group. We are purely concerned with making the real truth available so that you - as a discerning, informed, and loving dog owner - can make the right choices for your friends. It is your right to disagree with the information we supply - but it is also your right to have access to it. There are many who have a vested interest in your decision, and who would prefer you didn't know.

Canine

Health Concern has valuable friendships with vets from around the world, as well as a number of ethical pet food manufacturers. For despite the fact that we say 'real food' is best . . . such as a dog would eat in the wild given the choice . . . even an improvement in the quality of processed pet foods, plus the addition of bones, vegetables, and good quality table scraps in a dog's diet, could save your friends from years of debilitating disease or unnecessary death.

Canine Health Concern is, incidentally, a non-profit-making organisation. All work done on behalf of CHC is voluntary, and all membership funds are re-invested so that more dog lovers can discover the truth - for at the core of Canine Health Concern is our desire to help you give your dogs the chance they deserve. Profits, such as they are, from book sales, are also re-invested for the sake of our dogs.

Which brings us round full circle: what can you do for Canine Health Concern? CHC exists for one reason only: to help you help your dogs. Resources are limited, so we need you - if you agree with our aims - to network and spread the word. By becoming a member, you are helping us to print newsletters and leaflets, produce cassette tapes, and generally give others the chance to hear how they can help their own dogs. Our philosophy is that individuals can change the world.

To participate in the Canine Health Census, please send a large self-addressed envelope (stamped in the UK, but with an international reply paid postal coupon if outside the UK), to

The Canine Health Census, PO Box 1, Longnor, Derbyshire SK17 OJD, England.

Further Selected References/Bibliography - and suggested further reading.

Vaccine Safety and Efficacy Revisited, W Jean Dodds DVM   Dodds, WJ, Current issues on vaccine safety and efficacy. Kennel Healthline, vol 8, 2-4.
Dodds, WJ, Vaccine, drug and chemical-mediated immune reactions in purebreds challenge researchers. DVM News magazine, vol 21, No 12, 1990.
Dodds, WJ, Killed versus modified-live virus vaccine. AKC Gazette, vol 108, 166, August 1991.
Tizard I, Risks associated with use of live vaccines. JAVMA, vol 196, 1851-1858, 1990.
Phillips, TR, Jensen, JL, Rubino, MJ, Yang, WC, Schultz, RD. Effects of vaccines on the canine immune system. Can. J. Vet. Res., vol 53,   1989.
Luck, D. Are we causing diseases by trying to prevent them? Vet Forum, 12 April 1991.
Ackerman, L. Wanted: Dead of alive. The vaccine controversy. Pet Focus, vol 3, February 1991.
Cantarino, JK. Do interferon levels interfere with vaccines? Vet   Forum, 12 December 1991.
Stockner, PK. ML vaccine causes immune-mediated symptoms in Great Danes. DVM Newsmagazine, vol 22, No 6, 1991.
Priest, SA, The vaccination quandry. Kennel Healthline, vol 9, 2-6 February 1992.
Vaccination - The Hidden Enemy, K Santos, MA, MRCVS.
An Holistic Viewpoint on Vaccinations. Stephen Tobin, Dr.Med.Vet.
Are we vaccinating too much? JAVMA, Vol 207, No 4, August 15, 1995.
1990 pdate on autoimmune diseases of purebred dogs, Dodds, WJ, DVM, AKC Gazette, Vol 107, No 7, July 1990.
Brooks, R. Adverse reactions to canine and feline vaccines. Aust Vet J, 1991.
Schultz, RD, Theoretical and practical aspects of an immunization program for dogs and cats. J Am Vet Med Assoc 1982.
Veterinary Sleuthing ncovers Bluetongue Virus in Vaccine, Society for the Perpetuation of Desert Bred Salukis.
Epilepsy: The link with diet and vaccines, Control Your Health Magazine, Vol 6, No 8.
Genetic Illness: the purebred dilemma, Dodds, WJ, DVM. Paper presented at AVAR Session, Veterinary Medicine - Issues and Activism', 132nd AVMA Convention, July 10, 1995
Dodds, WJ, DVM. The immune system: guardian against diseast. Dog World (SA), March 1995.
Dodds, WJ, DVM. Thyroid can alter behaviour. Dog World (SA), Vol 77, No 10, October 1992.
Dodds, WJ, DVM. Nutritional approaches for a healthy immune system.
Berry MJ, Larsen PR, 1992. The role of selenium in thyroid hormone action. End Rev 13(2).

Burkholder WJ, Swecker WS Jr, 1990. Nutritional influences on immunity. Sem Vet Med Surg (Sm Anim) 5(3).

Vaccinosis. Tiger Tribe September/October 1992.

The informed Parent bulletin, various.

Leading edge Vaccination News and Discoveries (http://www.cco.net/~trufax/vaccine/mmr.html)

Stephens, Sue. A different approach to influenza immunity, Veterinary Times, November 1996.

Tom R Phillips, Ronald D Schultz, Canine and Feline Vaccines, Current Veterinary Therapy XI, 1992.

Esh Cunningham JB, and Wiktor TJ: Vaccine-induced rabies in four cats. JAVMA 180:1336, 1982.

Nara PL, Krakowka S, and Powers TE: Effects of prednisolone on the development of immune response to canine distemper virus in beagle pups. Am J Vet Res 40:1742, 1979.

Pedersen, NC, Emmons, RW, Selcer, R, et al: Rabies vaccine virus infection in three dogs. JAVMA 172:1092, 1978.

Phillips, TR, Jensen, JL, Rubino, MJ, et al: Effects of vaccines on the canine immune system. Can J Vet Res 53:154, 1989.

The Merck Veterinary Manual, seventh edition, 1991.

The Merck Manual, 1998

The International Vaccination Newsletter, June 1996.

J Barthelow Classen, Childhood Immunisation and diabetes melitus, New Zealand Medical Journal, 24 May 1996.

Medical Review, Vol 9, No 5, June 1996: Voting against policy of compulsory immunisation.

Medical Observer, 29 October 1995: Immunisation - parents lack faith.

Animal Research Takes Lives: diseases of cats and dogs.

S Marston: The Vaccination Connection, Prism, 1993.

Dr John Fudens DVM: Vaccinations. Natural Pet, Mar/April 1994.

Your child's measles jabs: has the Health Ministry got it wrong? The Mail on Sunday, September 22, 1996.

R Malik, M Dowden, PE Davis, et al, Concurrent Juvenile Cellulitis and Metaphyseal Osteopathy: An atypical canine distemper virus syndrome? Aus Vet Practit 25(2) June, 1995.

Sad cat's warning for us all. Daily Mail, August 15, 1996.

Jab that damaged our child. Daily Mail, August 20, 1996.

Yvonne Roberts: A Shot in the Dark. Sunday Times, 17 December 1995.

DVM Vaccine roundtable: safety, efficacy heart of vaccine use; experts discuss pros and cons.

Tizard, Ian: Veterinary Immunology 4th edition.

Pitcairn, Richard H, 1993 Proceedings of the American Holistic Veterinary Medical Association: A new look at the vaccine question.

R Brooks: Adverse reactions to canine and feline vaccines. Australian Vet J, Vol 68, No 10, October 1991.

Port Macquarie News: Some can get virus even after being vaccinated.

What do you see as the problems associated with the use of routine vaccines? Wolf Clan Magazine, April/May 1995.

Birchard, SJ, and Robert G Sherding. Saunders Manual of Small Animal Practice: Erythrocytes, leukocytes, and platelets, pages 149-153.

James P Thompson: Systemic Immune-Mediated Diseases, Saunders Manual of Small Animal Practice.

Merck Physicians' Desk Reference, 1992 supplements for revisions, 1495.

Vaccination: do you know the risks? Independent, 12 April 1994.

Jean Lyle: Damage following immunization. Afghan Hound Rev, April 1988.

Jean Lyle: Bloat, seizures, stained teeth . . . do North Americans inflict them on their dogs? Mastiff Club of America Journal, 1992, Number 4.

C Wilford DVM: Vaccines. Gazette, January 1994.

Mason, Dr C: They shoot horses but vaccinate dogs. Positive Health, Feb/Mar 1996.

Cured to Death, Arabella Melville & Colin Johnson, New English Library (ISBN 0-450-05637-6).

Vaccination, The Medical Assault on the Immune System, Dr Viera Scheibner.

The Homoeopathic Treatment of Small Animals, Christopher Day, CW Daniel Company Ltd (ISBN 0 85207 216 3).

Dirty Medicine, Martin J Walker, Slingshot Publications (ISBN 0 9519646 0 7).

Vaccination, Social Violence and Criminality, Harris L Coulter (SIBN 1-55643-084-1).

Thorsons Complete Guide to Vitamins and Minerals, Leonard Mervyn (ISBN 0 7225 2147 2).

Quantum Healing, Deepak Chopra MD, Bantam Books (ISBN 0553173324).

Recommended diet-related books:

Lets Cook for Our Dog, Dr Edmund R Dorosz (ISBN 0-9696884-0-7), also available from Abbeywood Publishing.
Feeding Dogs the Natural Way, Second Edition, C E I Day (ISBN 0 9520071 6 9), also available from Abbeywood Publishing.
How to Have a Healthier Dog, Wendell O Belfield, DVM and Martin Zucker (ISBN 0-9629947-1-5).